WRITING PORTFOLIO ACTIVITIES KIT

Ready-to-Use Management Techniques and Writing Activities for Grades 7-12

Mary Ellen Ledbetter

THE CENTER FOR APPLIED
RESEARCH IN EDUCATION
West Nyack, New York 10994

DEDICATION

For my mother and father who taught me the beauty of words.

Library of Congress Cataloging-in-Publication Data

Ledbetter, Mary E. (Mary Ellen)
    Writing portfolio activities kit : ready-to-use management
techniques & writing activities for grades 7–12   /   Mary E. Ledbetter.
        p.   cm.
    ISBN 0-87628-938-3
    1. English language—Composition and exercises—Study and teaching
(Secondary)—Handbooks, manuals, etc.   2. English language—
Rhetoric—Study and teaching (Secondary)—Handbooks, manuals, etc.
3. Portfolios in education—Handbooks, manuals, etc.   I. Title.
LB1631.L336   1998
808'.042'0712—dc21   97–40860
                                                              CIP

© 1998 *by* M. E. Ledbetter

Printed in the United States of America

10 9 8 7

ISBN 0-87628-938-3

ATTENTION: CORPORATIONS AND SCHOOLS
The Center for Applied Research in Education books are available at quantity discounts
with bulk purchase for educational, business, or sales promotional use. For information,
please write to Prentice Hall Special Sales, 240 Frisch Court, Paramus, NJ 07652. Please
supply: title of book, ISBN number, quantity, how the book will be used, date needed.

**THE CENTER FOR APPLIED RESEARCH
IN EDUCATION**
West Nyack, NY 10994

On the World Wide Web at http://www.phdirect.com

ACKNOWLEDGMENTS

The author thanks **Nora Clark** for her graphic layouts, her expertise, and her support—she truly gave the book wings to fly.

The author also would like to thank her **student writers** who, by sharing their visions, might cause us to consider an issue, reconsider a point of view, or create whole new worlds of our own.

GRAPHICS are from the following sources:

©Corel Corporation, 1994, Corel GALLERY Clipart Catalogue—Version 1.0 (First printing) and Corel GALLERY 2, 1995.
©1987-1995, T-Maker Company, Incredible Image Pak and ClickArt Studio Series Design Group.
©Novell, Inc. 1994, WordPerfect, Version 6.1.

ABOUT THE AUTHOR

Mary Ellen Ledbetter was born in Texas City, Texas, attended Texas Lutheran College, and graduated from Western Michigan University with a B.A. in English and Speech and from Michigan State University with a Master's degree in English. She has taught in public schools in Michigan and Texas as well as at San Jacinto College in Pasadena, Texas. Ms. Ledbetter has been an instructor in the Writing Process Workshop for teachers, a presenter at TMSA and NCTE, has received Goose Creek CISD's Board of Trustees' Bell Award for Outstanding Teacher in 1995 and 1997, and is currently a presenter/consultant for the Bureau of Education and Research, Bellevue, Washington.

LETTER TO TEACHERS

Dear Colleagues:

As educators, we all know that students learn more effectively when they perceive real-life relevance, when they are interested in the subject, and when they are able to see their own growth. As Language Arts/English teachers, we realize that all too often our loaded curricula seem to prohibit our motivating and interesting our students; we tend to get caught up in covering the many aspects that make up Language Arts. We separate the skills in an effort to analyze them when we need to integrate them in order for them to make sense. We sometimes forget that students need to be taught to view **writing, grammar,** and **literature** as a whole.

If, for instance, we are teaching the writing of a persuasive essay, students must be taught that the essay can move an audience only if it is well organized. They must be taught that it cannot incite action or passion or allegiance to a cause if it is grammatically incorrect. The final connection comes when they realize that it cannot even be written without its author having first felt the excitement in other pieces of a similar mode, voice, style, or structure—hence writing and grammar and literature as **inseparable pieces in the language arts puzzle.**

The question then becomes how do we teach integration? How do we put the pieces of the puzzle together? Students have always rebelled at "exercises" in isolation, the arbitrary dissecting of the errors of others or analysis for the sake of analysis alone, but students and teachers as students—all of us who study the written word—can see relevance in working with our own ideas, our own sentences, our own errors. And that's the starting place. **Grammatical concerns** such as fragments, run-ons, and subject-verb agreement errors become more meaningful, more urgent when they threaten to lessen our chances of being understood. The **literary elements** of tone, conflict, characterization, and theme, to name a few, become more than some abstract concepts to be applied to some abstract works. We suddenly see them as integral aspects of our own narratives, necessary parts of the **whole story** we must tell.

When we allow students the opportunity to consistently work with concepts applied to models and THEN to their own works, they tend to understand the connection in the many facets that make up our language. Through **literature** examples students are shown the goal, they understand where they are headed, and they start their own **writing process,** armed with **proofreading skills** that continually improve as they learn to adjust and readjust their ideas. They learn techniques of self-assessment, their peers are there to give opinions and suggestions, and they are constantly being given more models, more skills, more chances to rethink. Students begin to value their own voices, they know there is a real-life audience for their ideas, and they want to be heard.

Sincerely,

Mary Ellen Ledbetter

ABOUT THIS RESOURCE

Writing Portfolio Activities Kit provides ready-to-use writing assignments for integrating **writing, grammar,** and **literature** in an easy-to-follow approach for establishing individual student portfolios. Teacher pages give suggestions ranging from grading assignments and involving students in the assessment process to creating minilessons for specific units. Reproducible pages for students in grades 7 through 12 are accompanied by student and teacher models and are designed for students to individualize assignments to fit their writing needs. It is organized into four parts:

Part One, "Getting Started," gives step-by-step directions for creating portfolios that serve not only as examples of students' growth in writing but document mastery of grammar and literature/reading skills as well.

Teachers can learn

- ➤ how to interest students in keeping a portfolio,
- ➤ how to teach students to manage their own portfolios, and
- ➤ how to involve students in **portfolio assessment.**

Also included are tips on the purpose, use, and grading of unique forms of **student-interactive rubrics** as well as ideas for the use of portfolio charts and various methods of organizing writing response groups.

Part Two, "Writing," covers all writing process stages for all writing modes
- ➤ from specific prewriting activities and **student-interactive rubrics**
- ➤ to higher-level assignment sheets, and
- ➤ **award-winning student models.**

Students learn to revise their writing by using specially designed rubrics that provide them and their teachers with an **in-depth analysis** of all aspects of the paper in progress. The rubrics for each writing mode help shape student writing by reminding them of the elements of each particular mode and by requiring **student-written proof** for including each element in their work.

Part Three, "Grammar," is an individualized, student-based approach to language usage and includes ideas such as

- ➤ An easy-to-grade correction sheet that can be a **personalized instructional follow-up** to all teacher-graded written assignments,
- ➤ Sample assignment sheets integrating literature and grammar,
- ➤ **Poetry ideas** incorporating various grammatical concepts, and
- ➤ Portfolio **assessment sheets** that provide students with an opportunity to review their progress.

Grammatical categories listed on the portfolio chart for this section indicate aspects to be studied throughout the year.

Part Four, " Literature," offers unique features for busy teachers, such as

➤ Generic Application Tests for any short story or novel:

✻ The reproducible "Bookworm" test, as "pop quiz" or end-of-unit major test, that can be given repeatedly with emphasis on various skills to stress the importance of applying literary terms to works.

➤ Individual Student-Interaction Reading Sheets to enable students to respond to a work as it is being read

➤ Sample group projects with vocabulary units and student models

➤ Ideas for incorporating research into literature units

➤ Independent Reading Assignments:

✻ Assignments that can be applied to any independent student reading.

➤ A comprehensive chart listing literary devices and skills to give students a test-by-test record of their progress in each area

Assignments in this section ask students to view literature from a writer's perspective by citing examples of literary elements that make a story/novel a successful piece of writing, by interacting with literature through write-to-learn assignments, and by creating their own "literary works" using various aspects of famous models as springboards for their ideas.

Using Writing Portfolio Activities Kit, students begin to comprehend the concept that writing, grammar, and literature work together to create the "ART" of language.

Mary Ellen Ledbetter

Table of Contents

PART 3: GRAMMAR   237

CHAPTER 4: LITERATURE   311

PART 1

GETTING STARTED

How to Interest Students in Keeping a Portfolio

① **INDIVIDUALIZING PORTFOLIOS:** Let students INDIVIDUALIZE their portfolios as much as possible. Provide students with a standard-size manila file folder or colored folders, or they may wish to purchase folders with dividers.

② **HOLDING CONTESTS:** COMPETITION usually creates interest among students, especially if extra points, small prizes, etc. are awarded to winners. Hold a PORTFOLIO CONTEST for the top three (or whatever number is feasible for a particular classroom) portfolios in the class. Give students a week to do the following:

a. **DETERMINE A THEME:** Each student may decide on a SINGLE "THEME" for his or her portfolio that best represents his or her personality, or the student may choose to create a COLLAGE OF IMAGES. For example, a football player might also be interested in writing as well as in classical music and would like his portfolio to reflect his varied pursuits.

b. **DECORATE THE COVER:** Each student DECORATES HIS OR HER COVER--outside and inside--with original art work, pictures cut out from magazines, newspaper clippings or headlines, memorabilia, etc. The idea is that whatever is on the cover somehow symbolizes WHAT is inside the student.

c. **EVALUATE THE COVER:** Let the students know that the cover will not only be GRADED BY YOU but JUDGED BY THEIR PEERS as well. Specify a minimum number of images for certain grades.

d. **PRESENT PORTFOLIOS:** STUDENTS ENJOY PRESENTING their portfolios, as it gives them a chance to explain the images to their classmates. After all students are finished with their presentations, place the portfolios on students' desks. Students should then circulate around the room to decide on their favorite three.

e. **DISPLAY PORTFOLIOS:** DISPLAY WINNING PORTFOLIOS in the room for a week as an added honor.

f. **PRESERVING PORTFOLIOS:** LAMINATE PORTFOLIOS for more durability.

HOW TO KEEP UP WITH PORTFOLIOS

①→ **_STORING PORTFOLIOS:_** Keep portfolios in colorful baskets around the room, divided by classes, for _EASY ACCESS._

②→ **_DISTRIBUTING PORTFOLIOS:_** _ROW LEADERS_ may help pass out portfolios on days they are needed, or students may retrieve their own portfolios by rows or individually as they finish an assignment.

③→ **_RECORDING ASSIGNMENTS:_** To increase _STUDENT RESPONSIBILITY,_ ask students to be in charge of recording all grades, dates, and assignments on the charts that may be kept in the front of each section of their portfolios. Since the grades will have already been recorded by you in the grade book, the charts serve more as student records.

④→ **_FAMILIARIZING STUDENTS WITH TERMINOLOGY:_** When an assignment that has been designated to go into the portfolio has been graded and passed back to the students, simply instruct students which section it will be filed in and what to record on the chart. By working with the charts frequently, _STUDENTS WILL BECOME FAMILIAR WITH THE TERMINOLOGY_ involved in the course and will soon be able to record their scores without teacher instruction.

⑤→ **_PORTFOLIO ASSESSMENT:_** Portfolios can be _ASSESSED_ at various intervals in terms of spot-checking student record keeping.

PURPOSE OF PORTFOLIO CHARTS

①→ **TYPES OF CHARTS**: Four PORTFOLIO CHARTS are included throughout this resource for your use, each chart providing room for the TITLE, DATE, and GRADE of a particular assignment.

    a. WRITING PORTFOLIO TABLE OF CONTENTS--A list of five modes of writing, a research section, and a section designated as "other" (possibly for recording literary analysis, poetry, special projects, etc.).

    b. GRAMMAR SKILLS--A list of skills related to usage (that students are required to master for standardized tests) rather than merely identification of functions.

    c. LITERATURE/READING SKILLS AND RECORD OF TESTS--A list of reading/literary skills included in most curricula and on most state-mandated tests.

    d. INDEPENDENT READING RECORD--A record of books read outside of class and any related grades.

②→ **CHARTS AS GRAPHS OF STUDENT PROGRESS:** The charts serve not only as HANDY REFERENCES during parent/teacher conferences or team/administrator meetings but as REMINDERS FOR STUDENTS of their progress in a given area.

③→ **CHARTS AS GUIDE TO CURRICULUM:** Another advantage of the charts is that they provide an ONGOING LIST OF SKILLS covered and those yet to be taught. A copy of the charts can be kept by the teacher as INSTRUCTIONAL GUIDELINES or blueprints of how skills can be meshed. For instance, a teacher might want to combine the writing of descriptive paragraphs (WRITING) with the study of adjective and adverb usage (GRAMMAR) and figurative language in a particular literary selection (LITERATURE).

©1998 M. E. LEDBETTER

NAME:_____ CLASS:_____ DATE: _____

WRITING PORTFOLIO
TABLE OF CONTENTS

MODE/ASSIGNMENT	DATE	GRADE
PERSUASIVE:		
COMPARISON/CONTRAST:		
NARRATIVE:		
DESCRIPTIVE:		
HOW-TO:		
RESEARCH:		
OTHERS:		

NAME:_____ CLASS:_____ DATE:_____

WRITING PORTFOLIO (SAMPLE)
TABLE OF CONTENTS

MODE/ASSIGNMENT	DATE	GRADE
PERSUASIVE: *"Bar Harbor, Maine"*	9/94	B+
COMPARISON/CONTRAST: *"Strawberry Ice Cream Soda"*	12/94	A -
NARRATIVE: *"The Mystery of the Lost Purse"*	10/94	A
DESCRIPTIVE: *"The Nutcracker"*	2/95	A
HOW-TO: *"How to Fly Behind the Stars"*	4/95	A
RESEARCH: *"Colorado, Spring Break '92"*	3/95	A
OTHERS: *Poems--refrain--"The Storm"*	5/95	A

PURPOSE OF RUBRICS

RUBRICS are designed to do the following:

♥*TO SERVE* as GUIDELINES for what is expected in a final product, including points on which a GRADE can be based,

♥*TO PROVIDE* students with a STRUCTURAL PICTURE of an excellent paper, and

♥*TO PROVIDE* an organized approach to REVISION, which is the key to a student writer's growth.

USE OF RUBRICS

① → ***ASSIGNING RUBRICS:*** Hand out rubrics AFTER THE INITIAL ROUGH DRAFTS are completed since rubrics can signal errors in structure--which necessitate deep revisionary strategies--as well as in mechanics, which could simply be a stage in the final proofreading.

② → ***COMPLETING ALL SECTIONS OF RUBRICS:*** Instruct students to COMPLETE EVERY ASPECT of the rubric, leaving no part incomplete. For example, if the rubric calls for five figurative language devices, the point is not for the student to include the two his or her paper currently contains and think that satisfies the requirement but to revise the paper accordingly to include three extra devices.

GRADING RUBRICS

①→ **SPOT-CHECKING:** Rubrics can be SPOT-CHECKED for effort and given a nominal grade. If a class has worked on certain skills (e.g., run-ons and fragments), only the section of the rubric dealing with those lessons may be graded. OR...

②→ **GRADING RUBRICS SEPARATELY:** Rubrics can be handed in and graded BEFORE THE FINAL DRAFT of the paper, serving as a sort of outline of the necessary components, and checked by the teacher in much the same way as rough drafts are often reviewed. OR...

③→ **GRADING RUBRICS AS INTEGRAL PARTS OF PAPERS :** One effective method is to grade rubrics on HOW SUCCESSFUL each aspect was in terms of producing a better product. For instance, if no errors in organization occurred in the final draft of the paper itself, no points would be deducted from the rubric for that section. If, however, mechanical errors such as run-ons or fragments detracted from the value of the paper, a designated number of points could be subtracted, indicating to the writer that more time needs to be spent proofreading for these sorts of errors and mechanics.

④→ **ORAL-CONFERENCING:** Rubrics can be used as ORAL-CONFERENCE grades--the student and teacher together focusing on problem areas, strengths, etc.

HOW TO USE
WRITING PROCESS "GENERIC" SHEETS

① **USING THE PREWRITING GUIDE:** Hand out the PREWRITING GUIDE as a reminder of the steps in the prewriting stage of the writing process, or require students to complete the sheet as a large or small group activity.

② **USING GENERIC RUBRICS:** In the rough draft stage, give students the following rubrics:

A. ELABORATION RUBRIC to remind students of the importance of supporting details,

B. SENTENCE STRUCTURE RUBRIC to ensure sentence variety, and

C. TRANSITION WORDS AND PHRASES sheet to provide students with transition options.

③ **USING RESPONSE SHEETS:** After students have completed their initial rough drafts, solicit peer feedback by handing out the following:

A. RESPONSE SHEET FAVORITE PARTS to give students **positive feedback** on their papers, by group members' quoting the passages they liked and explaining the appeal and

B. THE RESPONSE SHEET SUGGESTIONS to offer **specific suggestions for improvement**. You may specify that students concentrate on a specific skill, such as sentence combining, or that they proofread for all errors.

© 1998 M. E. LEDBETTER

12

✳The RESPONSE SHEET provided could serve as a **model** for students to make their own response sheets out of **notebook paper** (tearing a piece of paper in fourths, leaving blanks to be filled in during the response time, and using the back for the suggestions), or it could be **reproduced for classroom copies.**

✳An organized approach to all response activities is to **use a timer** set for a designated time for each response--perhaps five to eight minutes. Instruct students to have **other work** with them (their homework, the next assignment, a library book) in case they complete their responses before the allotted time.

ORGANIZING RESPONSE GROUPS

Effective methods of **ORGANIZING RESPONSE GROUPS** are the following:

① **ROW RESPONSES**--Ask students to pass their rough drafts to the students behind them, who will respond to the papers and pass them back to the next student and so on. This method provides a quick check with a minimum of student movement.

② **GROUP RESPONSES**--Students may number off for grouping purposes. Once the groups are established, papers may be read aloud or passed around, students responding as they listen or read.

③ **MUSICAL CHAIRS**--Students enjoy a chance to play "musical chairs," which allows them to move to any student's desk to read the paper that has been left out for response purposes.

✳FOR THIS METHOD, ASK STUDENTS TO FOLD THEIR COMPLETED RESPONSE SHEETS and leave them on the author's desk so that the writer can compare the responses.

④ **CLASS CIRCLE**--Arrange the desks in one large circle around the room. Students pass to the right, mark the rough drafts as a teacher would--praising the strengths and noting the errors--and pass to the next student. Papers will probably not be read in their entirety in this method, but it allows students to compare their writing to that of all class members and to receive feedback from a larger group.

✳Students should keep response sheets for revision purposes and turn them in with the rest of the rough draft material along with the final paper.

✳You may wish to participate in any of the groups, passing your paper or a sample paper to be read as a model.

RESPONSE

GROUP

PREWRITING GUIDE

① → Individually, **BRAINSTORM** ten topics on your mode of writing:

a. _____   f. _____

b. _____   g. _____

c. _____   h. _____

d. _____   i. _____

e. _____   j. _____

② → Share with the class your favorite idea and list any topics from the **CLASS EXCHANGE** that you might like to write about:

a._____

b._____

c._____

③ → Choose your topic and **WEB** it in order to decide on your **THREE MAIN IDEAS** and **SUPPORT** for each. (*For comparison/contrast, you may use your chart instead of the web.)

(Draw web with central circle, three main circles, and three circles under each main one.)

NAME_____ CLASS_____ DATE_____

ELABORATION RUBRIC

To prove that you have **SUFFICIENT ELABORATION** for your essay, choose

ONE BODY PARAGRAPH on which to do an elaboration outline.

Keep in mind that all body paragraphs must have enough detail to illustrate your point.

BODY PARAGRAPH #_____

① → **TOPIC SENTENCE** that states main idea of paragraph:
(Remember not to give elaboration within the topic sentence itself.)

_____

_____

② → **FIRST SUBPOINT** stated in a sentence:

_____

_____

③ → **ELABORATION** stated in a sentence (or sentences):

_____

_____

④ → **SECOND SUBPOINT** stated in a sentence:

_____

_____

⑤→ **ELABORATION** stated in a sentence (or sentences):

_____

_____

⑥→ **THIRD SUBPOINT** stated in a sentence:

_____

_____

⑦→ **ELABORATION** stated in a sentence (or sentences):

_____

_____

© 1988, M. E. LEDBETTER

SENTENCE STRUCTURE RUBRIC

To ENSURE that your writing has sentence structure variety, REVISE your work to include at least one example of each of the following:

①→ List your **BEST SENTENCE THAT CONTAINS A "MAGIC 3"** (Three nouns, verbs, etc. **AND** their modifiers). Example: I could see old BLACKIE asleep on the sidewalk, 100-year-old PINES like sentinels guarding our house, and CLAUDIA playing hopscotch with her friends across the street.
UNDERLINE YOUR "MAGIC 3."

_____

_____

_____

②→ List your **BEST NOUN ABSOLUTE** (Noun followed by a present or past participle). Example of **PRESENT PARTICIPLE**: MY HANDS SHAKING, MY VOICE QUIVERING, I whispered what I hoped to be the one word he wanted to hear. Example of **PAST PARTICIPLE**: Daddy studied me across the dining room table, HIS GLASSES LOWERED, HIS FORK POISED MIDAIR.
UNDERLINE YOUR NOUN ABSOLUTE.

_____

_____

_____

③→ List your **BEST PARTICIPIAL PHRASE** (an "-ing" verb used as an adjective). Example: My arms and legs strained to the tempo, WANTING TO PERFECT EACH AND EVERY MOVEMENT, WANTING SO DESPERATELY TO PLEASE.
UNDERLINE YOUR PARTICIPIAL PHRASE.

_____

_____

_____

④→ List your best sentence that has been **"EXPANDED" BY USING A FIGURATIVE LANGUAGE DEVICE.** Example: Always that face and that smell I waited for were Mama as she'd hug me tight to her, Mama and her wonderful smells, LIKE FIELDS OF LAVENDER JUST FOR ME.
*UNDERLINE YOUR FIGURATIVE LANGUAGE DEVICE.

_____

_____

_____

⑤→ List a sentence that has an **UNUSUAL STRUCTURE** (in other words, not the usual subject/verb pattern). For example: "ONE, TWO, THREE, FOUR...ONE, TWO, THREE, FOUR," I RECALL HER VOICE RINGING SHARPLY, CLEARLY, LIKE A FAMILIAR, EXPECTED CADENCE. (The subject is "I," and the verb is "recall," but the sentence does not begin with the subject.)

_____

_____

_____

TRANSITION WORDS AND PHRASES
Phrases to begin paragraphs

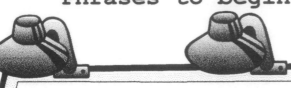

1st Body:
First
One example/instance/method/way

Middle Body:
Another	Besides
In addition to	Next
Moreover	Not only
Second, Third, etc.	Then

Final Body:
A final example/instance/method/way
Finally
In conclusion
Last
To conclude

Within Body Paragraphs:
Also	For example
For instance	Furthermore
In addition	Specifically
In particular	Moreover
That is	To illustrate

SPECIAL TRANSITIONS FOR COMPARISON/CONTRAST

By contrast	By the same token
Conversely	However
In spite of	Yet
Likewise	Nevertheless
Unlike	On the other hand
Similarly	Still
On the contrary	In the same manner/way

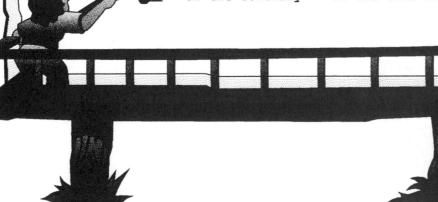

© 1998 M. E. LEDBETTER

RESPONSE SHEET: FAVORITE PARTS

(CUT ON ALL DOTTED LINES)

Name of Responder:_____

Name of Author:_____

Title of Paper:_____

My three favorite parts:

☺

☺

☺

What I liked best about the paper in general:

Name of Responder:_____

Name of Author:_____

Title of Paper:_____

My three favorite parts:

☺

☺

☺

What I liked best about the paper in general:

Name of Responder:_____

Name of Author:_____

Title of Paper:_____

My three favorite parts:

☺

☺

☺

What I liked best about the paper in general:

Name of Responder:_____

Name of Author:_____

Title of Paper:_____

My three favorite parts:

☺

☺

☺

What I liked best about the paper in general:

RESPONSE SHEET: SUGGESTIONS
(CUT ON ALL DOTTED LINES)

Name of Responder: _____

Name of Author: _____

Title of Paper: _____

Three specific suggestions for improvement:

1

2

3

The area that needs the most work:

Name of Responder: _____

Name of Author: _____

Title of Paper: _____

Three specific suggestions for improvement:

1

2

3

The area that needs the most work:

Name of Responder: _____

Name of Author: _____

Title of Paper: _____

Three specific suggestions for improvement:

1

2

3

The area that needs the most work:

Name of Responder: _____

Name of Author: _____

Title of Paper: _____

Three specific suggestions for improvement:

1

2

3

The area that needs the most work:

HOW TO USE GROUP GOALS/ASSESSMENT SHEET

①→ **HOLDING GROUP MEMBERS ACCOUNTABLE:** Groups may be given the goals/assessment sheet at the onset of any group assignment or project.

    A. Ask *EACH STUDENT* to fill in the sheet to turn in with the final project, emphasizing that each group member is an essential part in the creative process.

    B. With all students' having access to an assessment instrument, students more often *STAY ON TASK*, knowing that their *PEERS CAN EVALUATE* their contributions.

②→ **FOCUSING ON PROCESS AS WELL AS PRODUCT:** The point of the exercise is to encourage students to analyze the *PROBLEM-SOLVING PROCESS.*

NAME_____
CLASS_____
DATE_____

Group Goals/Assessment

GROUP MEMBERS:

① _____   ③ _____

② _____   ④ _____

SKILL: _____

PROBLEM TO BE SOLVED: _____

STEPS IN SOLVING PROBLEM:

① _____

② _____

③ _____

SPECIFIC DUTIES OF MEMBERS:

① _____

② _____

③ _____

④ _____

SUMMARY OF SOLUTION:

_____

_____

_____

ASSESSMENT OF SOLUTION/REASONING: _____

_____

ASSESSMENT OF GROUP AS A POLITE, ON-TASK PART OF THE CLASSROOM/REASONING:

_____

_____

PORTFOLIO ASSESSMENT

① → **EXCERPTING STUDENT WORKS:** Students enjoy reviewing the works in their portfolios and citing their *FAVORITE PARTS* from their favorite pieces.

② → **REVIEWING TECHNIQUES:** The "Portfolio Assessment: Stylistic Devices" not only provides students with a concise listing of some of their best excerpts but offers a *REVIEW OF THE DEVICES* that made the writing special.

③ → **CREATING CLASSROOM DISPLAYS:** As an addendum assignment, ask students to make a *POSTER, MOBILE, BOOKMARK, ETC.,* incorporating three of their favorite excerpts, complete with the title of the work, illustrations, and an author autobiographical blurb.

④ → **WRITING AUTHOR AUTOBIOGRAPHICAL BLURBS:** Ask students to compose a "factual" blurb containing at least three interesting points about their lives, and a "creative" blurb giving insight into the imaginary life of the author. Blurbs should be accompanied by author's picture.

⑤ → **PRESENTING BLURBS:** Students may present blurbs and three best passages to the class as a culminating oral assignment.

©1998 M. E. LEDBETTER

PORTFOLIO ASSESSMENT: Stylistic Devices

A+

ASSIGNMENT: In an effort to assess your growth as a writer, review the works in your portfolio, citing your best example for each of the following devices. In an internal footnote, include the title of the work and the page number.

EXAMPLE: SIMILE:

And always that face and that smell I waited for were Mama as she'd hug me tight to her, Mama and her wonderful smells like fields of lavender just for me ("All My Favorite Places," Part 2, Section 4).

① SIMILE:

_____

_____

② EXPLICIT METAPHOR:

_____

_____

③ IMPLICIT METAPHOR:

_____

_____

④ PERSONIFICATION:

_____

_____

⑤ ALLITERATION:

_____

_____

⑥ ASSONANCE:

_____

_____

⑦ HYPERBOLE:

_____

_____

⑧ REPETITION FOR EFFECT:

_____

_____

⑨ THREE SPECIFIC DETAILS FOR EFFECT:

A. _____

_____

B. _____

_____

C. _____

_____

⑩ THREE SENSORY IMAGES:

A. _____

_____

B. _____

_____

C. _____

_____

HOW TO USE
CHECKLIST FOR PUBLICATION

① → **ASSESSING WORKS:** To encourage students to gain more experience in *REAL-LIFE PUBLICATION,* require them to send off their best piece of the year to a publication of their choice.

② → **REVIEWING STUDENT-WRITTEN PUBLICATIONS:** Classes enjoy reading magazines whose stories, poems, essays, etc., not only reflect student interests but are student-written as well. Early in the year, set aside several class periods to *ANALYZE TYPICAL TYPES OF WORKS* contained in various publications as well as outstanding aspects of students' favorite pieces *(unusual story beginnings and endings, interesting character development, realistic dialogue, etc.)*

③ → **PREPARING MANUSCRIPTS:** *THE CHECKLIST FOR PUBLICATION* will remind students that attention to details plays an important part in the final preparation of manuscripts.

④ → **REVIEWING LETTER FORM:** Students will gain practice in writing an informative/persuasive *COVER LETTER* whose purpose is to interest an editor in a student's work.

⑤ → **REVIEWING ENVELOPE FORM:** Students will learn about *SASE's* (self-addressed, stamped envelopes) and gain experience having their manuscripts weighed and mailed.

Checklist for Publication

Put a CHECK in the blank after each step has been completed.

I.   Work to be submitted (Bound with paper clip--not stapled)

_____**A.   TYPED, DOUBLE-SPACED** (except poetry)

_____**B.   MARGINS**
1. 1 1/4 inches on top and bottom
2. 1 inch on each side

_____**C.   TOP LEFT-HAND CORNER OF FIRST PAGE:**
Name
Address
Area Code and phone number
Social Security number
Word count (or word count and date in top right-hand corner)

_____**D.   CENTER:** (1/3 of the way down the page, centered)

            TITLE (all caps)
                by
            Your Name

_____**E.   ALL PAGES AFTER FIRST:**
1. Last name in upper left-hand corner
2. Key word or phrase from title on same line in center
3. Page number on right-hand corner

_____**F.   END OF MANUSCRIPT**
1. Space two lines from end.
2. Type "The End."

II.   Cover letter
_____**A.   HEADING**
Your address
Your telephone number (with area code)
Date of mailing

_____**B.   INSIDE ADDRESS**
Name of editor
Name of publication (underlined or all caps)
Address of magazine

_____**C.**   ***SALUTATION***= Dear _____: (editor's name or the word <u>Editor</u> followed by a <u>colon</u>)

_____**D.**   ***BODY***--written like a short personal letter or business letter stating the name of the piece, any interesting fact regarding it, or any interesting fact about you as an author or how the piece relates to you

_____**E.**   ***CLOSING***
    1. Type the word <u>Sincerely</u> followed by a <u>comma.</u>
    2. Skip approximately four spaces.
    3. Type your name as you wish it to appear in the publication.
    4. In between <u>Sincerely</u> and your typed signature, sign your name in blue or black ink.

III.   Envelopes

_____**A.**   ***S.A.S.E.*** (Self-Addressed, Stamped Envelope)--folded in half to fit inside mailing envelope

_____**B.**   ***MAILING ENVELOPE*** addressed to magazine

STOP

Parts I - III must be completed by _____ so that I can record your effort.

DO NOT MAIL PACKET UNTIL I HAVE RECORDED IT, OR YOU WILL NOT RECEIVE CREDIT.

IV.   Mailing--Parent signature verifying the following:

_____**A.**   ***STUDENT*** himself or herself had experience at the post office having envelopes weighed and stamped.

_____**B.**   ***ENVELOPES*** were actually mailed.

Date: _____

Parent Signature: _____

Publication(s): _____

PART 2

WRITING

Section I:

PERSUASIVE WRITING

How to Use the Structure Rubric

① VISUALIZING THE STRUCTURE OF AN ESSAY: The **STRUCTURE RUBRIC** gives students a **PICTURE** of a well-organized essay and can be kept in their notebooks for easy reference.

② MARKING THESIS AND THREE ASPECTS:

A. After prewriting activities, ask students to begin the **INTRODUCTORY PARAGRAPH**, reminding them that the introduction usually ends with the **THESIS STATEMENT**, which should include their three points to be covered.

B. Instruct students to use a colored marker to **BRACKET** the thesis and another color to put **CHECKS** on their three points. Thus, students match their structure with that of the rubric.

③ MARKING TRANSITIONS, MAIN IDEAS, AND SUPPORTS: When assigning each **BODY PARAGRAPH**, ask students to refer to the rubric for the appropriate structure.

A. Students should use the **LIST OF TRANSITIONS** and be reminded that **LINKING PHRASES** in the topic sentence are often more effective than simple transition words. To ensure that each body paragraph is linked to the next with the appropriate phrase, ask students to **CIRCLE** the transition device with a colored marker.

How to Use the Structure Rubric, page 2

B. Next, students must state the **MAIN IDEA** in the topic sentence for each body paragraph and draw a **BOX** around it to match the structure of the rubric. Suggest that a different color be used for the boxes, which will further emphasize their importance in the overall essay.

C. As students progress through their rough drafts, the **STRUCTURE RUBRIC** serves as a constant reminder that each body needs **AT LEAST THREE SUPPORTS**, which they should check, using yet another colored marker.

④ MARKING RESTATEMENT OF THESIS: Finally, by once again referring to the **STRUCTURE RUBRIC**, students will realize that the **CONCLUDING STATEMENT** should restate the thesis and the three points covered.

➤ Since students benefit from **TEACHER- AND STUDENT-WRITTEN EXAMPLES** of essays in the same mode, several have been included.

STRUCTURE RUBRIC

✔ ✔ ✔

I. [THESIS STATEMENT] Containing 3 aspects to be covered

II. *TRANSITION WORDS* |MAIN IDEA|

✔ SUPPORT

✔ SUPPORT

✔ SUPPORT

III. *TRANSITION WORDS* |MAIN IDEA|

✔ SUPPORT

✔ SUPPORT

✔ SUPPORT

IV. *TRANSITION WORDS* |MAIN IDEA|

✔ SUPPORT

✔ SUPPORT

✔ SUPPORT

V. [CONCLUDING STATEMENT] Containing 3 aspects to be covered

✔ ✔ ✔

Let's Head to Seaside!

Hungry for fresh mahi mahi? Longing for white sands and crystal clear water? Tired of all work and no play? Then let's head for Seaside, Florida. *Thesis Statement* *Three Aspects* ✓ [We can visit our favorite restaurant, enjoy the world-famous ✓ scenery, and participate in activities ✓ that will put Baytown light years away.]

Transition Word (First,) in terms of [cuisine,] *Main Idea* aren't we ready for a change? How many times lately has our collective refrain been "This again?" when hot dogs, TV dinners, and everything and anything microwavable have been plopped down on TV trays in front of the six o'clock news? Then Bud and Alley's is for us. We'll be dining beach side in an open-air bungalow. Exotic fish, ✓ vegetables ✓ *Support* al dente, and salads ✓ with such unusual ingredients as arugula, endive, and shiitake mushrooms will be served with that perfect wine ✓ that we always enjoy. And don't forget espresso ✓ or cappuccino in the gazebo afterwards. What could be more romantic?

(Besides) all the culinary delights, Seaside's scenery would be a welcome relief. Instead of Gulf Coast's refineries rising in our polluted skies like giant, soot-blackened tinker toys, we'd have an unobstructed view of nature's best--clear blue skies broken only by steep-pitched rooftops of homes that are not only award-winning for their uniqueness but reminiscent of days long ago. Gone will be the monotony of neighborhoods we're used to, where each house resembles the next except for a curlicue here and a doodad there, and in its place will be winding, red-bricked streets and rainbow-colored houses, some with gables and dormer windows, rooftop decks, and tri-level porches. And the terrain itself is unparalleled. When was the last time we've seen yards sprouting misshapen scrub oaks like some sort of beach-side modernistic sculpture? And grass, your dreaded enemy, is almost a thing of the past in Seaside. Instead, wildflowers and sea grasses and sand--miles and miles of it--make this town truly a Seaside paradise. Ready for some sightseeing?

If fine dining and unprecedented scenery aren't quite enough to fill our postcards, (then) the activities will be truly something we can write home about--if we have time, that is. Your endless complaints of a thirty-mile drive to an "uninspired" municipal golf course will be forgotten. Seaside's neighboring town, Destin, offers courses challenging enough for even the most jaded players. Soon you could be teeing off with the rich and famous, one picture-perfect hole after another as your backdrop. What about biking? ✓ How many times have we dreamed of following the ocean wherever it may lead--just you and I, and our trusty Schwinns. We could pack a picnic lunch, and the day would be ours--coasting along the seaside highway or following countless bike trails in and out of the city itself. Who knows, we just might strike up a conversation ✓ with Prince Charles, a fellow Seaside visitor and cyclist, as rumors go. And what's more relaxing after a hard day at the links or out on the road than a swim ✓ in one of Seaside's pools or in the ocean itself? Galveston's murky waters would fade from memory as we'd swim and play in Seaside's surf. For once we'd be able to see all the treasures the Gulf holds. Just think of the possibilities!

Concluding Statement

What do you say? [Let's put away those frozen dinners, get out those travel brochures, and plan the itinerary for the best trip of our lives.] Tennis anyone?

Helmuth Mayer
National Contest Winner
Assignment: What's Right About My Life

I LOVE YOU!

From
Your Mother

Enjoyments of My Life

Participial Phrase
SITTING UNDER AN APPLE TREE, WITH A LITTLE

PICKET FENCE SURROUNDING ME AND MY SOUL, I think about
Repetition for Effect
what's right about my life. Was it the **FIRST TIME** I took a step, the

FIRST TIME I was a winner, the **FIRST TIME** I ate a freshly picked orange, squishing

it between my teeth to let the juice slide down my chin? Or was it plain just being

born?
Personification
Then a gust of wind blows and the **TREES HOWL AND STRETCH MY MIND**

beyond the limits. To hear my parents' car drive up in the driveway, to have a friend

call and ask to play, these are things right about my life. I hear the **LEAVES**
Personification   *Implicit Metaphor*
RUSTLING UP A GROWL so I look up and a **GRANDPA RAINDROP** falls on my nose.

Gasping for air, I hustle to the house to stay out of the rain. What's right about my
Hyperbole
life goes spinning through my head **A MILLION TIMES**. Was it the first drop of rain

that fell on me? Was it having the rain splatter on the pavement while I was under
Vivid Verb
the protection of my home? It was being loved by nature. As the rain **KERPLUNKS**
Parallel Structure
heavily onto the ground **DROP BY DROP**, I get older **SECOND BY SECOND**, to finally

have a beautiful rainbow gleam in the midst of the air. Was that the call of God

telling me that fate had arrived into my life? As I walk into the kitchen, I see a ham

Dialogue Inclusion

sandwich on the table with a note that says, **"I LOVE YOU! FROM YOUR MOTHER."**

I then realize that everybody loves me. That is right about my life.

Next, my curiosity is right about my life. My parents have always said I am

a smart kid with questions. They have told everybody they have ever met that I have

Hyperbole

a **FEVER FOR QUESTIONS**. Nature loves me. I talk and talk to the trees and bushes

and play chase with the leaves as they blow and I run after them. I'm not sure but I

think fate also had its laughs. I ask; it rains. I don't ask; it doesn't rain. I ask

quietly and politely; it rains gently with a rainbow. I'm not sure if fate hates my

Personification

curiosity all the way up its **SPINE,** but that is right about my life.

Implicit Metaphor

Finally, **I CATCH IT IN A MITT AND A GLOVE.** I find out that being right about

Magic 3's

my life is having fun. **PLAYING KICK WITH A SOCCER BALL, THROWING A**

BASEBALL BACK-AND-FORTH, OR PLAYING MONOPOLY MY WAY IS RIGHT. Having

fun with nature is a breeze. Playing hide-n-go-seek with the trees or planting a new

tomato plant for the season is right. Friends also come along in the fun, going to each

other's house and playing Yahtzee till we are bored out of our pants.

Magic 3's

What's right about my life will go through my head as I get **KISSED BY MY**

MOM GOODNIGHT, ASK MORE QUESTIONS, OR PLAY MONOPOLY AGAIN. Living

a life of love, curiosity, and fun is right about my life.

Christy Alexander
Persuasive Writing

OH, FOR A SWAN

The night thickens, and frogs start croaking their mournful cries. Marsh reeds whistle out a ghostly tune, and I start to shiver in the cold autumn air. No love, no grace, just the darkness engulfs me. With one last breath, the pontifical night begins to fade, whispering that I can do no better than what I have now. But as dawn begins to sing, filling the land with the sounds of morning, I know what is missing--a swan. Oh, for the beauty of the swan. I'd never get bored, and the responsibility isn't more than I can handle.

Just think about the beauty of it. The flowing curve of the neck, like a rainbow streaming across the sky, would be there every time I looked. Soft, smooth, white feathers, as soft as a pillow made of downy fluff, would cover its body. To watch it glide through the water, gracefully skimming the top of that blanket of blue, would be pure pleasure. Oh, just think about its beauty.

Besides its esthetic value, I'll never get bored with her. In the hot summer sun I'll watch her splash showers of droplets, like tiny crystals, onto the snow-white feathers that surround her. Then, in late fall, when Jack Frost is biting, I'll be there to watch the swan make its bed of golden straw and see winter pass by like sand in an hour glass. When spring comes, I'll watch her little cygnets--those fluffy brown, black, and yellow marshmallows--grow and swim. Don't you see, I'll never get bored with that rose I'll hold so dear.

If its beauty and constant source of pleasure aren't enough, the responsibility is an issue. It's not more responsibility than I can handle. As long as cats hunt and as long as trees grow, my swan will have food and water. I will talk to her and play with her and not leave her forgotten on those cold December nights. Will I give her medicine? I will remember to give my swan her medicine those days she feels like a wilted rose and revive her strength to live again. You know I can handle the responsibility.

As a symbol of love and grace, a swan skims the water of a nearby lake. With a sudden burst of energy it emerges onto the picture-perfect canvas of blue sky. The swan lights up the night with its radiance and beauty and slowly lands on that old tree in the middle of the yard. As I stand there watching, my face starts to glow, and I say to myself, "I can't believe she's all mine." Oh, for the beauty of the swan.

How to Write a Narrative Scenario Introduction and Conclusion

A PICTURE IS WORTH 1,000 WORDS!

① → **WRITING A NARRATIVE SCENARIO** INTRODUCTION: One type of introduction to a paper is called the *"BRIEF ANECDOTE"* or *"NARRATIVE SCENARIO,"* which arouses the reader's interest by painting a specific picture that helps make the author's point.

② → **HELPING THE READER VISUALIZE THE THESIS:** For instance, in a persuasive essay whose thesis deals with proving the strengths of portfolio assessment, the author could choose to write an INTRODUCTION that presents a **TYPICAL SCENE** in a school where portfolio assessment is not used, emphasizing the weaknesses of traditional assessment methods. The reader, then, can easily *"VISUALIZE"* the problem by having been witness to this *"SCENE."* Instead of pedantic generalizations, the reader can be shown the problem in a more real-life *"SNAPSHOT."*

© 1996 M. E. LEDBETTER

③→ **WRITING A NARRATIVE SCENARIO** *CONCLUSION*: The author may use the *CONCLUSION AS A CONTRASTING PICTURE*. In the case of the portfolio assessment, the conclusion may present the same school scenario with one change--the use of portfolios. By then, the reader has *"SEEN"* the problem, has been given the documented/supported reasons, and is ready to *"SEE"* the plan carried out.

④→ **ACTING OUT THE PLAN:**   The scenario conclusion, like the introduction, does more than *"TALK"* a good game; *IT ACTS ON IT*, and the reader is there to see it.

Cathy Facundo
Sample Introduction and Conclusion
Persuasive Research Paper

Portfolio Assessment: The Wave of the Future

Introduction:

Just one hour before the social studies test, nine-year-old Abbey is seated at the breakfast table. Her mother tries to coax her to eat, but she's much too nervous. She has studied the Eskimos and their customs and knows it all forwards and backwards. And she also knows what will happen. It always happens. Her mother's words echo in her tiny ears, "Mommy and Daddy will be so proud of you if you make straight A's." Abbey can feel her stomach beginning to knot up and her palms grow wet with perspiration. Now, just moments before the test, Abbey sits at her desk in school. Mrs. Bishop is passing out the tests, and Abbey looks into space as if she were in a trance. It's happening again. She'll forget half of what she knows, and when she brings home her test to be signed, Mommy and Daddy will be very angry. Stress is a word that should not be part of a nine-year-old's vocabulary.

In progressive times, public schools need to use progressive methods of assessment. Portfolio Assessment fits the bill. With numerous benefits, three of the most obvious are that portfolios are process-oriented; they help develop a partnership between students, parents, and teachers; and they relieve some of the pressure put on students by conventional testing methods.

Conclusion:

It's the day when Abbey is going to be assessed in social studies, and she's at the breakfast table wolfing down her oatmeal. Why isn't she displaying the stress-related symptoms she has had in the past? Maybe it's because Abbey is the one doing the assessing. Abbey's school has adopted a program that uses portfolio assessment. Abbey no longer has stomachaches the night before a test because conventional testing is only a bad memory. Abbey no longer feels the pressure to excel, and her parents don't stress that any longer either. With this new portfolio assessment method, Abbey and her teacher have become partners in the learning process in which Abbey is succeeding. Abbey and her fellow students work cooperatively, and she really enjoys school now. Abbey is one of the brightest children in her class. And she has deleted the word <u>stress</u> from her young vocabulary.

Portfolio Assessment has proven, in many school districts, to be a remedy for ineffective testing in public schools. Portfolios create a process-oriented assessment, better cooperation between students, teachers, and parents, and alleviate pressures faced by students.

© 1998 M. E. LEDBETTER

Lisa Gonce
Sample Introduction and Conclusion
Persuasive Research Paper

Welfare Reform: A Time for Change

Introduction:

The welfare office lobby is teeming with individuals of vastly different ages, ethnic backgrounds, and personal histories. The room hums with the droning sound of their voices as they kill time waiting for their names to

be called for the screening process. Betty, a veteran welfare recipient who abuses the system, is busy drilling newcomer Veronica on how to beat the system. Oblivious of all the distractions, the room full of people network while noisy children run amuck on the dirty floor. Meanwhile, infants wail at emptied bottles and exhausted diapers, and their cries produce echoes that reverberate throughout the building. A disgruntled clerk at the front desk snaps at the unsupervised children. She detests serving these individuals whom she considers parasites of the system. The only small bit of satisfaction she gets is the power and control she wields because she decides who sees a caseworker and who does not. Approaching the desk, another young woman distracts the clerk to inquire about her appointment with a caseworker. This is Amy, a former recipient of welfare benefits, who temporarily used the system to obtain certification as a legal secretary. Now that she is able to interview for a job, she is hoping this will be her final visit to the welfare office.

Betty's, Veronica's, and Amy's situations show how the welfare system can create dependence, cause bureaucratic ineffectiveness, or work as an advantage. For these reasons, now is the time that federal and state governments should reform our current welfare systems.

Conclusion:

Congress has passed the welfare reform bill. President Clinton's signature gave approval for sweeping changes now known as the Welfare Reform Act of 1994.

Reform has changed welfare offices into efficient, streamlined places of business. New guidelines have eliminated abuse of the system by prosecuting and penalizing perpetrators like Betty. The rules now allow for Veronica to draw benefits for a maximum of two years so she can obtain education or training to support herself in the future. She is assured day-care benefits for her three young children. Additionally, she qualifies for assistance from child-support enforcement agencies to secure monthly payments from the children's father. Having completed the government program to achieve welfare independence, Amy is now working as a legal secretary and no longer receives the AFDC and food-stamp benefits she once needed to make ends meet.

Federal and state governments should reform welfare programs because of the advantages to welfare recipients, agencies, and governments. Furthermore, reform abolishes the opportunity for individuals to abuse the system or for the system to disservice individuals through its ineffectiveness.

NAME:_____ CLASS:_____ DATE:_____

Rubric for Narrative Scenario Introduction and Conclusion

I. INTRODUCTION

A. State the *THESIS* of the paper and the *PLAN OF DEVELOPMENT*:

_____

_____

_____

1. Are the *VERBS ACTIVE?* List them:

_____

_____

_____

2. Are the *THREE POINTS TO BE COVERED STATED IN PARALLEL TERMS?* If so, write them below and label the parts, proving that they are indeed parallel. If not, correct the error by rewriting the sentence on this sheet.

a. _____

b. _____

c. _____

B.   How have you used the narrative/descriptive scenario to MAKE THE THESIS MORE PERSUASIVE?

_____

_____

C.   List what you feel to be the MOST EFFECTIVE SENTENCE in the scenario.

_____

_____

D.   Do you feel the scenario NEEDS WORK in any area? Maybe one part rambles or appears to get off the subject. Or maybe one part needs to be expanded in order to "set the stage" for your reasoning that is to follow. Explain the problem that you will work to correct.

_____

_____

_____

II. CONCLUSION

A.   How have you used the concluding scenario to BENEFIT THE PAPER?

_____

_____

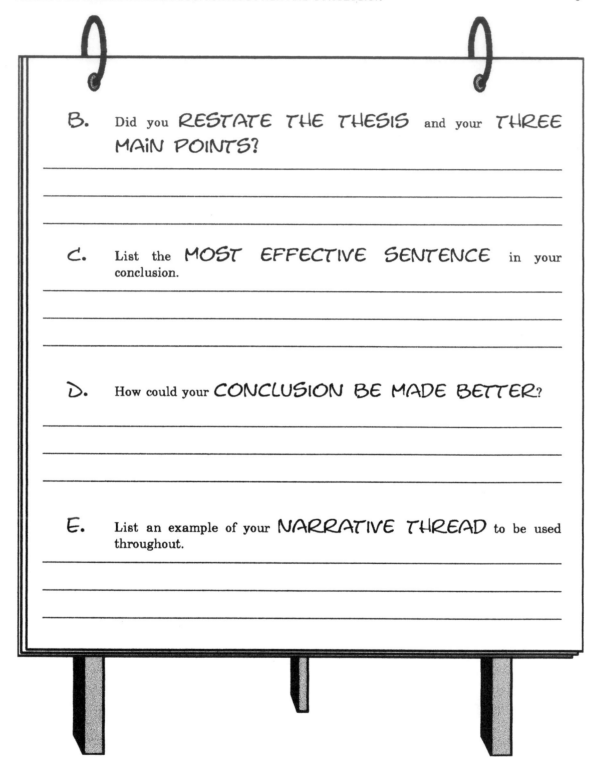

B. Did you RESTATE THE THESIS and your THREE MAIN POINTS?

_____

_____

_____

C. List the MOST EFFECTIVE SENTENCE in your conclusion.

_____

_____

_____

D. How could your CONCLUSION BE MADE BETTER?

_____

_____

_____

E. List an example of your NARRATIVE THREAD to be used throughout.

_____

_____

_____

PERSUASIVE WRITING STRATEGIES

INTRODUCTION--Introduce your **five-paragraph essay** with a **DESCRIPTIVE SCENARIO**. Give the reader a **BRIEF SLICE-OF-LIFE SCENE** that illustrates the point you will be making. Be careful not to confuse the reader by writing too much narrative. Your goal is to **paint a picture** that will make your reader see that your topic is important. **Grab the reader's attention!**

Example 1:

This morning you overslept. Your dog knocked over your steaming hot cup of coffee onto your neatly ironed shirt. You locked your keys in the car. Your boss yelled at you . . . again. After this hard day at work all you want to do is sit back and relax with a quiet evening of television. This idea crumbles like the Berlin Wall as you turn on the TV only to be whisked away to the siren-filled world of brutal, bloody violence. A man frantically waves his arms as he is pushed from a ten-story building. TV violence. A young child is an innocent victim in a drive-by shooting. More TV violence. A majestic lion viciously attacks an antelope. Even more TV violence. As you flip rapidly through the channels, you are filled with disgust as you realize that children could be watching this. **TV violence contributes to teenage crime by the increased number of shows depicting violent acts, by the increased number of violent acts per show, and by the numbing of the audience to the acts themselves** (Michelle Cruz).

(The writer has given a picture of how common TV violence is through specific examples of what we all see all the time. Her scenario ends with her **thesis**, which she will prove in her paper.)

Example 2:

Picture yourself here: white sandy beaches; beautiful hotels; clear, blue skies; the best Mexican food you can eat. This is where Fred Banda is today, sitting in Mexico's finest restaurant about to order some sizzling fajitas with extra onions. Unfortunately, the waitress only speaks Spanish, and Fred is having trouble communicating with her. "Es una senora gorda y fea! Como es usted? Ya odio a usted, es usted maravillosa! Quiero esto! Que?" Fred says politely to her. Suddenly her face turns a vivid red, and her eyes get as big as golf balls. The waitress grabs him by the ear and throws him out the back door of the restaurant. Fred can't help but wish he had paid more attention to his Spanish class in high school. If he had, he would have learned a very important lesson. **Taking a foreign language has many advantages** (Allisa Brill).

(Great **CREATIVE** introduction. Adding her proposed three main points to the thesis would strengthen her argument because readers would be able to see the **ORGANIZATION** that will follow.)

Example 3:

Ten, nine, eight, seven, six, five, four, three, two, one! Blast off!

One man stands over the controls, his face illuminated by a rainbow of fluorescent radars, knobs, and buttons while he stares in a trance through a half-meter-thick glass. A shower of stars flashes by the space station as it accelerates through the void of space, leaving the bright blue and green ball of Earth far in the distance. Beyond transparent windows, the astronauts can see the palatial world of planets and craters all intertwined with this special mission. If we dare to gaze into the mysterious eyes of one astronaut--look deep into his pupils for a reflection--we might catch a glimpse of a dream. We'll see flying vehicles inhabiting the air, buzzing past Mars at the speed of light and raised, insulated buildings decorated with rays of color popping up throughout the space cities on Jupiter. We'll see other universes where the "Jetsons" are considered a realistic cartoon. This incredible fantasy can become a reality with space travel. **The United States should allocate more funds to the space program because it won't fail, the future relies on its great accomplishments, and it will benefit the Earth** (Karen Suire).

(**SOPHISTICATED** introduction. The author's opening sentence creates interest, and her descriptions of the "glimpse(s) of a dream" sustain it.)

Structure:
Draw the structure that you will use and mark your scratch accordingly to make sure no element is missing:

[Thesis]

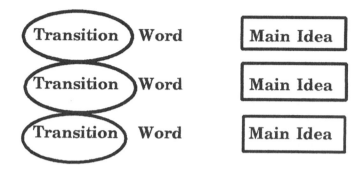

[Restatement of Thesis]

Problems to watch out for in introductory paragraph:

1→   Present a concise scenario; DON'T RAMBLE.

2→   DON'T REFER TO YOUR WRITING by saying, "In the following paragraph," etc.

3→   DON'T USE FIRST-PERSON SINGULAR ("I," "me," "my").

4→   DON'T WRITE, "My three reasons are . . . ." Instead, JUST SAY, "Three reasons are . . . ."

5→   Be sure to INCLUDE your THESIS STATEMENT and THREE REASONS at the end of the introductory paragraph.

BODIES--Your essay will have ***THREE BODY PARAGRAPHS***.

①→   Begin each with a ***TRANSITION WORD*** (such as first, next, and finally) or a transition phrase.

②→   For each paragraph, give the ***MAIN REASON*** in the topic sentence.

③→   Each body paragraph should contain ***THREE SUBPOINTS*** and detailed ***SUPPORT FOR EACH***.

④→   You may use a narrative thread in your body paragraphs to remind the reader of your introduction. For instance, in the second body paragraph of Allisa's paper, she refers to Fred again when she writes the following: As in Fred's school, some high schools require students to take foreign language classes because . . .

⑤→   Be sure to WEB FIRST to organize your ideas.

© 1988 M. E. LEDBETTER

CONCLUSIONS--A concluding paragraph should come **full circle** by referring to the introduction. Usually it will give the *opposite view or picture*, showing the reader what can happen if the writer's plan is put into effect. Concluding paragraphs will be *brief* and will end with a <u>restatement</u> <u>of</u> <u>the</u> <u>thesis</u>.

Example 1:

Today was a good day--no spilled coffee, no keys locked in the car, no confrontations with your boss. When you finally sit back--feet propped up on end table, remote in hand--your TV program options now reflect your idyllic day. You tune in to families laughing and playing together, adventure without graphic violence, and suspense without brutality. You and your children can choose television shows where people learn to <u>solve</u> their problems instead of pushing them off ten-story buildings. Finally society has learned that <u>**TV**</u> <u>**violence**</u> <u>**does,**</u> <u>**in**</u> <u>**fact,**</u> <u>**increase**</u> <u>**teenage**</u> <u>**crime**</u>. Finally we have found alternatives (Michelle Cruz).

Example 2:

If Fred Banda had paid attention during class, he would have realized that he had told the waitress, "You ugly, fat lady! How be you? I hate you; you're wonderful. I want this!" So instead of enjoying a nice hot plate of quesadillas, Fred ended up out on the street, all because he did not realize that <u>**learning foreign languages has many advantages**</u> (Allisa Brill).

Example 3:

As they disembark from the space station, the astronauts enter the palatial world of a whole new universe. Their dreams have become at last their reality. The bright blue and green ball of Earth is only a memory, for today it is Mars, tomorrow Jupiter, and the day after that--well, the possibilities are endless. Man can now conquer what before he could barely visualize--all because the <u>**United States government allocated more funds to the space program**</u> (Karen Suire).

Allisa Brill
UIL Ready Writing District Winner
Persuasive Writing

SMOKING BAN
Caution: Cigarettes Can Be Hazardous to Your Health

Absentmindedly, Fred brings the lighter to the rolled-up paper in his mouth, barely missing his bushy black moustache. Then, coming up behind him, his secretary taps him on the shoulder, not noticing how preoccupied he seems to be. Startled, Fred swings around in his chair, momentarily forgetting the lighted tobacco he has moved to his hand. For Fred's employees' sakes, the smoking law should be passed because it can take time away from business, be dangerous in the work area, and leave bad impressions on visitors to the office.

To begin with, Fred is taking time out from his work every time he stops to light up a cigarette. This can really hurt him and his coworkers in the long run. If someone is always busy concentrating on getting his lungs to burn, he can't be concentrating on much of anything else. That means his work is going to suffer. Or, if worse comes to worse, no work is going to be done at all. Also, how can people smoke and do other things at the same time? Can you imagine a shelf stocker carrying heavy boxes around with a cigarette dangling from his lips? One trip, and BOOM! the thing goes right down his throat, and his esophagus turns into burnt firewood. It would also be kind of awkward to have to worry about putting a cigarette out all the time. "Hey! Boss wants to see you, man!" Worker has to put his cigarette out. "Could you please come help me with this load?" Worker has to put his cigarette out. "Do you know how to fix this thing? It's acting up again." Again the inconvenience of the cigarette. At least these actions would make the trash can or ashtray feel more useful-- poor Fred, he must go through two or three a day.

Second, smoking should be banned because it can be dangerous to the work area. The effects of secondary smoke can last a lifetime, which fellow employees are running out of. The smoke from one person's cigarette can make almost everyone in the room sick. In fact, about fifty percent of the people who die from heart attacks have smoked or been around someone who smokes a lot. So, every time someone lights up, one of his or her coworkers could be the one suffering for it. But, smoking during business hours can also hurt the smokers. For every cigarette they burn, their lungs are looking more and more like chopped-up rat's fur. Next, when smoking, they always stand the chance of burning a building down. If they accidentally drop the flaming wrapper of killer poison, it could easily catch the carpet on fire and WHAMMO! They can hear sprinklers going on and sirens blaring. Maybe Fred should think about this the next time he so carelessly throws a charred cigar into the trash can, waiting for the three-point buzzer to ring.

Last, when a visitor leaves Fred's office, he may go away with a bad impression of the people who work there. No one can have any respect for people who continually try to commit suicide by sticking that "thing" into their mouths. They know better, they've been taught better, and they can do better. But, still they continue smoking. When visitors see ashtrays lying around the business place, full of cigarette stubs, it gives what could be a nice, pleasant atmosphere, a dirty, unclean appearance. If people don't like their work well enough to make it look attractive, it must not be worth it. Then, when someone walks in and sees all of the employees with their feet propped up on the desks and cigarettes in their mouths, it makes it look like no work ever gets done, which could be true. It is hard for Fred to get things done with a suicide machine sticking out of his mouth.

Sadly, Fred and his secretary watch their office go up in flames. If only Fred had been more careful as to watch out for the plant sitting next to him. But, obviously, fire and chlorophyll don't mix. Now, Fred wants smoking banned because smoking can take time away from work, be dangerous to the work area, and leave bad impressions on visitors.

Monica Prince
UIL Ready Writing District Winner
Persuasive Writing

NO PASS, NO PLAY

Kids bash their helmets together, fighting to get the football that is spiraling over their heads. Soccer balls zoom past the sweaty head of the number one goalie from Lee High School and into the white mesh net behind him. Sand flies as a player dives and hits the volleyball, forcing it back into play. All of these sports are fun, but should they be a necessity or a privilege? With the "No-Pass, No-Play" rule in effect, those who want to play will work hard, have a chance at a good future life, and be the "good kids" that get privileges.

First of all, kids have to work hard to show their skills off in a tennis match or to run through the white ribbon first at a track meet, the crowd screaming, cheering them on. Hard work is the only way for everyone but Einstein's daughter to get A's to engulf her report card. With a little bit of determination, kids will soon see that homework stacked a mile high can quickly recede to a regular pile. Homework done, books put away, heads held high, guys walk out to the field.

Those who should have been home studying for midterms look guiltily away as the thought of them at home studying flashes through their minds. The "No Pass, No Play" rule should convince these kids to go home and study. Only through effort will papers and tests become increasingly simple. Only through effort will everyone have a chance at good grades. Once 90's - 100's cover a report card, the player could be allowed to be quarterback, giving him a reason to work even harder in his sport. Sitting at home, television off, books open, every player will finally realize that if he doesn't pass, he doesn't play.

Also, with grades sky-high, kids will have a better chance of having a more productive life ahead of them. From all the lonely hours spent at home studying, they will have developed good study habits. Papers will be easily researched, for now the hard-working athletes know that the library holds many books containing the information they need. With these study habits in place, they will know exactly how to accomplish their goals. Futures for these kids will hold more than a short football career followed by nothing at the age of forty. Instead, doctors, lawyers, and veterinarians will thrive, making the world a safer place. Adding to this safer world will be the lack of gang activity. Fewer kids will have the time or the desire to be in a gang, as it will be more apparent than ever that gangs are for those with nothing to do, with no goals to work toward.

Finally, the trouble-makers, the ones who do not value education, will be separated from those who do. The kids with the desire to achieve will come every day to play basketball as a reward for their good grades. On the other hand, those who are unwilling to advance academically must stay away from the court, only watching the star of the Sterling High School team rack up points. The score going up by three's, the team is happy, playing only for fun. Without those who are unwilling to participate in the total educational program, sports can be more fun. No threats come flying at the good guys, engulfing them, all for making a lay-up. Fewer injuries will follow a rebound when only the good kids are playing.

"98, 100, 91, 93, 99, 98 . . . and 97!" Good grades will allow athletes to play the sports that interest them. Good grades will let them steal the ball from #20 at Lee High. Good grades will make it possible for the winning shot to go hurling towards the goal. Should sports be made a privilege or a necessity? With the "No Pass, No Play" rule, kids will try harder, have a chance at a better future life, and receive the privileges they deserve.

© 1996 M. E. LEDBETTER

Bryan Woods
UIL Ready Writing District Winner
Persuasive/Descriptive Writing

Being a Good Neighbor

The dog is barking, the TV is blaring, the kids have to go to school, and you are already five minutes late for work. Then the phone rings, "Hi, Betty, it's Jane. Listen, I've noticed things have been a little hectic around your house lately so if you'll send the kids over, I'll take them to school." Once again your neighbor has thrown you a ladder on which to climb out of the pit of endless responsibility. A good neighbor repeatedly helps you out, is considerate, and knows you well.

One thing about a good neighbor is that she never ignores a problem and is always eager to solve it. She would watch your kids in a heartbeat just so you could see your sick aunt. And the next day, instead of wanting something in return, she bakes you a pie so that you'll feel better. And she never thinks a thing about it.

 A good neighbor is always considerate. When you accidentally leave the backyard gate open, who comes over and locks it so the dogs won't get out? Or when in the middle of the night someone is lurking around your house, who gets out of bed to make sure it's not a robber? Your neighbor, that's who. And even better, a good neighbor doesn't call the police or fire department for every little thing that you do wrong.

Probably the most important quality of a neighbor is that she knows you well. She doesn't mind lending you a cooking pan because she knows you'll bring it back. And she doesn't care when you park your car slightly in her way so your kid can play basketball. Or when you've got an extra ticket to a ball game, you know that good neighbor will always go.

A good neighbor always seems to know when some things go wrong and always  seems to care. When it's your birthday, Christmas, or you're just having a bad day, a good neighbor always takes time out to do that perfect little something just for you.

How to Use
Rubrics for Persuasive Essay

TWO FINAL RUBRICS are included for possible use.

① **THE FIRST RUBRIC FOCUSES ON AUDIENCE APPEAL** and can be used to help shape any persuasive essay but is particularly useful for those that will be judged in events, sent to contests, or entered for publication purposes.

A. Students must expound on the CREATIVE ASPECT of their papers, concentrating on STYLISTIC DEVICES used for effect.

B. This rubric also asks student authors to concentrate on the APPEAL of their INTRODUCTIONS and CONCLUSIONS, forcing students to explain their attention-getting techniques.

C. Finally, students must prove that they have PROOFREAD for various mechanical errors, such as run-ons and fragments.

How to Use
Rubrics for Persuasive Essay, page 2

② **THE SECOND RUBRIC** is less detailed and concentrates on **ORGANIZATION** and **MECHANICS**.

A. Students must list transition words, main ideas, and supporting details in an effort to prove their understanding of the basic STRUCTURE of the essay.

B. The second rubric also requires the inclusion of FiGURATiVE LANGUAGE/DESCRiPTiVE PASSAGES as one method of elaboration.

C. Once again, students must focus on CORRECT SENTENCE STRUCTURE, detailing their efforts to rid their papers of run-ons and fragments.

RUBRIC I FOR PERSUASIVE ESSAY

After writing the rough draft of your paper, use the following rubric to help with your **revising/editing stages.**

I.   Creativity--

A. Write a short paragraph explaining how your paper could be given points in terms of creativity.   **Box in three specific creative aspects.**

_____

_____

_____

_____

_____

_____

_____

B. **Stylistic devices--**Mark your **rough draft** for all stylistic devices (repetition for effect, figurative language, unusual sentence structure, etc.). List three of your best examples:

① → _____

② → _____

③ → _____

II. Organization--

A.   Draw a **detailed web of your paper, showing your three specific aspects** and at least **three supports** for each aspect.

B.   Introduction

①→ Explain how your **introduction will capture the reader's attention.**

_____

_____

_____

_____

②→ List your **three aspects** stated in the introduction: Make sure they are stated in parallel structure (the same part of speech--all noun phrases or all verb phrases, etc.)

a. _____

b. _____

c. _____

C.   Conclusion

①→   Explain how your conclusion will leave your readers
        feeling good about your paper.

_____

_____

_____

_____

②→   Did you remember to restate your three aspects?
        _____

D.   Briefly, explain how you organized your paper.   (Did you use
        emphatic structure, beginning with the least important point and
        ending with the most important?)

_____

_____

_____

_____

E.   Give a sample persuasive statement for each aspect:

①→   _____

②→   _____

③→   _____

III. Mechanics--To prove that you have proofread for grammatical errors, fill out the following:

A. Spelling--List five **spelling/vocabulary words** from your paper and their page numbers in the dictionary.

① → _____ (   )

② → _____ (   )

③ → _____ (   )

④ → _____ (   )

⑤ → _____ (   )

B. Run-Ons--To prove that you have checked for run-ons, write a **sample sentence** from your paper that you had to check for possible merging errors.

_____

_____

C. Fragments--Do the same for fragments.

_____

_____

D. Repeated Words--Repeat words only for effect. Check your paper by writing any repetition for effect.

① → _____

② → _____

③ → _____

RUBRIC II FOR PERSUASIVE ESSAY

A **rubric** helps you organize your paper by reminding you of the types of errors you should be **proofreading for**-- like a checklist. **Prove** that you have proofread your paper carefully by doing the following checks.

I.   Organization
     A. Transition words/phrases--Remember transition words/phrases are used at the beginning of body paragraphs to indicate to the reader that a point is going to be made. Transition words include words such as *first*, *next*, and *finally*. Write the transition words/phrases that you have used for your three main paragraphs.

①→   Transition word/phrase for first body paragraph:

_____

②→   Transition word/phrase for second body paragraph:

_____

③→   Transition word/phrase for third body paragraph:

_____

     B. Main ideas/reasons--In a persuasive paragraph or essay, you will use three main reasons to persuade someone to do something. List your three main reasons below. Remember that they should be stated in **parallel terms**. In other words, they all should be nouns or similar parts of speech.

① → 1st reason:_____

② → 2nd reason:_____

③ → 3rd reason:_____

C. Elaboration--Choose one of your body paragraphs and prove that you have sufficient elaboration by listing your subpoints below. Remember to check each body paragraph for appropriate convincing details.

Body #_____   **Details:**

① → _____

② → _____

③ → _____

II. **Figurative Language/Descriptive passages**--Each paragraph should contain at least one example of a SIMILE, METAPHOR, PERSONIFICATION, OR OTHER FIGURATIVE LANGUAGE DEVICE and/or an **EFFECTIVE DESCRIPTIVE PASSAGE**. Prove that you have revised your paper to include these by listing your best passage from each paragraph.

A. _____

B. _____

C. _____

D. _____

E. _____

III. Mechanics

A. Run-ons--A run-on sentence is two or more sentences put together without the proper punctuation. The ways to correct a run-on are as follows: period, semicolon, comma and conjunction, or clause signal (BECAUSE, SINCE, ETC.)
Prove that you have checked for run-ons by writing the longest sentence from your paper or the one where you have added the most details. Make sure it is punctuated correctly. Don't stop proofreading with this sentence. Check the whole paper. Sometimes run-ons are the shortest sentences.

_____

_____

_____

B. Fragments--A fragment is a piece of a sentence. Sometimes fragments are the longest sentences because we don't finish them. Check your paper for fragments by writing the most suspicious sentence on your paper--the sentence that might not be a complete thought. Make sure to write it correctly now.

_____

_____

_____

C. Spelling--Read your paper carefully and put a check mark by any word that you might have misspelled. Then list at least five of the words on this sheet, putting their dictionary page number to the side. If you have more than five words checked, add the others to the back of the sheet.

Name of dictionary: _____

    ① → Word: _____   dictionary page _____

    ② → Word: _____   dictionary page _____

    ③ → Word: _____   dictionary page _____

    ④ → Word: _____   dictionary page _____

    ⑤ → Word: _____   dictionary page _____

Section 2:

COMPARISON/CONTRAST WRITING

How to Use the Comparison\Contrast Chart

① **CHARTING VS. WEBBING:** Students may **WEB** ideas for a comparison/contrast paper, or they may wish to make a **CHART**, which makes the comparison or contrast for each point more apparent. Explain to students that the concept of the chart is the same as that of a web or an outline; the difference is that the chart provides **ROOM** for a point-by-point comparison.

② **PREWRITING:** Students should do **PREWRITING ACTIVITIES** of **BRAINSTORMING** for topics about which to write. One way is to ask students to brainstorm several **PEOPLE** (e.g., two friends, mother and father, two literary characters), **PLACES** (two cities, two favorite places, two schools), **THINGS** (two books, two computer games, two types of meals), and **IDEAS** (winter and summer, beauty and ugliness, love and hate). Ask students to choose a topic they would like to chart and to place the topic on the "Topics Compared" line.

③ **DETERMINING CATEGORIES & FORMULAS:** Students should decide on their **CATEGORIES** and **FORMULA** next. Remind students that since most writing prompts ask for points of comparison **AND** contrast, they should determine if their topics are predominantly similar or different. If mostly similar, their formula will be S, S, D. If mostly different, they will use D, D, S.

④ **PROVIDING SUPPORT:** The **SUPPORT** or **DETAILS** should be addressed in parallel terms (i.e., if the clothing style for one individual is discussed, then clothing must be explained for the other as well).

⑤ **PLAYING GAME:** Students may begin writing their rough drafts on the subject of their choice or play the **HERSHEYS VS. SKITTLES GAME** that follows.

COMPARISON/CONTRAST CHART

FORMULAS: SIMILAR, SIMILAR, DIFFERENT or DIFFERENT, DIFFERENT, SIMILAR	CATEGORIES: APPEARANCE, PERSONALITY, etc.	_____ (1) TOPICS COMPARED (people, places, things, ideas)	_____ (2) TOPICS COMPARED (people, places, things, ideas)
_____ FORMULA	_____ CATEGORY	1. 2. 3.	1. 2. 3.
_____ FORMULA	_____ CATEGORY	1. 2. 3.	1. 2. 3.
_____ FORMULA	_____ CATEGORY	1. 2. 3.	1. 2. 3.

HERSHEYS vs. SKITTLES Game

① USING CANDY AS TOPICS: As **PREPARATION** for writing a comparison/contrast paper on a subject of the student's choice, ask students to compare/contrast **Hersheys Kisses** and **Skittles**.

② DETERMINING CATEGORIES: Before passing out the candy, decide the **CATEGORIES** and **FORMULA**. Since most things/people/places can be compared and contrasted on the basis of APPEARANCE and PERSONALITY, suggest to students that these would be good categories with which to experiment on this initial assignment. The third category will obviously be TASTE.

③ DETERMINING FORMULA: Students will easily understand that the appearance and taste of the two candies are different, and they will want to come to the conclusion that the personalities are different as well. Remind them, though, that the exercise prepares them to write a paper on topics that are compared as well as contrasted. The **FORMULA**, then, will be as follows:

        APPEARANCE = D

        TASTE = D

        PERSONALITY = S

HERSHEYS vs. SKITTLES Game, page 2

④ SUPPORTING WITH FIGURATIVE LANGUAGE: As you pass out the candy, tell students that for this assignment you want them to think **METAPHORICALLY**. For instance, instead of the Hersheys being **GOLD** (literal), they might describe it as being **golden like the sun on a scorching summer day** (figurative). This encourages them not only to think on another level but to expand their ideas as well.

⑤ AWARDING PRIZES: This can be done as a group activity, as a class, or individually. **PRIZES** may be given for the best answers. Students enjoy winning extra candy, pencils, erasers, etc., for unusual, clever phrases.

COMPARISON/CONTRAST CHART
(SAMPLE)

FORMULAS: SIMILAR, SIMILAR, DIFFERENT or DIFFERENT, DIFFERENT, SIMILAR	CATEGORIES: APPEARANCE, PERSONALITY, etc.	HERSHEYS ALMOND KISSES (1) TOPICS COMPARED (people, places, things, ideas)	SKITTLES (2) TOPICS COMPARED (people, places, things, ideas)
DIFFERENT FORMULA	APPEARANCE CATEGORY	1. SIZE: LIKE A DOLLHOUSE-SIZE REPLICA OF A PYRAMID 2. SHAPE: LIKE A TEARDROP 3. COLOR: GOLDEN LIKE THE SUN ON A SCORCHING SUMMER DAY	1. SIZE: AS TINY AS A BABY'S BUTTON 2. SHAPE: LIKE A MINIATURE SPACESHIP 3. COLOR: LIKE EASTER EGGS FRESHLY DYED
DIFFERENT FORMULA	TASTE CATEGORY	1. OUTER: SMOOTH, LIKE A RIVER OF CHOCOLATE 2. INNER: CRUNCHY, LIKE CHEWING ON WOOD	1. OUTER: SWEET, LIKE A 1000 SUGAR KISSES 2. INNER: SOUR, LIKE ACRES OF LEMONS
SIMILAR FORMULA	PERSONALITY CATEGORY	1. BOTH ARE LIKE POLITICIANS, ONE THING ON THE OUTSIDE, ANOTHER ON THE INSIDE. 2. BOTH ARE CHEERLEADERS: PEPPY, PERKY, FUN TO BE AROUND. 3. BOTH ARE LIKE GRANDMOTHERS; THEY SPOIL YOU ROTTEN.	1. SAME 2. SAME 3. SAME

Ways to Use Model Essays

① → ANALYZING MODEL ESSAYS AS A GROUP ACTIVITY: One prewriting activity is to ask students to analyze teacher- and student-written essays in terms of **STRUCTURE**. Give students **BLANK CHARTS** and several **MODEL ESSAYS**, divide the class into **GROUPS,** and ask them to determine the structures on which the essays were based as well as the details used for support.

② → ANALYZING ESSAYS AS AN INDEPENDENT ACTIVITY: Another approach is to ask students to analyze various essays **INDEPENDENTLY** and then put students into groups to compare their charts and to check one another's findings.

③ → USING RESPONSE SHEETS: Besides determining the structure, students may use **RESPONSE SHEETS** to critique the essay in terms of **FAVORITE PARTS** and **SUGGESTIONS**.

Resûmay

Teacher Model
Comparison/Contrast Essay
Marked Using Structure Rubric

REAL VS. IMAGINED LIFE

Question Intro

WHO hasn't dreamed of another life? **WHO** hasn't gotten up, gone to

school or to work--day after day, year after year, one routine after another--only

to realize that life, at least the one they had envisioned for themselves, is passing

them by? [Maybe we haven't realized that our real lives differ dramatically from

Three Aspects   ✔   ✔

our imagined lives in terms of housework and work in general but are similar in

✔

the hope they both provide.] *Thesis Statement*

Transition Phrase

If we are honest with ourselves, we realize that our very real days, the

Main Idea

ones we actually get up to each morning, bear no physical resemblance to the

ones we often escape to in our minds. When we're young, we have our **BEDS** to

Support

make, our **ROOMS** to clean, our **CHORES** to be done, and when we grow up we

Repetition for Effect

don't escape. The routine simply escalates. Then suddenly there are more beds

to make, more rooms to clean, more chores to do. Where meals were once

grabbing a sandwich for ourselves, as adults we're faced with **SHOPPING** for,

PREPARING for, and **CLEANING** up after others. Somehow in the real world we

Special Transition

are never released from the bonds of housework. Oh, but how different it is in

our imagined worlds. The fantasy luxuries depicted on the cartoon "The Jetsons,"

combined with very real ones reserved for stars of "The Lifestyles of the Rich and

Famous," pale in comparison to those in our own private dream worlds. Gossip

columns had for years chronicled the details of Jackie Onassis's extravagant demands: satin sheets changed every time her expensively coifed head hit her down pillow and a maid to hang up her designer outfits carelessly thrown atop her designer duvet covers. Sandwiches? Cleanups? World-famous chefs worried about her next meal. She had only to make a request, and, like magic, five-star gourmet food miraculously appeared. And whether most of us would **PUSH BUTTONS** like the Jetsons or **PULL STRINGS** like the rich and famous, if we had our own way, in the most perfect of worlds, housework would no longer be a worry. (It would be relegated to the dusty pages of some unabridged dictionary with the annotation "archaic" crouched in proximity.) *Transition Thread*

If a life without housework could be so different, we can only imagine what a life without work in general would be like. Emotionally the two lives would be worlds apart. We would no longer "burn the midnight oil"; nor would our candles be "burnt at both ends." All the work-ethic adages would be replaced by soothing, comforting messages encouraging a stress-free environment. The McDonald's slogan "You deserve a break today" would become "You deserve a break this hour." Or this minute. Or, heck, break from what, we'd wonder as we'd return to our **MASSAGES**, our **TENNIS GAMES**, our **YACHTING**. Arguments over **DEADLINES** and **JOB TITLES** and **MONEY** would give way to where to **LUNCH**, when to book that **FLIGHT** to Paris or Tokyo or Rome and just which **BEST SELLER** to curl up with this time. (Our dictionary would have another entry from bygone years--several perhaps--namely, "stress" and all its work-

related synonyms.**)** *Transition Thread*

Somehow, (though,) our real lives and our imagined lives do have

something in common. We overlook it or we don't admit it, but if we look hard

enough, if we examine closely enough, we can find it, *Simile* {**like a perfect white**

pearl hidden in a crusty old oyster}--the one similarity, the ⬚ hope. What we

really know as we *HIT* the snooze alarm for the third time, as we *MAKE* our beds

that we'd give a day's salary to crawl back into, as we *EAT* our Kellogg's Corn

Flakes when we'd rather have eggs Benedict, as we *SIT* in classrooms or *WORK*

in chemical plants or *CRUNCH* numbers on Wall Street or sell anything salable,

as we do whatever it is that we have to do, we all the while realize that there

are those times we do have it all, when our real lives have just as much hope

and promise and downright fun as those lives we think we've been deprived of.

A truckload of bonbons delivered from all points East and West can't replace the

Magic 3 Support

FIRST MEAL we ever cooked for someone we love. And reading those best selling

novels can't hold a candle--burnt at both ends and the middle--to what it feels

like to write the *PERFECT SENTENCE* or the perfect paragraph or the perfect

story that someone else would someday curl up with and read and tell a friend

about. Trips to Paris and Rome are the makers of memories, but then so are

Implicit Metaphor

TRIPS in our own backyard, {**gathering dandelions and sunshine and more**

memories still.} [So if we were honest, our dictionary would have to include a phrase, the most important phrase of all, "awareness" we'd call it or "insight." Or "hope.")] *Transition Thread*

So when we dream of another life, when we get up, go to school or work--day after day, year after year, one routine after another--[we need only to pause, *Concluding Statement* just for a moment, and realize that maybe, just maybe the life we find ourselves in isn't so different from what we've always imagined.] It might look and feel a little foreign. Oh, but if we look just so, there it is--that perfect world. There it has been all along.

Liz Alexander
Comparison/Contrast Writing

 and

The *?* and *!* are very different. They each have their own appearances and moods, even though they are found in the same habitat.

First of all, *?* and *!* have different appearances. The most noticeable feature of all is, of course, *?*'s poor, poor posture. He is always slumped over, while *!* is perfectly straight. *?* also often has his head hanging down. And some people, oh dear, don't even draw him with one on. *!*, on the other hand, stands on his head with perfect ease. *?* and *!* are different heights. Don't believe me? Well, if only *?* would straighten up a bit, you would see how tall he really is. *?* and *!* have very different appearances.

Second, *!* and *?* have extremely different moods. *!* is usually happy, but seems shocked by this and that. However, *?* is almost always confused and poking into other people's business, asking them everything. *!* has a strong feeling toward things. It's NO!!! and YES!!! But dear little *?* can never make up his mind, always wanting to know what other people think. Sometimes *?* is doubtful, while *!* is sometimes sarcastic. With such different personalities, they can never get along.

Finally, these species, though having very different appearances and moods, live in the same habitat: English papers, paragraphs, ads, and the like. You may find an occasional one in a nonfiction book, but it is rare. If you would like to find them, the best place to look is in advertisements. They are filled with Wow!'s and Zap!'s and What?'s and Why?'s. Another good place to look is by CAPITAL LETTERS since they, *?* and *!*, are their good friends. Also occasionally *!*, and more rarely *?*, are found in groups having parties. They are often found gossiping to the ever-so-talkative *"*. Other good places to try are posters, books (not math), schools, and almost any place q,w,e,r,t,y,u,o,p,a,s,d,f,g,h, j,k,l,z,x,c,v,b,n,m,l,3,(), and : are found.

As you can see, *?* and *!* are two creatures with very different moods and appearances found in the same habitat.

Sarah Kohles
Comparison/Contrast Writing

Loud Vs. QUiET

Loud and QUiET are very different, yet still the same. They differ in the sounds they make and the moods created by each, while they are alike in the way both have the ability to enclose you, body and soul.

One way **loud** and QUiET are very different is in the sounds they make. QUiET is the sly, frozen hand of death that comes to steal happiness when you're not looking and leaves silent sorrows behind. Sometimes QUiET can be the sound of prayer, a prayer that your mind dwells heavily upon, like a sack of potatoes on your back weighing you down. Each potato in the sack is another prayer that steals into the quietness and interrupts every thought. Yet **loud** is birthday parties that erupt into giggles at the sight of a funny-looking clown. Sometimes **loud** is even a shriek of terror at the sudden drop, jerk, or twist of a topsy-turvy roller coaster car on the most dreaded ride in the entire theme park.

Another way QUiET and **loud** differ is in the mood of each one. QUiET's mood is peaceful and allows you to be a pixie sipping tea while watching the world's every movement. QUiET's mood also lets your mind wander into new places. It can take you deep into the sea to watch the amazing creatures of a world of water, or it can let you soar above the earth, higher and higher, farther and farther away from life itself. However, **loud**'s mood is the craving for fun, the fun of being on that roller coaster, feeling your stomach in your throat as you drop into nothing, then finding that your feet are back, safe and sound on the ground just where they belong. **Loud**'s mood is also the headache-causing atmosphere with speakers blaring music, laughing faces and just plain noise that comes from all around. It feels like your eardrums will burst with the continuous pressure of loud coming at you, giving your head a powerful throb of pain. Even so, you wouldn't change it for anything.

The one way in which QUiET and **loud** are similar is the way they both have the ability to surround you. They both come to enclose you, to press down on your head, not allowing you to escape from their powerful hand, always there beside you, either one or the other squeezing the life out of you, not letting you go. The more you fight their presence, the tighter the grip of their ever-powerful fist. They also have the power to control your opinions on whatever the subject may be. They don't allow you to change your mind or point of view. QUiET and **loud** never leave your side to capture someone else.

Loud and QUiET are alike and different in many ways, some of which are the sounds they make, moods they create, and their effect on people.

Robert Rizzetto
Comparison/Contrast Writing

Hanging Up the Spikes

My passion for baseball began at a very early age. I can still vividly remember the day my father took me to see the Giants play at Candlestick Park. I believe it was on this day that baseball and I became one. There was a period of time when my interest in baseball changed, and my attention was diverted in new directions. Lately, my interest in baseball has been rekindled, and I now realize how much I have missed it. The images and sounds of baseball have not changed much from when I was a child; however, my perception of the game has changed.

Primarily, the images of baseball have not varied over the years. When I was a child, the ball park was an icon of wonder that promised an exhibition filled with insurmountable skill and energetic performance. I still view the ball park as a great hallowed temple that satisfies the sportsman in all of us. Inside these grand architectural marvels, the game itself takes place. From the first pitch to the last out, baseball will forever be the game of the towering homerun and the blinding-fast double play and the no-hitter and the fleet-footed shoestring catch. The ball field has not changed much either. To this day, the cool, green grass of the playing field lends us the likeness of a pure diamond in the midst of a sea of emerald green.

Likewise, the sounds of baseball are both joyful and triumphant. The reverberation of a baseball contacting a heavy-barreled wooden bat instills a sense of raw power as the ball is lifted to a new dimension. Upon that crack of the bat, a loud roar comes over the stadium like a hungry lion awaiting his noonday meal. This roar of the crowd has remained in its primal state since the days of Babe Ruth,

Ty Cobb, and Mickey Mantle. And who can forget the memorable sounds of the peanut vendors hocking their wares for the multitude of starving fans? "Peanuts! Get your hot-roasted peanuts!" has always echoed throughout the stadium, bouncing left, then right, then sideways as if to taunt reluctant customers.

In contrast, since I have grown older, my perception of a game of boys has turned into a multi-million dollar business of men. As a child, I considered baseball a game to be played, a game to determine who is best. Now I am older and I see baseball as a game of who has the most high-dollar players on the team. I also have seen the wizardry and magic of the game vanish from my youthful imagination, only to be replaced by a slew of statistics and calculations only an adult can relate to. Thus, my identification with the game has changed. When I was younger, I couldn't wait to be old enough to play, and now I wish I were young enough to play.

In retrospect, the images and the sounds of baseball have not changed since I was a child. The only thing that has changed is the way we all perceive baseball as we age. Even though the magic of baseball for me is absent, one thing is for certain, the game of baseball will never yield to the phrase "Going, going, and it's gone!"

Russell Gifford
Comparison/Contrast
in Narrative Framework

THE FARM–
IMAGES AND FEELINGS OF NOW AND THEN

On a vacation trip back to my hometown of Ashland, Kentucky, I decided to travel out of the city to my uncle's old farm. I had a purpose in mind as I ventured out of the city and into the shadows of the Appalachian Mountains. I had lost my senior class ring out there, and I wanted to try to find it. As I was driving out of Ashland on Highway 60, images of my childhood appeared in my thoughts. I started recalling the past in vivid detail. As I child I had taken this trip many times with my family, never needing a special reason to go. All I needed was that good feeling of anticipation, the excitement of the unknown in the foreboding, ominous thousand acres of forest I knew as my uncle's farm. My feelings were still the same; the place was still a mystery to me. There were lessons learned here and experiences never to be forgotten.

The trip to the farm was uneventful. The memories were still prevalent, though, as I thought of the past. Old Highway 60 was a beautiful stretch of road, winding in and out of the mountains. The lush, green carpet of forest ran right up to the edge of the road. The two-lane road was now a four-lane highway. The natural landscape was destroyed as the highway ran through filled-in valleys and cut-down mountains. The forest had been cut away to be replaced along the highway by multiservice gas stations.

The trip was complete as I drove onto the access road of my uncle's farm. The scene had changed dramatically. My memories pictured my uncle's sleepy, dull-grey house sitting in the middle of the pasture. The house was no longer there. It had been replaced by a large red brick barn with a shiny black roof. My uncle had sold the farm many years ago to a close friend. The new owner had torn down the

 house and built the barn. I pulled up to the barn and stepped out to witness the beauty of my surroundings. The serene atmosphere was a welcome respite from my hectic adult life. It was just as I had remembered it as a child, as a teenager, and now as an adult. The place was still largely unspoiled and uncluttered by man. As I stood there, the feelings of exuberance and excitement again overtook me. Freedom of spirit abounded, but my maturity had lessened the exciting, challenge-filled, indestructible feelings of my youth.

Hiking up into the edge of the woods, I came upon the old barn built by my uncle. Memories returned. I saw ten or twelve high-spirited, prancing horses in the

corral, all milling about, waiting, with that occasional glance at me, for the hay they knew I'd throw out for them. Here was where I lost my ring, the ring that represented so much to me. It was the accumulation of all I had accomplished in my young life. It was extremely cold that day, and my fingers were almost numb as I grabbed the golden baled hay from the barn. The ring felt loose on my finger. As I threw the hay to the waiting, impatient horses, I felt my ring slip off my finger. I watched, as if played in slow motion, the ring sail out with the hay and land in the hoof-deep mud under the still-prancing horses. The more I urged them to stop, to move away, the more excited they became. There I was on my hands and knees in the mud, the horse manure, and the hay, searching for my cherished ring. Today the horses were gone, and no smell of fresh hay or associated horse odors lingered. My life and my priorities have changed since those times. The intensity of youth has been replaced by the confidence and realism of maturity. If that were totally true, though, what was I doing here looking for that silly ring again?

The search began with shovel in hand. On my frequent breaks, I slipped back in time. Looking out over the pasture, I remembered practicing the barrel pick-up event with my best friend, using this stud quarter horse of my uncle's. The horse's name was Ol' Red, and he lived up to his stud reputation by being the meanest, no good piece of horseflesh I ever encountered. But Ol' Red was fast, and my uncle thought that with a little work and training my friend and I could win the barrel event at the local horse shows. Looking back, I'm not sure my uncle thought we could actually train this horse; I think he just got pleasure from watching us try. The event itself required a rider to ride his mount at full gallop from the starting line to a barrel one hundred feet away, pick up his partner, then gallop back to the starting point. It was the pick-up rider's responsibility to grab onto the saddle horn and swing into the saddle while Ol' Red did his best to stomp, trample, bite, and kick him. There was no challenge too great for my friend and me. My uncle always brought along a bottle of Old Crow whiskey when we went to the weekly summer horse shows. He always let us have a little sip for good luck, but what we didn't know was, he was giving Ol' Red a swallow too. Remembering all of this, I looked away from the pasture.

Would I do something like that now, in my complicated, established lifestyle? This experience taught me that seemingly impossible goals can be accomplished with the right motivation. I was impressed by the whole idea of training a supposedly untrainable horse; I am now less inclined to be as impressed by such wild, uncontrollable challenges. Experience has also proven that not all efforts have a

good ending. There is sometimes pain associated with uncontrolled choices, and we tend to insulate ourselves from taking too many risks.

I grew tired of digging and decided to take a walk up into the forest. It seemed nothing ever changed there. The paths up the hillside were still there. I remembered horseback rides and hikes up into the wilderness. Halfway up the mountain the path broke open into a wide, flat expanse created by strip mining from years ago. The scars of the eroded soil and cut tress, left by the indiscriminate mining for the black gold of the hills, had all but disappeared under new foliage. The path of the strip mines meandered along the side of the mountain, bordered by a sharp high cliff on one side and a steep drop-off on the other. It was beautiful, peaceful, tranquil, with the only difference being the occasional crackle of electricity from the high power electrical lines that transgressed the property. I would, on occasion, ride up there. I remembered deciding one day to take a chance on Ol' Red and ride him up there. Bad decision. Ol' Red peeled me out of the saddle on the way up the mountain by walking under a low tree branch. As I lay on the ground, Ol' Red turned and looked at me; I would have sworn he was grinning. After I remounted, without being bitten, stepped on, or kicked, Ol' Red instantly traveled to the closest briar bush where he proceeded to buck me off into the middle of its sharp, thorny grasp. It was a good thing I hadn't brought my squirrel gun because I would have shot Ol' Red right there. Okay, okay, I'm not giving up I told myself, as I wiped the blood off my arms and pulled the thorns out of my body. Again, I remounted and continued my journey. We reached the strip mine area and proceeded to follow the winding, flat open space. Finally everything was fine with the world. Ol' Red seemed to pick up the pace slightly, but I didn't mind. Just as I was relaxing in the saddle, Ol' Red changed directions, and I found myself on the back of a crazed horse galloping off the side of the flat and down the steep slope of the mountain. There I was, lying flat out on this hell-bound, devil of a horse with my face at the wrong end yelling, "Whoa! Whoa!" How I remained in the saddle I'll never know. At the bottom I dismounted and walked Ol' Red back to the barn. From that day on I always rode mares up the mountain.

I now understand from experiences at the farm that we all have choices in life and we should draw from our experiences the knowledge we need to make the right choices. My trip to my uncle's farm did not yield the much-valued ring, but it did reinforce my feelings of gratitude for the lessons I learned there, as a child, as a teenager, and now as an adult.

© 1998 M. E. LEDBETTER

Karen Solis
Comparison/Contrast Writing

FOR THE RIDE OF A LIFETIME

It occurred to me, as a matter of course through my daily reflections, that a number of similarities exists between life and a roller coaster. As I look back on what has been and consider what is yet to be, I realize that the experiences, events, and attitude with which we "ride" through life determine, to a great extent, how we "unboard" at the end.

The journey starts out innocently enough as we find ourselves standing in line for the roller coaster. Like a twinkle in our father's eye, we are merely there, not quite aware of the experiences life has in store for us. After we board, we are locked in snug and tight. Secure as a newborn baby wrapped in swaddling cloth, we have no idea of what's ahead. Then it begins--that palm-sweating, gut-wrenching, butterflies-flying feeling in the pit of our stomachs as anxious anticipation builds while waiting, waiting for the ride to begin. It reminds us of the first time we went to visit the dentist--the smell, the sounds, the nervous laughter all around us as we waited to go in. Or that time in softball when it was our turn to bat, and the bases were loaded, only one out to go, and it was the last inning of the game,

and we were trailing one run behind. Or that first date, when we wondered if we looked all right, or what we would say, or whether we would kiss, or worst of all--what if our date didn't show! Or that time we bent the bumper on the family car, right

after we got our driver's license, and Mom said, "Wait till your father gets home!" It's that old, frantic feeling of familiarity that overwhelms us while awaiting the unforeseen.

Then, attempting to prepare us for the eventful voyage ahead, the roller coaster slowly begins its arduous ascent. It rises, rises like a concert's crescendo, and the wedding march continues as we walk up the aisle, and suddenly we realize we're not so sure this was a good idea. We must be crazy; we want to turn back, but the roller coaster just keeps click, click, clicking up the precariously pitched incline of its predetermined path. As we reach the top, a scream builds in our throats, releases, and then, whoosh, we're falling, falling endlessly. Through the clouded realm of our minds, we are vaguely aware of the joyous shouts around us as they announce, "It's a boy!" We momentarily relax, relieved, relishing the brief interval before it returns to its previous pace. Picking up speed, seemingly out of control at times, it twists and turns through the choices, the decisions,  like buying the first house, or which car, or which dentist, or what if . . . ? As it courses through the ups and downs, the laughter, the tears, the excitement, the worries, we hang on for dear life, then realize the ride is almost over. The roller coaster banks slowly around the last curve, and then, gliding, gliding, through the golden years, we near the end. With children grown, life's decisions made, a contented, peaceful feeling comes upon us as the roller coaster finally comes to a stop.

Yes, life is like a roller coaster, but with a few subtle differences. With a roller coaster, we can swap out our ticket for another ride, ride it some other time, or ride it over and over again. With life, we get only one "ride" from start to finish. We can experience life with hands held high in the air, as we welcome the opportunity and embrace the adventure. Facing its challenges with our heads thrown back and lips parted in joyous expression, we are jubilant through the twists and turns, gloriously triumphant as we reach the end. Or we can cower, knuckles white, teeth clenched, as we tremble through every change of course, dreading the road ahead. Miserable as we wait for it to end, we finally unboard, broken and defeated.

Although with life we cannot choose to experience another "ride," or necessarily be in control over the events surrounding the "ride" we're on, the attitude with which we "ride" is another matter. So climb aboard and make the best of it, because when it's over, it is over.

Patricia H. Eaton
Comparison/Contrast
Advantages & Disadvantages

THE ADVANTAGES OF BEING A WOMAN

Hey, ladies, remember the battle of the sexes? The whole thing seemed so important at the time. Does anyone know who won? Did anyone win? We thought we were striving to better ourselves. We thought we were being left out. We thought we were missing something. But, as we have always known deep down inside, our gender is an advantage. Our options in lifestyle and appearance are vastly superior. However, there are some misconceptions that remain regarding our collective personality traits. All in all, it is comforting to know that the more things change, the more they stay the same.

Perhaps our most apparent advantage is that we enjoy a lifestyle that men can only look upon with envy. We can have them change our flat tires for us, check our oil and water, and haggle with the garage mechanic because, as everyone knows, we are as helpless as kittens when it comes to car repairs. Doesn't it do our hearts good when we need to move the sofa or to take out the garbage, and he'll just jump right in there? He knows we are as weak as watered-down tea, and we might "hurt ourselves." We can be as pampered as princesses, not opening a door or lifting a package. Who among us has not been at the Circle-K, walking toward the store, and there he is, falling over his feet to get in front of us, so that he can hold the door open? Then, there are those cute sackers at Kroger's. They'll take one look at our forty-pound bag of dog food and case of Diet Coke and offer to help us to our car. Oh, and the shopping privileges are endless! We get chills just thinking about Foley's Red Apple Sale! Just like the Mervyn's commercial, we are there at the break of dawn, chanting, "Open, open, open." We have elevated shopping to an art form. We shop with the skills of an NFL quarterback reading the field, faking to the left, lobbing to the right, double-teaming the opposition, and always reaching the goal line with our prize.

Likewise, our creative approach to appearance is one that men have never mastered. We can keep them waiting for hours while we primp and preen like peacocks. How can they object? We just want to look our best for them. Besides, we construct our ensembles with all the dedication and intensity of architects and commandeer all available storage space in the house for our treasures. We load our handbags with the skill and precision of airline baggage handlers, leaving behind nothing of importance. We are not restricted to a pitiful little wallet and whatever we can stuff in our pockets. We can change our hair style and hair color like changing TV channels. And, as an added bonus, when we go to the beauty parlor to get a "complete makeover," we can catch up on all the latest gossip and what's in <u>People</u> magazine, with nary a mention of truck carburetors or sports statistics or lawn care or the comparative merits of Craftsman versus Snap-On wrenches.

On the other hand, we have a small image problem concerning our collective personality traits. Men think our moods and our minds change as quickly as the weather, and with just about as much notice. They attribute this to our "hormones," or "that time of the month." Have you ever asked one of them about a mechanical or technical principle, or, God forbid, questioned the way they were doing something? They will lower their voice and start

talking slowly and carefully, as if we were three years old, explaining, "Well, honey, this is a carburetor and this is a screwdriver. You put this screwdriver on this screw on the carburetor and turn it and you get more gas to the engine. You need gas to get the engine to run." It can be a truly humbling experience. Perhaps, the workplace is where we are most misunderstood. Have you ever noticed, when a man is aggressive, he is a leader? When a woman is aggressive, she is a . . . well, you understand. Sisters, we have some work to do in this area. There is a way we can strike a balance, here. We just need to figure out how to do it.

In conclusion, as we know, we have always had an advantage. We are not, and have never been, the weaker sex. We are the organizers, the shoppers, the care-givers and the nurturers. We received some concessions in the battle of the sexes. Did we need them? Did we want them? Did we get them? While we have the versatility in our lifestyle and appearance, choices that makes us much more interesting and colorful, we need to work on that personality perception problem. As it is, though, we really have the best of both worlds.

COMPARISON/CONTRAST RUBRIC

Use the following **CHECKLIST** to assist you with the organizing, revising, and proofreading of your comparison/contrast essay.

I. Organization

A. *INTRODUCTORY PARAGRAPH*

1. **THESIS**--Write the thesis of your paper.
   Put **BRACKETS** around the thesis statement on your rough draft.

_____

_____

_____

2. **FORMULA**--Write the formula that you used: _____, _____, _____

   S/S/D (Similarity/Similarity/Difference)
   D/D/S (Difference/Difference/Similarity)
   A/A/D (Advantage/Advantage/Disadvantage)
   D/D/A (Disadvantage/Disadvantage/Advantage)
   G/G/B (Good points/Good points/Bad points)
   B/B/G (Bad points/Bad points/Good points)

3. **STATEMENT OF THREE POINTS TO BE COVERED**--
   Write your three points of comparison/contrast and put check marks on them in the introduction of your paper (e.g., appearance, personality, interests).

   _____, _____, _____

B.   *BODY PARAGRAPHS*--For your three body paragraphs, list the *MAIN CATEGORY* (which should have a separate sentence of its own from the support sentences) and the *DETAILS*.

CATEGORY: 1. _____

DETAILS: a._____

              b._____

              c._____

CATEGORY: 2. _____

DETAILS: a._____

              b._____

              c._____

CATEGORY: 3. _____

DETAILS: a._____

              b._____

              c._____

*For paragraphs explaining a *DIFFERENCE* (as opposed to a similarity), you might find it easier to give all the details for one of your subjects in that category *BEFORE* giving any of the contrasting details for the other subject. In other words, in the category of *APPEARANCE* of your mother versus your father, for example, describe your mother's hair, clothes, and body type before mentioning the same elements for your father.

C.   *CONCLUSION*--Using brackets and checks, mark the following on your paper:

    1. *RESTATEMENT OF THESIS*

2. *RESTATEMENT OF THREE POINTS COVERED*

II. Figurative language/descriptive passages--

Quote *FIVE EXAMPLES* from your paper. Remember that these passages must be appropriate in tone to correspond with the tone of your paper.

A. _____

B. _____

C. _____

D. _____

E. _____

III. Mechanics

A. *RUN-ONS*--To prove that you have checked for run-ons, list the most suspicious sentence on your paper, one that might in fact need one of the following corrections: a period, semicolon, comma and conjunction, or clause signal (because, since, etc.). Be sure to write it correctly on your rubric.

_____

_____

B. *FRAGMENTS*--To prove that you have checked for fragments, list a sentence that could possibly be a fragment, such as "-ing" word groups, clauses beginning with which, that, etc. Remember that most fragments can be corrected by attaching them to the preceding or succeeding sentence.

_____

_____

C. *SENTENCE VARIETY*--For one of your body paragraphs, analyze the types of sentences you have created.

1. *EXPLAIN HOW YOU HAVE ATTEMPTED TO ACHIEVE* variety in length/sentence structure:

_____

_____

2. *GIVE SEVERAL EXAMPLES OF* variety in sentence beginnings:

a. _____

b. _____

c. _____

3. *TO AVOID NEEDLESS REPETITION, WORDS/PHRASES SHOULD BE REPEATED ONLY FOR EFFECT. LIST ANY* repeated phrases used for emphasis:

a. _____

b. _____

D. *SPELLING*--To prove that you are proofreading for spelling, *LIST FIVE WORDS THAT YOU NEED TO LOOK UP* in the dictionary and write the page number and name of dictionary where the word was found.

NAME OF DICTIONARY: _____

1. _____ ____   4. _____ _____

2. _____ ____   5. _____ _____

3. _____ ____

IV. **Partner Check**--Your partner must read your paper and comment on the following:

A. *BEST OF THREE BODY PARAGRAPHS AND REASON:*

_____

_____

© 1998, M. E. LEDBETTER

_____

_____

_____

_____

B. *ORGANIZATIONAL ERRORS:*

_____

_____

_____

_____

C. *MECHANICAL ERRORS:*

_____

_____

_____

_____

D. *SIGNATURE OF PARTNER:*_____

A+

Section 3:

NARRATIVE WRITING

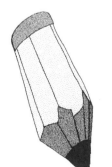

HOW TO USE STORY STARTERS

① → TEACHING IMPORTANCE OF STORY BEGINNINGS: Students gain a better understanding of the importance of narrative beginnings if they are asked to **CREATE SOME STORY STARTERS OF THEIR OWN** to be shared with the class.

② → WRITING STORY STARTERS: Require students to **SUBMIT FIVE TO TEN STARTERS**, varying their approach. For instance, you may suggest that they include one with **DIALOGUE**, another with **SETTING**, a third with **CHARACTERIZATION**, etc.

③ → TEACHING TYPES OF NARRATIVES: Story starters may also include a **LESSON ON TYPES OF NARRATIVES**--mysteries, romances, adventure, slice-of-life, etc.

④ → EXCHANGING STORY STARTERS: Students may **EXCHANGE** starters, **PASS** them around the room--each student writing one possibility--or **CHOOSE FROM A COMPILED LIST** of teacher-chosen favorites.

STUDENT-WRITTEN

ASSIGNMENT:

Choose **ONE** of the story starters below. Write a **THREE-PAGE** (minimum) story using the student-written starter as a "prompt."
INCLUDE AT LEAST ONE QUOTE FROM A BOOK OF QUOTATIONS.

EXAMPLES OF QUOTE INCLUSION:

① → For instance, in your story, a character might be watching a **CAT** stretched out in the sun and comment that "Cats are intended to teach us that not everything in nature has a function" (Garrison Keillor).

② → Perhaps your character is facing **PEER PRESSURE** and is having trouble being independent. He could read or be told this piece of advice that might even serve as your **CLIMAX**: "We forfeit three-fourths of ourselves to be like other people" (Arthur Schopenhauer).

③ → Maybe your character has decided that she alone can solve her problems--with a little help from **CREATIVE ENERGY**. She tells herself something she has read once: "The creative act, the defeat of habit by originality, overcomes everything" (George Lois).

➡ Be sure to use **QUOTATION MARKS** and give **ATTRIBUTION** (tell the source of the quote).

➡ If you use the quote in **DIALOGUE**, you must use a **QUOTE WITHIN A QUOTE**: "Listen, honey," Mother said to me, " 'to thine own self be true' " (Shakespeare). **DOUBLE QUOTES ARE FOR DIALOGUE; SINGLE QUOTES REPRESENT THE SAYING QUOTED**. The **AUTHOR** is placed in parentheses at the end (as in an internal footnote) and the **PERIOD** follows.

OTHER CONSIDERATIONS:

➡ Remember the **IMPORTANCE OF STORY BEGINNINGS**; you must prove your writing ability early so as to interest an editor. You might want to use **FIGURATIVE LANGUAGE, DETAILS FOR EFFECT, AN UNUSUAL SETTING, OR AN ATTENTION-GRABBING CONFLICT** early in the story.

➡ Also remember the importance of **"TYPICAL" STORIES**--ones that many people can identify with, stories such as "Sixteen" and "Eleven."

➡ Consider the **TENSE** of your story. **BE CONSISTENT**. If you begin using past tense, stay with past tense unless there is a reason for changing.

STORY STARTERS:

1. The inside of the bus was hot and dusty and had that bitter, stale smell only sweat has.

2. The car rolled merrily down the road, its passenger concentrating on the wide stretch of gravel that went on for miles.

3. He sat on a boulder, watching the lazy waves create mysterious little pools in low tide. He had so much to think about.

4. It was a satin dress with a flared skirt that skimmed the knees. Lavender-colored and tight down to the waist, her satin dress. That was his reason.

5. I had to admit that my heart did skip a beat when I had first met him. But now I don't like him, not in the least.

6. Multicolored hands dangled from the ceiling. Room 117 was the number. Fun was the description.

7. It was a perfect day for nevers. It was such a dreamy day, until I got that phone call. It was such a perfect day, until I got that phone call. It was a day for living, until I got that phone call.

8. The silver heart necklace tumbled out of his hands. . .

9. I watched as the pitcher of red Kool-Aid tumbled. . .

10. The sand edged its way in between my toes as I walked carelessly down the beach.

11. Kids swarmed all around me, jumping like restless frogs in and out of the water. GEEZ, I hate Saturdays!

12. Sue McQue tossed her hair onto my desk during science today. I know that doesn't sound odd, but I absolutely hate it when she does that.

13. Anna yawned as she woke up. She listened to a Nirvana song blaring from her radio/alarm clock as she looked around the room with her eyes open just enough to make everything hazy. "What?" she thought when the radio guy announced it was the tenth. It was supposed to be the eleventh!

14. It was a warm, sunny summer day. Samantha had been sure that this was going to be a great day for a picnic, but by the look on her mother's face, suddenly she wasn't so sure.

15. The twirling skirts, the full dance cards, the white gloves --all these made Dolly want even more to be just like them.

16. The paper was blank, the pen was out of ink, and the clock ticked on.

17. "All right! Who ate the last of the cottage cheese?"

18. The bright sun dips under the clouds, the fishermen cast their last cast, and the women flock into the houses.

19. I hate these goofy braces. They always slice my fragile lips.

20. A hush falls over the room as she walks in. Mouths drop. Eyes go wide.

21. As the bright, golden sun rises over the mountain range . . .

22. When I opened my eyes, everything was purple. So it was true, just like he said it would be.

23. I lift my eyes to the sun, smiling, thinking of home and the people there waiting for me.

24. Coming home from work, I found a note pinned on the door of my car. It read: BEWARE OF THE DRAGON.

25. I lift my chin stubbornly, holding back tears. They can't see me cry. They will never understand. I must keep smiling.

26. "Okay, everybody, take out your #2 pencils and begin. You will have three hours to complete the test."

27. Being telepathic, she answered the phone, knowing it was ➡him.

➡**NOTE**: A more formal, grammatically correct sentence would read: it was <u>he</u>; however, this would sound too stilted for fiction.)

28. Yesterday my girlfriend (boyfriend) broke up with me.

29. My chestnut curls flow freely in the wind, back and forth, in some kind of rhythmical pattern.

30. As my brother dropped to the floor--the past ran through my head like an old freight train, never stopping, and never going back.

STORY STARTER VARIATION

①→ EXPANDING STARTERS USING TITLES & KEY LINES:

A. Suggest that students write a specified number of **TITLES, STORY STARTERS**, and lines that could serve as **REPETITIONS FOR EFFECT IN A NARRATIVE**.

B. The class then chooses from the list of student-written suggestions, such as the following:
1. **TITLES** --"I Belong on the Beach"
2. **STARTERS** --"I sat staring at the names carved into my desk. . ."
3. **REPETITION** --"Red is not my favorite color"

C. Students **INCORPORATE** their favorite title, starter, and repetition into their own narrative.

②→ EXPANDING STARTERS USING LITERARY ELEMENTS:

A. To serve as a **REVIEW OF SHORT STORY ELEMENTS** and to create an entertaining assignment, ask students to write several possible choices for the following:

1. Setting   2. Character   3. Conflict   4. Dialogue   5. Theme

B. Students exchange with a neighbor, share in small groups, or choose from a **TEACHER-COMPILED** list of best samples.

C. To ensure that students write **DETAILED, EXPANDED SUGGESTIONS**, explain that each student's contribution could result in a grade or that the best selections will receive extra credit, a prize, etc.

Shelly Lopez
Narrative Vignette

I Belong on the Beach

Story Starter

I sat staring at the names carved into my desk, my mind already confused. My head was like a bowl of swirling soup, and in that watery substance I heard my teacher's voice droning on and on about algebra and saw all the names that had been scrawled on my desk with an electric-blue marker: Julie and John, and James and  Rebecca, and Katie and Michael . . . all twirling around some part of my head that felt as if it were about to leak.

Today is not a great day, even if it is Friday.

Maybe I got that impression from the moment I heard my mom's aggravating voice from a distance. I had been smiling wistfully in my sleep at Josh Farrington. I was practically drowning in his ice-blue eyes that seemed to hold so much but say so little. I wanted to run my hand through his ink-black hair and brush my fingertips over his soft, sun-kissed skin and touch his cherry-red lips with my gentle hands. But his gorgeous face faded away into nothing as I heard my mom's voice telling me to get up. Her annoying words shattered his ever-so-clear image in my head, banishing his face to a place where other unfinished dreams and fantasies roam. I groaned and rolled over. It was right then that I fell off my bed, entangled in covers in every shade of red.

Red is not my favorite color. *Repetition for Effect*

I stood up and yelled that I was awake before slipping back into my bed. Wishing sleep to come, I sat there for a minute, closing my eyes tight . . . but no matter how hard I tried, Josh wouldn't pop back into my mind.   I sighed, exasperated, staring gloomily out my window.

And to make matters worse, the sun was glowing a brilliant gold, and the sky was crystal-blue, and the wind whispered seductively: I should be at the beach, not crammed up in the house getting ready for school. I wanted to slip on a green polka-dot bikini, not a green plaid skirt. I wanted to feel the sand between my toes, not my socks bunching up in the front of my Reeboks.

But no, I had to go to school. And as I said before, I had to listen to my math teacher preach about numbers and letters and figures for forty-five minutes. I was tired of hearing her annoying voice lecture about "a=b divided by x." I glared at the small black hands on the clock, silently threatening them to go faster. But they didn't listen, and I caught myself wishing I were in a bathing suit again, walking carelessly on white sand and looking down at almost transparent pale-blue water with Josh at my side. . .

I don't belong in some dumb math class. I belong on the beach, where I can soak my feet in caressing water and let the wind wander its way through my chestnut-colored hair and sip Doctor Pepper all day long. I want to grip a straw all day, not a mechanical pencil that will try unsuccessfully to write the answers to unsolvable questions. The only thing that kept me from going off the deep end was the handsome hunk in front of me . . . Josh. His midnight-black hair and piercing blue eyes were enough to make me stay in math class till the end of time, but he was also blessed with that smile that made his eyes light up like blue-white fire. Then again, those two-inch-in-diameter dimples that appeared on the sides of his lips when he grinned also contributed to saving me from ultimate boredom.

But the beach seemed to beckon me, restlessly calling me to walk on its feather-soft sand and swim in its magical water. So I focused my eyes on charcoal-colored hair and tried not to think of anything else. He turned around suddenly, probably feeling my gaze on the back of that perfect head.

"Sorry to bother you, Sharon, but do you have another red pen? Mine just busted."

At first all I could think was that he knew my name, and then as he showed me his lobster-red checking pen, red ink flew all across my pearl-white shirt. I looked down and saw red splatter-painted all over my ivory shirt. I took a deep breath and sighed.

Red is not my favorite color. *Repitition for Effect*

Slowly I laid my head on the desk that had Julie and John, and James and Rebecca, and Katie and Michael scrawled all over the top with an electric-blue marker. *Full-Circle Ending*

"I'm sorry, Sharon. Gosh, how can I make it up to you?"

Shaking my head, I mumbled that it was all right. I looked up to show that I was okay. "Don't worry, it's just been a bad day." I poked around in my purse until I found another red pen. I handed it over to him and smiled wearily.

"I still feel kind of bad. Hey, it's Friday, and I love the beach. Why don't I take you right after school? You could relax there. The sand is super soft, and the wind seems to purr, and the water seems to cure all your aches and pains." He grinned, and the two-inch-in-diameter dimples appeared.

I smiled.

How to Design the Rubric to Fit the Assignment

① → EMPHASIZING REQUIREMENTS OF ASSIGNMENTS: Students should see rubrics as **"RED FLAGS"** that highlight the **IMPORTANT COMPONENTS** of a paper. Rubrics remind students what to watch out for--what to revise if necessary--and what will be considered in the assessment of the paper.

② → VARYING ELEMENTS OF RUBRICS: When constructing a rubric, you may choose to **VARY THE RUBRIC** for various classes and even for different assignments within the same mode.

    A. For instance, the **FIRST RUBRIC** that follows is more suitable for **STUDENT-WRITTEN SHORT STORIES**, as it concentrates on elements of the story---setting, characterization, plot/conflict, theme, tone/mood, etc.

    B. The **SECOND RUBRIC** is more "generic" and was designed to accompany a **SLICE-OF-LIFE NARRATIVE**-- a narrative vignette. Besides its more fundamental nature, it is evident that it follows a comparative study of similar assignments. This rubric not only provides for peer interaction but also for the student author's assessment of the writing process involved.

③ → ADAPTING RUBRICS FOR INDIVIDUAL ASSIGNMENTS AND STUDENT NEEDS: The point is that the rubric is a **LEARNING TOOL** for both students and teachers and should be varied when necessary to address the assignment as well as student weaknesses.

RUBRIC FOR SHORT STORY

AFTER WRITING THE ROUGH DRAFT OF YOUR NARRATIVE, USE THE FOLLOWING RUBRIC TO HELP YOU IN YOUR REVISING/EDITING STAGES.

① → Title

a. What is your title:_____

b. Explain how it is **EFFECTIVE**:

_____

_____

② → Beginning

a. Remember that all stories need **EFFECTIVE BEGINNINGS**. Write the first sentence (or the first few sentences) of your story below:

_____

_____

_____

_____

b. Explain why it will get the **READER'S ATTENTION**:
(Remember that often an editor will stop reading after an introduction that has failed to interest him or her.)

_____

_____

_____

③→ Setting

a. Quote an example of how you have **ESTABLISHED SETTING EARLY** in the story:

_____

_____

b. How is the setting **ESSENTIAL** in your story?

_____

_____

④→ Characterization

a. Readers need to identify with or be interested in the characters. Quote a passage from your narrative that proves that a **READER SHOULD CARE ABOUT THE PLIGHT OF ONE OF YOUR CHARACTERS**.

_____

_____

_____

b. Explain the **APPEAL**:

_____

_____

⑤→ Theme--Readers want some sort of **MESSAGE** from your story, something they can say they've learned about life or human behavior.

QUOTE OR EXPLAIN your theme (your message):_____

_____

_____

⑥→ Plot/Conflict--Draw a **PLOT GRAPH** of your story, showing at least three rising actions, one climax, and one falling action. **REMEMBER THAT READERS WANT TO SEE CONFLICT, IF ONLY INTERNAL**.

⑦→ Style--To prove that you've tried to develop a style of your own, quote examples of the following:

a. **SPECIFIC DETAILS** for effect:_____

_____

b. **FIGURATIVE LANGUAGE:**_____

_____

c. **ANOTHER STYLISTIC DEVICE:**_____

_____

⑧→ Tone/Mood--What is the tone/mood of your story?

_____

⑨→ Mechanical Errors--Prove that you've proofread for these by citing examples of words or passages that have been revised:

a. **SPELLING**--List 3 words you have looked up:

1. _____

   2. _____

   3. _____

b. **RUN-ONS**--List 2 examples of run-ons or sentences that you thought could be run-ons.

   1. _____

   2. _____

c. **FRAGMENTS**--List 2 examples of fragments or sentences that you thought could be fragments:

   1. _____

   2. _____

d. **TENSE CONSISTENCY**--Explain what tense you have used and list 3 examples:

   1. _____

   2. _____

   3. _____

⑩→ Effective Ending

a. **WRITE** the ending of your narrative:

_____

_____

_____

_____

b. **EXPLAIN** how it is effective:

_____

_____

NAME:________________________________ CLASS:____________ DATE:________

Rubric for Narrative Vignette

AFTER WRITING THE ROUGH DRAFT OF YOUR NARRATIVE, USE THE FOLLOWING RUBRIC TO HELP YOU IN YOUR REVISING/EDITING STAGES.

①→ List the ***TITLES OF THE STORIES*** you ***READ*** during individual reading time in preparation for your narrative writing.

a.____

b.____

②→ Specifically how has your ***READING HELPED YOU REVISE YOUR STORY?*** What ***CHANGES*** have you made because of your reading?

____

____

____

③→ Prove that you have considered the ***SPECIAL PROBLEMS*** involved in writing a vignette or short story by using examples from your piece:

a. ***INAPPROPRIATE TENSE SHIFT:***

➼What tense are you using?____________

➼List examples:

1.________________ 2.________________ 3.______________

b. ***PARAGRAPHING:***

1. ***HOW MANY*** paragraphs do you have?__________

2. Do you have ***DIALOGUE?***__________Did you remember to change paragraphs for each new speaker?_______

c. **SPECIFIC DETAILS:**

➤ Are you using specific details rather than general information?
_____

➤ List three good examples of **SPECIFIC DETAILS** you have used and the **LESS EFFECTIVE GENERAL WAY** they could have been written.

SPECIFIC:

1._____

2._____

3._____

GENERAL:

1._____

2._____

3._____

④→ Prove that you have **FIGURATIVE LANGUAGE OR DESCRIPTIVE WRITING** in your paper by listing three of your best examples:

a._____

b._____

c._____

⑤→ Based on the **ERRORS MARKED ON YOUR PREVIOUS PAPERS**, list the two types of mistakes you have made most frequently:

a._____

b._____

⑥→ Explain **WHAT YOU ARE DOING TO AVOID THESE TYPES OF ERRORS** on this paper and give a specific example for each:

a._____

EXAMPLE:_____

b._____

*EXAMPLE:*_____

⑦→ We have studied **EFFECTIVE BEGINNINGS**. How is your beginning effective? Give two specific reasons.

a._____

b._____

⑧→ Have two **PROOFREADERS** sign this paper and comment on the content and mechanics:

a. **READER ONE:**_____

COMMENT:_____

_____

_____

_____

b. **READER TWO:**_____

COMMENT:_____

_____

_____

_____

⑨→ What is your **FAVORITE PART** of your story?

_____

_____

_____

⑩→ Explain the **WRITING PROCESS** you went through.

_____

_____

_____

_____

➤What **GRADE** should you make and **WHY**?_____

_____

_____

First-Day Impressions

① → WEBBING: Ask students to make a **SENSE WEB** of their first-day-of-school impressions, concentrating on specific SIGHTS, SOUNDS, SMELLS, TASTES, and FEELINGS. Encourage class sharing of each sense, writing various phrases on the board or overhead to serve as a "resource pool" of ideas.

② → FREEWRITING: Give students 5-10 minutes to **FREEWRITE** about actual--or imagined--happenings involving their first day at school. They may choose to include many of their webbed images and to develop others as they freely associate.

③ → USING MODELS: Students should share their freewriting, perhaps **READ THE MODELS THAT FOLLOW**, and revise their drafts into a narrative vignette that paints a picture of that memorable day.

THE DARK-BROWN LACE-UPS

I had just gotten the shoes the week before--dark-brown lace-ups like Tiny Tim's in <u>A</u> <u>Christmas</u> <u>Carol</u>. I hadn't really given it much thought the year before in sixth grade when Mrs. Hockersmith showed us the film right before Christmas vacation. But I knew then, that seventh-grade year, my feet encased in their stiff prisons, exactly how Tiny Tim must have felt, but then it wasn't his first day of seventh grade, and he at last could walk. For him it was a miracle, like Scrooge's kindness. But for me, my feet had only been pronated, wayward, lazy, leaning inward slightly, but because of the shoes, they would be soldier straight, and I would be made fun of.

Already it was happening. My new navy and maroon fall Bobbi Brooks dress with its bright white Peter Pan collar and my freshly bobbed haircut couldn't make up for the fact that on my feet weren't the stylish feminine slippers or penny loafers the other girls wore. I wore army boots when army boots weren't in. And I was aware of them every minute that first day.

Crossing over the school's logo, our DJHS displayed in the tiled floor at the entrance of the school, I found myself looking at everything from the bottom up. Would I ever notice faces again, or would my gaze be forever focused on feet? For the first time I realized school was nothing more than a stampede of paired feet. Parked like guards to the palace were the tennis shoes of what surely must have been Coach Dismukes and the three-inch stiletto heels of what surely must have been our unmarried, sexy French teacher, Miss Pivito. Their first hall duty of the new year, I assumed without looking up. Then I was bombarded with the masses of summer sandals, Weejuns, flats, Mary Janes--all very "in" shoes, all belonging to everyone but me. Some were huddled near lockers in groups, some in pairs en route to the commons, or others already on their way to their classes. Every pair of feet seemed to have another pair of feet as companions. Everyone, that is, except me.

When I dared look up past feet--at knees, at midriffs, at faces--I saw almost immediately what I had feared. I <u>was</u> being made fun of. I saw it. I knew it. And I knew I would die. There, down the hall, was Suzanne Beady, her hand drawn up to cover her mouth, as if what she was whispering to another girl, whose hand was in the exact same position as Suzanne's, was a national secret of some sort, so top secret that five adolescent fingers and a rudely cupped palm were required to intercept the offending air waves lest the enemy detect the message.

Her hand might have hidden her words, but somehow the object of Suzanne's ridicule was always apparent. If your hairdo didn't meet her approval, her eyes

never left the top of your head. If your skirt was too long or too short, she transfixed her eyes to the appropriate length, either farther up or farther down your leg. You could almost judge how many inches off you were if you stared at her staring long enough. So, of course, today I knew where those laser orbs would stop--at my feet, my cowering feet, if feet can actually cower.

And I wasn't wrong. I froze at the top of the "J" in the middle of our tiled DJHS. And right there, almost my first step of my seventh-grade year, I thought of what Daddy had said when I had shown him my dark-brown lace-ups, shoes unlike any other seventh-grader's shoes.

"So what?" he had said. "You want to be a carbon copy of everyone else?"

I had thought at the time that he hadn't understood. What did he know, I had reasoned; he was my father. But right then, at the top of the "J," my first day in seventh grade, I decided he was right. The shoes were mine for a whole year, and there was nothing I could do about it. Nothing that is except realize that if it hadn't been the shoes, it would have been something else. Right then and there, at the tip-top of the "J," in good old DJHS, right then, my dark-brown lace-ups stiff and unfamiliar and unwelcome on my feet, I realized that girls like Suzanne Beady would always need something to talk about.

And from then on I decided that girls like me wouldn't care-- dark-brown lace-ups or not.

Nelda Cruz
Narrative Writing
Assignment: First-Day Impressions

Some Things Never Change

It was August 15, 1994, and as I set foot on the walkway to the entrance, I knew nothing had changed. The flags still clicked against the pole when the wind blew air out and almost as quickly swallowed it back up, the flower bed still lay alone and neglected, and the orange and white painted horseshoes on the sidewalk were so old and worn you could almost see the hundreds of thousands of footprints in them.

As I opened the glass door, I immediately noticed that the same Lysol smell lingered stiffly, and, as usual, the air conditioning was chilling everyone in the office but was broken everywhere else. In the commons the plants looked freshly cut and the flowers pruned, and the message board was brightly displaying "Welcome Back!"

Many people were walking around restlessly, probably wondering if they were ever going to wake up from this horrible dream, but sadly, it was all so true. As people poured in from the buses, I was reminded of the wedding saying "something borrowed, something new, something old and something blue." The borrowed was lunch money, the new was clothes, the old was eighth graders, and the blue was, of course, blue jeans.

There were new kids I was especially glad to see, but, naturally, there were still some of the old ones that I could have lived without. Without batting an eyelash, I saw Bryan and stopped dead in my tracks. He was a towering five-foot-nine, his eyes were pools of green, and his hair flopped over his ears just playfully enough to give him the teddy bear look but just suave enough to give him the look that would make him into a tall, dark, handsome lawyer. Well, I must have been staring because he came up and asked me what I was staring at. I was just about to let the words spill out of my mouth when the bell rang. With a wave of the hand and a "Catch ya' later," he left me standing in the commons, people all around me rushing to their advisory classes.

As I walked down the eighth grade hall, people were shoving and pushing and shouting. In the middle of the commotion, my best friend Stephanie was standing next to my best friend Jennifer trying to tie her shoe, fix her hair, and hold her books all at the same time so it looked like she was trying to direct traffic.

I gave a quick hello and slid into Mrs. Barron's room just as the tardy bell rang. Sitting alone with twenty people jabbering about who wore what, who was going out with whom, and how Jaime broke up with Blake as fast as Carl Lewis ran the 100 was kind of like being trapped inside a telephone wire.

I never even glanced up, but I could already tell that Carrie Housberger and Jenny Tatom were already studying everyone's outfits and every move they made. I already had my heart set that I wasn't going to be trapped into their little game. I just stood up and started walking toward their desks.

No one laughed, no one pointed, and no one told secrets when I tripped over Jenny's purse and tumbled to the ground. Instead, Carrie gave me her hand and said, "Cute outfit, want to sit with us?"

Well, after that, we became friends, and soon Bryan was a very good friend of mine, too. And although some things never change, maybe some of the best things do.

Rituals

① → Read the teacher sample *"MORNING RITUAL."*

② → Discuss the components of the piece, using the *ANALYSIS SHEET*.

③ → After reading *STUDENT SAMPLES*, ask students to brainstorm their own *PERSONAL OR FAMILY RITUALS* →

FAMILY PICNIC

Morning Ritual

Those childhood mornings before Pettie would rise from bed, it was always the same.

At first it would be that single strip of light easing its way between the shade and Mama's lace curtains, and it would always be the same spot-- the bottom right-hand edge next to the guardian angel who, Pettie's mama said, watched over Pettie when her mama couldn't. Or maybe it would be the sounds, the constant gentle rumblings--soothing sounds-- like a giant tabby cat's purr or the sound of the sun warming up for the day or maybe just the peacocks, the bishop's peacocks calling down the lane, Argus and his one hundred eyes, Pettie would think. Something else to watch over her as she slept, Pettie's daddy would always say.

Pettie could never really be sure what would actually call her from sleep those mornings just as she could never be sure the nights before which of her favorite dreams she could look forward to that night.

Maybe it would be the one where she climbed the great oak in Mrs. Fagin's backyard--oh, how many steps there were--hand-hewn steps fastened painlessly to the sprawling tree so that neighborhood kids could rise to its height, position themselves on a makeshift platform, attach their eager little hands and feet to their beloved trolley and sail down the tree, down the hill, down the other side of the world, it seemed, and land smack-dab in Mr. Fagin's squash or tomato plants--anywhere they could to relish the thrill of it all.

Or perhaps the dream would be the one where Pettie played hide-and-seek with her daddy. He'd call her name over and over. "Where's my little Pettie?" he'd sing and she would try to hold her breath, try not to give herself away, but it was always her giggles that did her in. Her daddy would come running, scoop her up from this nook or that cranny and off they'd go. Sometimes Pettie and her daddy would climb fallen trees, hundred-year-old pines making way for progress, and in her dreams the trees would grow bigger and bigger still, rising like mountains in the vacant lot next to their house. And from their very tiptops she could see all the way to China, Pettie always said. And in her dreams Pettie and her daddy would play longer and run faster and laugh and laugh and their adventure would never seem to end.

But whichever the dream on any particular night, she would ease from it gradually like the light finding its way up and over the angel, cutting a bold, confident path almost to Pettie's bed. On those childhood days one minute Pettie would be up in that old oak or at the top of her fallen pines and the next, she'd hear them--the peacocks--the bishop's peacocks down the lane. And before she would even turn over, before she would even stretch, her nighttime body still tucked lovingly under layers of the past--Grandma Rollo's cross-stitched sheets, Aunt Frieda's quilt and at her feet Gertrude's throw knitted in just three months for Eileen's wedding--before Pettie really woke to the world, she would hear her mama.

From Pettie's antique four-poster bed--acquired from Pettie's Grandma Wilson--she'd hear her mama in the kitchen, sizzling bacon, plunking down silverware and plates and cups to be filled with thick, steaming, chicory coffee like her daddy liked. But most especially Pettie would hear her. Her mama. The rise and pitch of her voice. Pettie couldn't hear the words, she could never hear the actual words, but that didn't matter. It wasn't what she was saying that Pettie needed to hear. She just needed to know that her mama was there, doing what she always did, drawing out the aunts and uncles and Cousin Kallie. Kallie, like the brother and sister Pettie never had, all rolled into one hundred stringy pounds.

Pettie would hear Kallie giggle at something one relative or another said or at a tomboy tale of her own, one Kallie would spin out of nowhere those early mornings while Pettie lay in bed.

And some mornings Pettie would stop to think about it all--Kallie practicing to perfect a story, like Aunt Frieda and Grandma Rollo and Gertrude must have practiced sewing and stitching and knitting. All those people busy weaving their lives with hers. And sometimes she would think she would hear Aunt Frieda in the kitchen starting up her pitch: "How're your potatoes comin' out, old man? ...They're not comin' out at all--you have to dig 'em out." Starting her famous--at least in their neck of the woods--knuckle rap: old lady sharp knuckles rapped on wood, like a vaudeville ending to a joke, something done in a minstrel show maybe, something done as a practiced finale to a practiced bit.

But it would be only Kallie that Pettie would hear, Kallie sounding like Frieda, but that was something still.

And Pettie would hear her daddy's bedside radio, a show-tune sort of station, a dash of Music Man cadence to most of the songs and a pinch of her daddy himself every once in a while. She'd hear his electric razor buzz up and over bone and flesh, around nose, then down. Four times down. Always four swipes for top of the lip. Then shaver would pause, humming like a bee midflight, before it would take its last two passes-- one sideburn, then the other, and then only the music.

Pettie would hear it all--the peacocks, Mama, Kallie, Daddy, the house. The whir of it all. She would hear them as they called out to her, wrapping her in their world, those mornings long ago.

Analysis of "Morning Ritual"

1. The author paints a picture of childhood mornings primarily using SENSORY IMAGES based on the sense of SOUND. Quote **FIVE PASSAGES** that represent five different sounds Pettie hears.

   A._____

   B._____

   C._____

   D._____

   E._____

2. Authors use SPECIFIC DETAILS FOR EFFECT rather than general, less vivid word choices so that readers can truly visualize a scene. Quote **THREE EFFECTIVE SPECIFIC DETAILS** from the piece.

   A._____

   B._____

   C._____

3. FIGURATIVE LANGUAGE is another way for authors to present their images to readers. Often authors show their readers what something **IS** and also what it is **LIKE**. The literal and figurative details combined add up to a more vivid, more interesting picture.

Quote **TWO EXAMPLES** of each of the following **FIGURATIVE LANGUAGE DEVICES**:

    A.   SIMILE: (Be sure to quote **BOTH** elements being compared.)

_____ & _____

    B.   METAPHOR: (Remember that **EXPLICIT** metaphors use a **"BE" VERB** and **IMPLICIT** do not.)

_____ & _____

    C.   PERSONIFICATION:

_____ & _____

    D.   HYPERBOLE:

_____ & _____

4.   QUOTE examples of the following and **EXPLAIN** their effect.

    A.   FULL-CIRCLE ENDING
       ❶ **QUOTE:** _____

       ❷ **EXPLANATION:** _____

    B.   ALLITERATION
       ❶   **QUOTE:**_____

       ❷   **EXPLANATION:**_____

    C.   DIALECT
       ❶   **QUOTE:** _____

       ❷   **EXPLANATION:** _____

5.   Quote an ALLUSION to mythology and an allusion to a certain type of performance. What **PURPOSE** do they serve?

     A.   MYTHOLOGICAL ALLUSION:

       ❶   *QUOTE:* _____

       ❷   *PURPOSE:* _____

     B.   ALLUSION TO PERFORMANCE:

       ❶   *QUOTE:* _____

       ❷   *PURPOSE:* _____

6.   A.   Quote two references the author uses to indicate a LINK between Pettie and her **PAST**.

       ❶ _____

       ❷ _____

     B.   How do these references help establish the **THEME** of the piece?

_____

_____

7.   Explain from what POINT OF VIEW the story is written and give **EVIDENCE** to support your choice.

_____

8.   Writers are concerned not only about WHAT their works say but about HOW they are written as well. An author's **SENTENCE STRUCTURE** helps create his or her **VOICE**. Quote passages that serve as examples of the following stylistic structures:

A. FRAGMENT FOR EFFECT: _____

B. MAGIC THREE: _____

C. PARTICIPIAL PHRASE: _____

D. REPETITION FOR EFFECT: _____

9. List **FIVE ASPECTS** of Pettie's RITUAL (e. g., "At first it would be that single strip of light. . .").

A. _____

B. _____

C. _____

D. _____

E. _____

10. BRAINSTORM a list of **FIVE RITUALS** from your own past.

A. _____

B. _____

C. _____

D. _____

E. _____

ANSWERS: Analysis of "Morning Ritual"

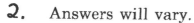

1. Answers will vary. Some possibilities are the following:
   - A. "the bishop's peacocks calling down the lane"
   - B. "sizzling bacon"
   - C. "plunking down silverware"
   - D. "The rise and pitch of her voice"
   - E. "her daddy's bedside radio"

2. Answers will vary.
   - A. "the bottom right-hand edge next to the guardian angel"
   - B. "Mr. Fagin's squash or tomato plants"
   - C. "up and over flesh, around nose, then down. Four times down."

3. Answers will vary.
   - A. "the sounds . . . like a giant tabby cat's purr" and "the trees . . . rising like mountains"
   - B. "Kallie . . . all rolled into one hundred stringy pounds" and "nighttime body still tucked lovingly under layers of the past"
   - C. "single strip of light easing its way" and "light finding its way . . . cutting a bold, confident path"
   - D. "down the other side of the world, it seemed," and "she could see all the way to China"

4. Answers will vary.
   - A.
     - ❶ "those childhood mornings . . . those mornings long ago"
     - ❷ The repetition helps to create a poetic quality and emphasizes that these sounds occurred with regularity; the mornings *were* the sounds.
   - B.
     - ❶ "tomboy tale"
     - ❷ Alliteration adds a certain internal cadence, a rhythmic quality within a sentence.
   - C.
     - ❶ "comin' . . . 'em"
     - ❷ The telling of the "joke" in its original, nonstandard form gives authenticity to the passage. The reader has a more accurate picture of the serious question and its humorous answer.

5. Answers will vary.

A. ❶ "Argus and his one hundred eyes"
　　 ❷ Pettie has been told the tale of Argus, a giant with one hundred eyes, and connects the sounds of the peacocks to safety, to her daddy, to home.

B. ❶ "like a vaudeville ending . . . something done in a minstrel show"
　　 ❷ Again, the link to the past is established. Pettie remembers her aunt's old routine, a part of their family's *personal* history, and we as readers realize it's a connection to our *collective* pasts as well.

6. Answers will vary.
　 A. "tucked lovingly under layers of the past" and "Pettie's antique four-poster bed--acquired from Pettie's Grandma Wilson"
　 B. The themes of security of home and a sense that the past and present are inseparably linked are evident in the fact that Pettie's present self is "tucked lovingly under layers" of her past relatives; even the very bed she wakes from daily has its own family history.

7. Limited omniscient--The author knows Pettie's dreams and the fact that "some mornings Pettie would stop to think about it all."

8. Answers will vary.
　 A. "The whir of it all."
　 B. "down the tree, down the hill, down the other side of the world"
　 C. "trees . . . rising like mountains"
　 D. "practiced finale to a practiced bit"

9. Answers will vary.
　 A. "the sounds, the constant gentle rumblings. . ."
　 B. "where she climbed the great oaks. . ."
　 C. "where Pettie played hide-and-seek"
　 D. "would hear her mama"
　 E. "would hear Kallie"

10. Answers will vary.

Teri Hagen
Narrative--Ritual
Published in <u>Creative</u> <u>with</u> <u>Words</u> 1993

A BLACKBERRY SUMMER

When we first moved into the house on Orchid Street, I didn't like it. My room was hot, cramped, and *STUFFY AS A* *Simile*

TRAIN IN THE MIDDLE OF THE SAHARA And the looming *SKELETON-LIKE GRAY* *Simile*

AND WHITE FRAME of the place scared me. I dared not imagine living there, *Repetition*

BUT THE BACKYARD, OH, THE BACKYARD. It was a huge, long mass of

plentifully growing trees and blackberries.

Goodness, how I loved them. The sour-sweet, kind of tart taste of them

appealed to my mouth ever so much. It made my mother so mad when Leann,

the girl across the street, her brother Timothy, and I would simply pick them

and eat them, without washing them. Mother said that we didn't know what

had been on those blackberries. *SHE SAID THAT LITTLE ELVES COULD HAVE* *Humor*

USED THE BATHROOM ON THEM. OF COURSE, WE DIDN'T BELIEVE HER. ELVES

HAD TOILETS IN THEIR UNDERGROUND HOMES.

Everyday, like clockwork, we would check for new, darker blackberries. *Personification* *Participial Phrase & Personification*
As the *WIND WHISPERED* around us, *MAKING THE TREES DO BALLET*, we ran.

We ran barefooted through the deep green grass. *Simile* **WE FELT AS IF THE WORLD**

Simile & Hyperbole
CRUMBLED BEHIND US, **AS IF WE WERE THE ONLY ONES LEFT IN THE UNIVERSE**

and the fence with the plentifully growing blackberries was our own world.

Nothing could harm us here. Not a parent, dog, cat, or any other being could

stop us. We were alone.

And the blackberry cobbler. One day out of the summer, Mother would

Participial Phrase
send us on a blackberry harvest. **ARMED ONLY WITH BUCKETS FROM RECENT**

Simile
VISITS TO MCDONALD'S, we trooped out into our own world. **IT WAS LIKE A**

CONTEST, the most blackberries, the most cobbler, but that really didn't

matter to us. We just enjoyed the right to freely pick every deep purple

blackberry we could find. **OUR LITTLE HUNT LASTED FROM AFTER "SESAME**

Specific Detail
STREET" WAS OVER TO WHEN THE "MUPPET SHOW" WAS DUE TO AIR.

The next day was considered a cooking day. **BLACKBERRY COBBLER**

Hyperbole
BY THE TONS sat itself all over our kitchen, but the smell was heavenly.

Noun Absolute
Those nights, lying in my bed, **MY STOMACH BRIMMING WITH THE**

SCRUMPTIOUS BLACKBERRY COBBLER, I thought of the many summers ahead

of me and the many summers behind me and slipped into my dreams.

Matthew Weber
Narrative--Ritual
Published in <u>Merlyn's</u> <u>Pen</u> 1995

CRAWLEY'S
FISHING
CAMP

FISHING: The Family Ritual

Fishing comes the first Saturday of summer. That's the day when we load up the boat and head for the bay. We wake up at 4:30 a.m. to the *Imagery* **AROMA OF FRESH BREWING COFFEE THAT FILLS THE AIR**. I get out the flashlight, chain up the dog, open the fence, and latch the boat up to the truck while listening to the *Simile* **CRICKETS SINGING LIKE A CHOIR**. My dad throws the morning newspaper in the back of the pickup, and we're on our way.

I turn on the radio, listening to the weather report while watching the rows of trees fly by. I see the *Metaphor* **CHEVRON PLANT PUFFING OUT CLOUDS OF MARSHMALLOWS THAT FLOAT THROUGH THE BLACK SKY**. I hear the huge *Imagery* **EIGHTEEN-WHEELER ROARING** as it passes by.

When we get there, Crawley's Fishing Camp is just opening at 5:30. We walk in, and we're greeted by the *Imagery* **ODOR OF FRESH SHRIMP AND CRABS**.

I pour the bucket full of shrimp into the live well, and we're on our way with the *Imagery* **WIND IN OUR HAIR**. When we get to our spot, we hook the shrimp and throw it into the *Simile* **WATER THAT LOOKS LIKE IT CAME OUT OF AN OZARKA BOTTLE**. I watch the cork until the fish pulls it under and then **MY HEART** *Simile* **STARTS BEATING LIKE A GREYHOUND RUNNING**. When I get it up to the boat, I recognize it's a four-pound trout. After I get the hook out, I measure it and *Simile* **PLACE IT IN THE ICE CHEST AS IF IT WERE A HUNK OF GOLD**.

When the fish stop biting, *Imagery* **WE PULL OUT THE MORNING PAPER, PUT IT OVER OUR HEADS SO WE DON'T TURN INTO PRUNES**, and take a siesta.

We wake up and decide to call it a day. When we pull up to the dock, I take one last smell of the water and air and decide I'll need to remember these moments forever.

Angela Benedict
Merlyn's Pen: April/May 1995
Ritual

SUMMER DAYS AND NIGHTS

Summer equals rituals and rituals equal summer, especially in the evening

Magic 3

when the **BIRDS FLY HOME, THE RACCOONS AND OWLS COME OUT TO PLAY,**

AND THE BUGS COME TO FEAST ON YOU FOR HOURS. No matter what you are

Personification

doing in the evening, outside the **BUGS WILL FEAST**--feast **WHILE YOU RUN,**

Magic 3

WHILE YOU SIT, AND WHILE YOU HIDE. And when everyone is gathered on

the porch after a game of kick-the-can, the bugs devour. While the kids are

making jokes, giggling and laughing, the adults sit and talk. They talk

about the day, the kids, and the night. But the kids still giggle and laugh,

without a care in the world.

But before the sitting and the talking, before the jokes and laughter,

that's when most of the fun comes. You play kick-the-can. You don't quit

because you are hot and tired--the night is cool. And you don't get tired,

because you are having too much fun to get tired. **BUT WHEN THE DARK**

Personification

CLOUDS OVERCOME THE SUN IN BATTLE and fill the night sky, it is time to

quit.

You know when it gets dark you have to go to sleep until **THE SUN'S**

Personification

RAYS PEEK BEHIND YOUR BLINDS AND QUIETLY WAKE YOU. The sun wakes

you so you can go out and play and soak up its warmth. **BUT NOT THE**

Personification

MOON. HE SHUTS YOUR BLINDS AND TURNS OUT YOUR LIGHT.

Inverted Sentence Order

THE SUN YOU LISTEN TO WITH ALL YOUR ATTENTION, and the moon

you ignore like the voice of your parents when they tell you to go to sleep.

But just as you obey your parents, reluctantly you obey the moon. But not

for long. You wait until they think you're asleep and **YOU STRIKE AS**

Simile

QUICKLY AS A KING COBRA BUT AS QUIETLY AS A MOUSE. You sneak up to

the living room door and eavesdrop on all their stories and tall tales.

Then the fun ends when you hear the adults telling each other good

night. You quickly but quietly return to your room and fall into a deep

sleep. You sleep for what seem only like seconds but is really hours on the

Metaphor

CLOCK OF GOD. But soon--very soon--the sun will peek through your blinds

and tell you it's time to start a brand-new day.

Jennifer Stephens
Narrative--Ritual
Published in <u>Stone</u> <u>Soup</u> 1995

GRANDMA'S BREAKFAST

Personification
THE TREES AWAKING, THE SUN COMING OUT FROM ITS NAP, AND THE
Magic 3
SWEET AROMA OF THE COUNTRY BREAKFAST SPREAD ALL OVER THE HOUSE.

Those were the days when my grandma lived in the country, and she always made coffee, biscuits, bacon, and scrambled eggs when I spent the night with her. I never had to have an alarm clock at her house because the *Imagery* **SMELL OF THE BACON** would wake me up. I would always get coffee while

I was *Imagery* **WRAPPED UP IN HER TERRY-CLOTH ROBE**. It made me feel like I was

older. We would sit on the big backyard screened-in porch to **EAT**
Magic 3
BREAKFAST, DRINK OUR COFFEE, AND WATCH THE SUN'S RAYS HIT THE FOG

ON THE GROUND. *Personification* **THE BIRDS WOULD BE FROLICKING** through the trees and

over the fog. Their two dogs would play around on the patio and chase my little sister. The Sunday morning comics were so funny. I liked Garfield the best. We would read the *Magic 3* weather to see if we could **GO FISHING, DRIVE TO GALVESTON,**

OR FEED THE DUCKS. If it were raining or hot outside, we would go into her

149

sewing room and work on a variety of things, such as her Christmas tree skirt. It didn't matter to me where we went as long as it was somewhere. Time was never wasted there. We were always doing something.

Since my grandmother has moved, we don't share those special moments *Full-Circle Ending* as often--**THE SMELL OF BACON, SCRAMBLED EGGS, COFFEE AND FRESH BISCUITS. IT'S JUST** *Metaphor* **ANOTHER PICTURE IN THE MOVIES OF MY LIFETIME.** The ones that mean a lot stay with you, and you will never forget them.

Since Grandma's country breakfast is part of my movie, it won't get lost.

Lance Brunson
Narrative-Ritual
Published in <u>Merlyn's Pen</u> 1995

Family Memories

Many precious memories come from simple family tradition or rituals. Special times I recall during our family's winter and summer vacations in the mountains. Whether it be **DRINKING RICH COCOA IN THE EARLY** *Magic 3* **MORNING, WALKING TIRELESSLY INTO THE RETREATING SUN, OR AWAKENING FOR THE EARLY MORNING GATHERING ON THE DECK OF MY FAMILY'S "GINGERBREAD HOUSE,"** the impressions left upon me have been great.

Without the early morning wake-up, there would be no riding of the *Participial Phrase* treacherous ski lifts, **DARING TO LET MY LIFE HANG IN BALANCE, SOLELY RELYING ON MY SEAT AND STRAP**. There would be no sitting in my *Simile* grandmother's soft blanket, **SINKING INTO HER LAP AS IF I WERE IN** *Imagery* **QUICKSAND**. There would be no listening to the **SERENE HUM OF THE HUMMINGBIRDS** as I slowly drink down the spiced cider that warms me.

As the vapors float gently, my mouth waters and I am drawn to the aroma that is partially waking me up. Then I begin the monotonous steps down the stairs. My eyes open as I clumsily reach the door. As I unlatch *Simile* *Participial Phrase & Hyperbole* and open it, **THE COLD ACTS AS AN ANESTHETIC**, **CHILLING MY BONES AND**

Noun Absolutes

FREEZING MY THOUGHTS. MY TEETH CHATTERING, MY HANDS SHAKING AS

Simile

IF FEEBLE, I stumble over to my grandmother's lap. There I sit, the **FLUFFY**

Imagery *Magic 3*

FOLDS OF HER ROBE CUSHIONING, COVERING, AND WELCOMING ME. HALF-

Adjective Placement

AWAKE, HALF-ASLEEP, I hear my mom and dad talking endlessly to relatives,

Personification

catching up on past experiences. The **SUN** rises, **STEADILY SWIMMING FOR**

MIDCOURT, and the hummingbirds slowly sip the juice from the feeder,

cooling their throats with refreshing nectar. **THEIR WINGS BEAT**

Implicit Metaphor

RHYTHMICALLY, WEAVING A SHARP SONG OF SECURITY AROUND OUR

FAMILY'S DECK. Love grows, and I know that not for an instant could our

family be separated.

Metaphor

As I fully awaken, the **MORNING HEATS AND SIZZLES WITH EXCITEMENT**.

We all part and go our separate ways, but I know we will all be together

again. We will make the sixteen-hour journey back to our gingerbread

house, knowing that the time will always be worth it.

Jabari Phillips
Narrative Ritual

THE GREATEST SHOW ON EARTH

A CIRCUS TRADITION

It comes every July. Frantic ticket sales. Sold-out performances.
Bumper-to-bumper traffic. And all for one thing, opening night at the
circus. Every summer, my mother, brother, and I go to the circus in mid-
July--a thing that I know I've outgrown. Every year I slap on a smile and
tone down my temper for one reason, "The Greatest Show on Earth." I have
to remind my brother that we're not in those front-row seats yet. Now is
just the first part of loud children, gummy floors, and wild animals: the
ticket sales line. Opening day draws an opening-day crowd for those who
will make special appearances that first night. After being nearly pecked
to death by the restless nest of ticket customers, we limp out barely alive,
but with tickets in hand.

A few days later, the big night arrives. After preening ourselves a
couple hundred times, we load up and start off. We leave an hour and
forty-five minutes early so we can have plenty of time to find a parking
space and not get caught by the vulturous crowd or traffic.

But no matter how hard we try, it always happens. Mind-numbing
traffic. Cars honking. Trucks honking. Truck-car combos
honking. Every year it seems like everybody thinks like us,
"Let's leave an hour and forty-five minutes early!"

Once the two-to-three-year wait in traffic is over, we finally
make it to the underground parking arena, a circus within
itself. Cars circling around and around. Little men in orange vests juggling

flashlights and pointing. We soon find a parking space among the act and join the crowd. The long but steady line to get in doesn't bother me, but it bores my brother to death. However, he survives, and yet not expecting his next test of courage, the circus toys. Every year he represses himself and says he's too old for that, although out of the corner of his eye he always spies a flag or a flashlight. We stop for a quick pick-up of popcorn and expensive drinks and nachos: all having a total at least six times my monthly allowance. We find temporary seats, but when people get seated, my mother suggests we find "better" seats that are a little closer to the action.

Finally, the lights dim. The first act is usually the clowns with their corny escapades. The roar of the kids' laughter is enough to drive us crazy. Every now and then we hear a food vendor bellow out his tune, "Popcorn, cotton candy, peanuts." The second act is sometimes a show of the elephants and an introduction to the animal acts. Once again those roaring kids and vendors, loud enough to wake the dead, make me wish I had brought ear plugs.

The final acts include the lions and tigers and bears along with the death-defying, don't-try-this-at-home stunts. Stunts so terrifying they always make me clutch the bottom of the arm rest to find that sticky pink surprise. When the show is over, we wait awhile to let the crowd die down. After about ten minutes we get up and start back home. Back to jobs. Back to family. And pretty soon, back to school.

THE GREATEST SHOW ON EARTH

© 1998 M. E. LEDBETTER

WHAT'S RIGHT ABOUT MY LIFE?

ASSIGNING A PERSONAL ESSAY: Ask students to write about what is right about their lives.

① **BRAINSTORMING ASPECTS:** Start by focusing students on different areas of their lives (e.g., school, favorite activities, home, church).

② **BRAINSTORMING IMAGES:** Next, instruct students to jot down sensory images beside as many aspects as they can:

"*PLAY CHASE WITH THE LEAVES AS THEY BLOW AND I RUN AFTER THEM*"

"*ATE A FRESHLY PICKED ORANGE, SQUISHING IT BETWEEN MY TEETH*"

"*GRANDPA RAINDROP FALLS ON MY NOSE*"

Students will soon find that their favorite areas will have an array of details surrounding them.

③ **NARROWING FOCUS:** Now that advantages, activities/people loved, and unique qualities of their lives have emerged, students should choose three aspects on which to elaborate.

④ **READING MODELS:**

A. The FIRST ESSAY that follows is a narrative/descriptive piece, where the author recounts one specific day that symbolizes one of many for him. Students should note the **contrasting images** ("COOL, CRISP SHEETS" VS. "CARDBOARD BOXES AND HANDMADE CURTAINS") and the **sensory details** ("RED OAK FLOOR...ITS ICINESS," "PREACHER'S BOOMING VOICE RANG OUT LIKE A BIG BASS DRUM").

B. The SECOND PIECE is a descriptive account of the author's love of nature. Students should notice that the writer employs **figurative language devices** in an effort to make her images come alive for the reader ("IMPRISONED SEEDS...PARACHUTE DOWN," "A DAY JACK FROST DROPPED BY," "WHISPERING WIND TELLING ME STORIES OF OLD SECRETS," etc.)

C. The THIRD WORK, "Enjoyments of My Life," is a NATIONAL CONTEST WINNER and has been included in Part 2, Section 1. It follows a prescribed **structure**, yet is **playful** enough to include images and techniques that are often reserved for more descriptive modes.

⑤ **WRITING ROUGH DRAFT:** After **sharing** their own images with the class or a partner, students should begin to tell their own stories of what is right about their lives.

Ryan Rogers
National Contest Entry
Assignment: What's Right About My Life

A Day To Be Thankful

I woke up that morning to the chirping of birds, the sizzle of pancakes and the aroma of bacon. I pulled back the cool, crisp sheets and jumped to the red oak floor, surprised at its iciness. I pulled on my slippers and ran to the kitchen. As I waited patiently for breakfast, I looked outside to see a man in ragged clothes walking down the street. "That man, unlike me," I thought, "probably doesn't have many things right with his life such as living necessities, family and friends, or a church to attend." My thoughts were interrupted as my mother set a stack of steaming pancakes on the cherry oak table.

After a delicious breakfast, we stepped outside, in our warm apparel, into the frigid air for a walk. The dew stood out like glistening diamonds, and icicles hung down from above. As we turned the corner, I suddenly noticed we were in a different environment, a dark, dreary one, one of cardboard boxes and handmade curtains. Then I noticed the faces: faces of those poorer than I, faces of those hungrier, faces of disappointment, of despair. The faces showed those colder than I , those in pain and in doubt, and those who had given up. They were faces of the homeless. We silently walked out of that area, but I never forgot those faces and how much they differed from my own.

The sun was just peeking out from behind a cloud as we drove to the park for a family/friend picnic. When we got there, I was out in a flash, running toward my friends. We had a wonderful time with sack races, snowball fights, and other picnic activities. I began to think how lucky I was to have such loving friends and family and how boring the picnic would be without them. We had just finished naming shapes of clouds and making snow angels when my mother announced it was time to go. With much reluctance, I waved goodbye to my friends.

The sun's rays set off beautiful colors as they passed through the stained-glass windows of the church. The preacher's booming voice rang out like a big bass drum. He talked of Jacob and his dream of the stairway to heaven. I rested my head against my mother's shoulder and let sleep slowly overcome me as the preacher's words of the dream comforted me. As I was approaching sleep, a loud yawn escaped my lips, much to the embarrassment of my parents. We decided to leave early, and I had a sense of peace as we walked together out of the great church and into the fading sunlight.

As my mother and I knelt beside my bed that night to pray, I realized just how revealing this day had been. We have enough living necessities, I have loving friends and family, and a church to attend. I drifted to sleep, remembering three important things right with my life.

Liz Alexander
National Contest Entry
Assignment: What's Right About My Life

The Magic of Tomorrow

I like to pick warm, fuzzy dandelion domes, turned cotton from gold, and release the imprisoned seeds as they parachute down from the land they once came from. I like to see the stars, hear the rain, and feel the crisp coolness of fall. That's what's right with my life.

I like to see the stars, to wake up before morning is born and see them, that they do exist beyond the city lights. Then I see steam rising out of the fence on a day that Jack Frost dropped by. And I wonder what it is and how there can be steam on a day that's so cold. But I won't ask anyone because deep down in my heart I don't really want to know so that the magic of tomorrow will still be there.

I like the rain singing me a lullaby at night, or a display of fireworks darting across the sky in booms and crackles. And on nights when there are huge bolts of gold, night--for a few seconds--turns into day, but not a yellow sunlight, a blue glow. I like the rain and lightning, but the best part of all is that, if I'm lucky, God will take a huge paintbrush and make all the colors into an arc in the sky for all to enjoy.

On the first cool night of fall, I like to open my window and then get under the soft, warm covers, only to wake up and be so cold I'll feel my way through the darkness and shut the pane of glass, so I won't have to be defrosted in the morning. I like the whispering wind telling me stories of old secrets. In summer's warmth it cools me and brushes through my hair. I can hear the trees sing in the wind, bowing down to him, their master. The wind blows golden fire leaves of fall to me. And I relax.

The dandelions of spring, the stars of morn, the cool fall nights, thunderstorms and rainbows--I enjoy them all. They all bring me pleasure. And that's what's right with my life.

Variations on the Drug Essay

①→ WRITING A SNAPSHOT NARRATIVE: Instead of a narrative about one drug-related instance, encourage students to present **THREE DIFFERENT "SNAPSHOTS"** that will paint one larger picture of the ill effects of drugs.

A. Ask students to **WEB THREE DRUG SCENES**, giving specific details for each scenario in their mapping.

B. Distribute copies of **"SILENT KILLER."**

* Discuss the **APPEAL OF EACH SCENARIO** with students.
* Ask students to note **SPECIFIC DETAILS FOR EFFECT**.
* Analyze the **UNUSUAL STRUCTURE** of the essay--the placement of the thesis at the end, after the three narrative scenarios which constitute the body of the essay.

②→ WRITING A PERSONAL NARRATIVE: Ask students to imagine the effects drugs could have on **THEIR OWN FAMILIES AND FRIENDS**.

A. Distribute copies of **"THE DAY MY OLDER BROTHER DIED."**

B. Ask students to mark their **FAVORITE PARTS** and analyze the **APPEAL**.

C. Assign a vignette about the **DAY** that drugs changed their lives.

© 1988 M. E. LEDBETTER

Liz Alexander
Narrative Writing
Second-Place District Winner 1995
Drug Contest

SILENT KILLER

A girl looks at the small square. LSD. Like that tiny dot could really hurt her. She tries it, promising herself not to become addicted. Little does she know that soon she will get hooked on the drug, and her life will be no longer her own. After several years a friend wakes her up and makes her realize that she needs help. After numerous rehabilitation centers, Kayla finally finds one that works. Even though she is off the drug, the rest of her life is haunted by terrifying hallucinations and the fact that she never graduated from high school. That little dot, that Kayla thought couldn't hurt her, killed part of her life. It burned her dreams and stole part of her soul.

At the same time, in another part of the country, Darren, an average student with an above-average heart and smile, is walking home from school. Even though he is only eight, all his relatives go on and on about how he's going to win the Nobel Peace Prize or find a cure for cancer. Sweet Darren. Lovable Darren. The Darren that gave Billy Johnson his last $2.27 in lunch money since Billy forgot to bring his. Happy Darren. Giving Darren. Dead Darren. It wasn't his fault that he died. It wasn't his fault that a drug dealer thought he was a kid that owed him money. It wasn't his fault that he looked like a lot of other kids at a distance or that the dealer had a gun. He would never fall in love. He would never ice skate. He would never win the Nobel Peace Prize. And none of his mother's tears and wails through the cold night could ever bring sweet Darren back.

At the same time, by the shores of a different ocean, a baby is born. It is the start of life. It is the start of hope. It is the start of dreams. It is so tiny; its hands and fingers are ever so small. Its toes are so itty-bitty. What a beautiful baby. Too bad that this pretty baby is a crack baby. Too back it won't ever have the chance of living a normal life. Too bad it suffers from numerous defects including a poor heart.

Each one of these victims had a killer or thief. It has a name. Its name is Drugs. Millions of people, just as precious as Kayla or Darren, fall victim to this silent killer. There are people shot, overdoses that lead to the end of life, DWIs that end in death for innocent children, and many, many more scenarios. And let us not forget all the babies who never had a chance because of cocaine or crack.

Beware, my child, take heed. Be cautious. Sleep with one eye open and don't forget to say your prayers, for a murderer stalks tonight. Its name is Drugs.

DANGER

Ardi Challenger
Narrative Writing
Gold Medal Winner <u>Scholastic</u> <u>Magazine</u> 1996

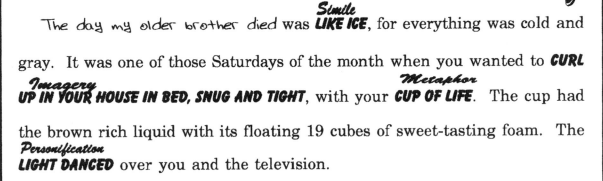

THE DAY MY OLDER BROTHER DIED

The day my older brother died was *Simile* **LIKE ICE**, for everything was cold and gray. It was one of those Saturdays of the month when you wanted to **CURL** *Imagery* **UP IN YOUR HOUSE IN BED, SNUG AND TIGHT**, with your *Metaphor* **CUP OF LIFE**. The cup had the brown rich liquid with its floating 19 cubes of sweet-tasting foam. The *Personification* **LIGHT DANCED** over you and the television.

The day my older brother died, he was outside playing basketball with his friends. They were playing on the cracked, graffiti-covered court of the playground. They performed magic again and again as they made the ball shoot from their hands and spin into the hoop. I got bored watching **MY** *Simile* **DRUNK-LIKE HAMSTER** waddle from side to side, back and forth, getting this seed and that seed, so I went to the courts. The day my older brother died I saw most of his friends--Toast, Slicky, Juice, Red, and Rock. Toast was small, 5 feet 3 inches, but he could jam. Slicky was tall, and he could move around and bend in all different ways. Juice was *Simile* **LIKE WATER**; he could go real fast or real slow. He could slip through your fingers like he wasn't even there. Red was one of the best. He always had a red bandana in his pocket. Rock was built *Simile* **LIKE A TANK**. He could bulldoze over you, for he was huge. But best of all was my brother Terence. He could **JAM**; he could

Rhyme
SLAM. He could do the Whimmy **WHAM**. If you didn't know what that was, it didn't matter because whatever it is you can't stop him from doing it. He and his friends were playing another group of kids from a couple blocks away from us. ✳The neighborhood where we weren't supposed to go. ✳The one with the drug dealers and the gang members. ✳The place where we went anyway. ✳*Fragments for effect*

The day my brother died was one of those games where you have to draw blood to have a foul called. The kind where you got so mad you *Hyperbole* wanted to **RIP SOMEBODY'S HEAD OFF AND KICK IT** to win the superbowl. My brother's team was doing their magic deeds as usual. They were shooting and spinning, hooping and juicing, slamming and jamming and other terms I didn't know at the time. Terence's team was up eight to six. While Terence was moving from side to side, distracting the player, Toast drove *Imagery* to the hoop and **FINGER-ROLLED** the ball inside. Terence's team went off. *Simile* Juice's basketball skills burst out **LIKE A BAD CASE OF PIMPLES**. His sweat *Vivid Verbs* **POPPED, SIZZLED, AND SMOKED** off his body. But once again Terence prevailed over the other players, even his own teammates. His rage spread toward *Simile* them **LIKE FIRE OVER GASOLINE**. It knocked them down, making a clear path for him to run through and lay it up for two more. My brother's team was *Simile* winning sixteen to ten. The ball looked **LIKE A BIRD THAT HAD BEEN LET GO**. The ball flew through the air to its nest, except this nest wasn't its home, *Repetition for Effect and Onomatopoeia* for it fell through the bottom to the world below. **SWISH, SWISH, SWISH** was all you could hear.

The day my older brother died, they were winning eighteen to fourteen. Slicky went up for the monster jam. He was rejected all the way to the street.

"Go get it!" Slicky yelled.

"Hell no!" the older boy said. I closed my ears so I wouldn't hear the rest. When I opened my ears, Terence had volunteered to get it, but that was a mistake. He didn't see the *Metaphor* **TORPEDO** coming at him. ✳The one with that metallic gray color. ✳The one with the plastic skulls hanging from the rearview mirror. ✳The one that could kill. ✳The one that did. ✳*Fragments for effect*

My brother was hit. I put his head in my arms, trying to give him strength, but he died in my arms. The day my older brother died *Full-Circle Ending* was **LIKE ICE**, for everything was cold and gray.

Section 4:

DESCRIPTIVE WRITING

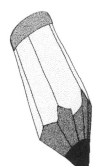

How to Use the Sample Integrated Lesson Plan

① → WRITING INTEGRATED LESSON PLANS: Since the idea of an **INTEGRATED LANGUAGE ARTS PROGRAM** is to present writing, grammar, and literature skills as a whole--not in isolation, it is important to devise **LESSON PLANS** that reflect this philosophy.

② → INTRODUCING A DESCRIPTIVE UNIT: Included is a sample integrated **LESSON PLAN** for introducing a **DESCRIPTIVE UNIT** and a **MODEL PARAGRAPH FORM** for student use as a prewriting strategy.

③ → USING TEACHER MODEL: Also included is a **TEACHER-WRITTEN EXTENSION,** elaborating on the images of sight, sound, and touch.

E-MAIL

SAMPLE LESSON PLAN FOR DESCRIPTIVE UNIT

PURPOSE/OBJECTIVE:
Students will be able to write a descriptive paragraph

I. **Review kinds of WRITING**--The introduction of each new mode can provide an opportunity to review modes covered and to show students the purpose of modes yet to be studied.

   A. Narrative--tell story
   B. Persuasive--convince
   C. Comparison/contrast--give similarities and differences
   D. How-to--list instructions
   E. DESCRIPTIVE--DESCRIBE

II. **Read passages from LITERATURE**--Students enjoy reading descriptive passages from literature, instead of passages from a textbook. The point is to emphasize the abundance of description in their everyday reading.

> We told Mother, my mother--not his--that we were going to a football game in football season or a basketball game when that was what we should have been doing or to any number of places that a mother could listen to, nod, and go on about her business. Not that my mother was the type who didn't care about her only daughter. She was the type who trusted her.
>
> We told my mother, not his, because one day when Mike was twelve, just a couple days after his birthday, his mom just sort of disappeared. Oh, she was still there, still doing what she had to do, but that was all. She'd make the breakfasts, pack the lunches, take the kids to school, run errands, dust and clean and wash and cook

and start it all over the very next day.   But there was, all of a sudden, nothing in between.

Mike said he remembered it vividly, like the shiny red bike he got when he was six, with tassels on the handle bars that would fly up as he sped around the neighborhood, tooting his new horn, and glowing after dark with the iridescent patches his mom had decorated both bumpers and the hubs of his spokes with.   The bike was his freedom and he remembered.   And the shotgun from his granddaddy he got when he was ten, that had been his permission to be a man, to be grown-up enough to be trusted with life and death.   But after that, he always said that for his twelfth birthday he got a new mom.

The old one used to sit with him for long hours on the porch and play whatever he wanted to play that day, stroking his hair and pushing his bangs up off his forehead, listening to stories of childhood injustices and dreams and anything that popped into his boyish head. Mike was so proud of having a mom who stuck up for him, who was on his side. A mom who understood.

III. **Analyze sentence structure--GRAMMAR--**To emphasize that grammar is a tool that real writers use to perfect their craft, ask students to analyze the reasoning behind certain "grammatical" decisions in literary excerpts.   For instance, in the piece above, students could explain the application of the following rules:

A. Comma for a series
B. Comma for an interrupter
C. Comma for an introductory word
D. A participial phrase for combining
E. Capitalization for a relationship and rule
F. Fragment for effect

IV. **Begin Invention/Discovery Strategies for PREWRITING--**
When students understand the concept/purpose of the writing mode, invention/discovery strategies such as the following can be done individually with you modeling at the board.

A. Brainstorm five favorite places

① →

② →

③ →

④ →

⑤ →

B. Web one of the places from the brainstormed list. As spokes off the central circle, list ***SIGHT, SOUND, AND FEELING/TOUCH***. Then, as spokes off those, list ***THREE SIGHTS, THREE SOUNDS, AND THREE FEELINGS***.

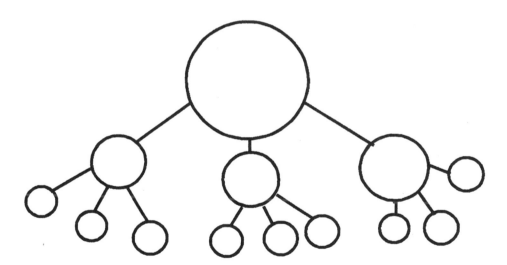

C. Add **details**. For the ***THREE SPECIFIC SIGHTS,*** write a SIMILE for each. For the ***THREE SPECIFIC SOUNDS***, list an ADJECTIVE for each. For the ***THREE SPECIFIC EXAMPLES USING TOUCH,*** write a CONCRETE IMAGE for each.

① → **Sight**--SIMILES

    a. _____

    b. _____

    c. _____

② → **Sound**--ADJECTIVES

    a. _____

    b. _____

    c. _____

③ → **Touch**--CONCRETE IMAGES

    a. _____

    b. _____

    c. _____

D. Transfer webbing to the **model paragraph**.

MODEL PARAGRAPH

<u>My hill in East Texas</u> is my favorite place to be. Here I can see <u>distant beckoning trees like friends in a crowd</u>, <u>fallen leaves like freckles on a face</u>, and <u>flickers of lightning like forgotten promises</u>. I can hear <u>singing katydids</u>, <u>murmuring thunder</u>, and <u>whispering memories</u>. I can touch <u>prickly cones</u>, <u>sharp needles</u>, and <u>lost dreams</u> as <u>I lean against my piney sentinel</u>. I can see, I can hear, I can feel in my favorite place, <u>my hill in East Texas</u>.

E. Students should **proofread** and **revise** their papers so that they'll be able to read them to the class. Remind students that revision means "re-seeing" a piece and that many times we "re-see" when we have to read aloud.

F. Students should participate in **oral reading**. Call on several students to read their favorite parts.

G. Participate in **individual response groups.** Trade with a neighbor.

① → Quote favorite sight image.
② → Quote favorite sound image.
③ → Give one more feeling/touch image that could have been used.
④ → List favorite sense and explain.
⑤ → List any mistakes.

H. Students should **revise once again**, using the information they received during the individual response groups.

① → Correct any errors the response partner might have found.
② → Use the dictionary for any possible misspelled words.
③ → Use the thesaurus for any synonyms.
④ → Add details where necessary--more images, etc.

NAME_____ CLASS_____ DATE_____

My Favorite Place

_____ is my favorite place to be. Here

I can see _____ like/as _____,

_____ like/as _____,

and _____ like/as _____.

I can hear _____,

_____,

and _____.

I can feel _____

while I _____.

I can see, I can hear, I can feel in my favorite place,

_____.

©1996 M. E. LEDBETTER

MY FAVORITE PLACE

School is over, the "dog days" have not yet begun, so I find myself once again at home in my parents' backyard. With iced tea by my side, my half-read novel momentarily forgotten, and Blackie curled up at my feet, I realize that this brown and white lawn chair in my parents' backyard is my favorite place to be.

Here, through the picture window, I can see Mama in the kitchen, fixing dinner, methodically moving from refrigerator to sink to stove, like an old dog chasing its tail or trying to settle in for the night. And there's Daddy in the study, reading, his head bent over his open book as if he were inspecting a long-lost treasure or committing to memory a secret he and I will share late one night when we're all alone. Everywhere, as far as I can see, from my vantage point of this brown and white piece of my past, are the tall, straight pines thrust into the earth like giant arrows having missed their mark. I close my eyes and listen.

I can hear the reassuring clatter of the pots and pans. Dinner will be done in no time, as it's always been, as it always will be, Mama turning water on and off, humming a tune of her own making, something I've heard a thousand times on days such as these. Off in the distance I can barely make out the faint sound of Daddy's radio, the lilting strains of the classical pieces he knows by heart and loves so well, and somehow I realize now, it's all connected, Mama and Daddy and the soothing sounds of the wind as it whips through the trees here in our backyard. I adjust this old chair one rung lower, unbend my knees, and stretch my body to its full length.

I can touch the frayed edges of this chair and run my hand up and over its weave. My family is patterned like this, I think, one strand connected to the next, woven strong and tight like this fabric. The fallen pine needles make such a soft, inviting blanket that I reach down, scoop up a handful, and select one perfect pine-needle cluster to braid, looping right over middle, left over right, till I've woven it, cord-like as Mama used to do my braids. And the grass--as I run my hand just so, my palm open--is prickly and dry and coarse like the burr haircut Daddy got once long ago. I would run my hand up and over it too, just for fun, just to feel a sensation I knew I would never forget.

So now Blackie has awakened, and as I take a sip of tea, leafing through my novel to find my place, I know that my real place is right here--in the brown and white chair in my parents' backyard.

EXTENDED SENSE WRITING

① → **BRAINSTORMING "SENSE" EXPERIENCE:** Ask students to recall an ***EXPERIENCE INVOLVING ONE SENSE*** (or a combination of senses). It could be the first time they ever tasted a new food (spinach) or a combination of tastes (their first Chinese meal). Or they could remember the sensation of playing with play dough when they were children--how it felt to mold the soft substance.

② → **USING CREATIVE PROMPTS:** To stimulate students' memories, try utilizing various sensory "prompts": ***CANDY*** (taste), ***SPICES*** (smell), ***COTTON*** (touch), ***SOUND EFFECT TAPE*** (sound), ***CLASSROOM-DISPLAYED OR INDIVIDUAL PICTURES*** (sight).

③ → **CREATING A SENSE VOCABULARY:** Students benefit from having ***LISTS OF WORDS*** for particular senses (specific colors, soft vs. loud sounds, etc.). Compile the lists as part of a class ***VOCABULARY ASSIGNMENT***, giving each group a different sense. Instruct students to footnote and define any unfamiliar words. ***MAKE CLASSROOM COPIES*** and keep as notes for future use or put on posters or colorful vocabulary "strips" hung around the room.

④ → **FREEWRITING:** Students' freewriting might yield a single paragraph or a multiparagraph ***DESCRIPTIVE OR NARRATIVE/DESCRIPTIVE PIECE***. The point is for students to be more aware of sensory images in future writing.

⑤ → **USING TEACHER MODELS:** Included are two teacher models. Students may web specific images from the pieces to reinforce the importance the importance of ***SENSORY DETAILS***.

BITTERSWEET PIECES OF SCIENCE

From my childhood I remember chocolate. Daddy and I would go for special treats, a Father/Daughter get-away to downtown Houston. How special I felt, just Daddy and me on our private forays into the metropolis. (I had learned that word from the Superman series and used it often to sound sophisticated and in-the-know, maybe like Lois Lane, Superman's girlfriend.)

On these once-a-month Saturdays our sweet tooths would prevail over what Mama called our good old horse sense, and we'd often sit at a coffee emporium on Westheimer, with its red-bricked walls and New York's Soho atmosphere, and slurp rich hot chocolate from oversized mugs topped with whipped cream and served with a cinnamon stick as a swizzle and a cherry for good measure, as Daddy used to say.

Once we even went to Maxim's, where amidst its red velvet splendor we ordered chocolate fondue, dipping plump fresh strawberries and delicate raspberries and heavy golden poundcake into a thick river of chocolate laced with Grand Marnier.

But my favorite times were spent at Foley's delicatessen, where we'd sample chocolate eclairs and truffles and homemade double fudge ice cream. On one occasion, though, after scouting the aisles for new delicacies, I came across an unprecedented, at least in our neck of the woods, culinary delight—chocolate-covered ants and grasshoppers. Since Mr. Phillips, my science teacher, encouraged unusual show-and-tells, and since Daddy and I were always game for exotic discoveries, I was allowed to buy enough small squares for my class.

I'll never forget Ken Warren with a grasshopper leg hanging precariously from the corner of his mouth. And Claudia Fagin would proclaim for weeks afterward that she, too, experimented with ants—the homegrown garden variety—in her mother's brownies. Of course, there were a few kids too timid to indulge, and Mr. Phillips himself looked a little green around the gills, as Daddy always said, but, nevertheless, I was a hit—or Daddy was—and so were my bittersweet pieces of science.

All My Favorite Places

As I nestle under the bed covers--hot, spiced tea by my side, Grandma Wilson's heavy, knitted afghan draped over my feet to ward off the inevitable midwinter chill I feel even in the warmest conditions--I am at once transported to my favorite place-- my memories, the recreations of times I'll always treasure. There I can see and hear and touch once again all the times I've ever loved.

"One, two, three, four . . . One, two, three, four . . . " I recall her voice ringing sharply, clearly--a familiar, expected cadence. My arms and legs strained to the tempo, wanting to perfect each and every movement, wanting so desperately to please. "Hear the music, feel the music, live the music," she instructed, and how I tried year after year. "Relevé, plié, pirouette" resound within my memory, lilting admonitions for a company of aspiring ballet students. Sometimes now--in my present--I can be walking aimlessly down a school corridor or on a country path or even to my neighbor's for a promised cup of coffee over innocuous neighborhood gossip, and I hear those waltzes from long ago. I walk a little lighter those days . . . in tune with my past.

Snuggling deeper in my bed, my tea half gone now, I remember--for reasons as strange as dreams that visit in the night--Mama and her scent, that perfumed, powdered fragrance that I waited for in another bed almost two decades ago. As a child, hospitalized for what seemed like an eternity, I'd long--on those long, lonely days--for a familiar face, someone besides the strange doctors and nurses and orderlies that surrounded me. Most especially I'd long for a sweet, familiar smell, not the antiseptic, medicinal smells I'd come to associate with my new environment. And always that face and that smell I waited for were Mama as she'd hug me tight to her, Mama and her wonderful smells, like fields of lavender just for me.

My tea all but gone, one final image comes to mind--the image of pine trees, the pine trees of my childhood. Wherever I've been since then, wherever I've called home, no place has truly seemed right, no place has ever felt like that two-acre piney woods of my past. There's something about a sky outlined with 100-year-old trees, like giant, pointed spears thrust into the earth. There's something reassuring about their presence, towering sentinels over those whom they must guard. It's those trees I missed when I was anywhere but home, and it's those trees I think of now, here in my bed.

My mind at ease, the pressures of my present erased, the dreams of the future left to another night, I pull up Grandma Wilson's afghan and remember ballet lessons and Mama and pine trees, and I know I'll visit these places often, these favorite places of mine.

RUBRIC FOR DESCRIPTIVE ESSAY

I. CONTENT

A. THESIS--Write your **THESIS STATEMENT**, which should include the **PERSON, PLACE, THING, OR IDEA BEING DESCRIBED**, the **DOMINANT IMPRESSION** (main idea or effect) on which the essay will focus, and the three aspects/details that will support this impression.

*For example, you might wish to establish a peaceful atmosphere when describing your favorite fishing hole; therefore, you will describe the calmness of the water itself, the beauty of the surroundings, and even the soothing effect of the process of fishing itself. Or you could recreate an **EERIE FEELING** when writing about the haunted house you visited as a child with its macabre sights, sounds, and feelings.

_____

_____

_____

_____

_____

_____

©1998 M. E. LEDBETTER

B. SENSORY DETAILS--List **SIX** of your best descriptive passages--**TWO FROM EACH BODY PARAGRAPH**. Label in the margin of your paper and below to which **SENSE** each appeals.

① _____

_____

Sense: _____

② _____

_____

Sense: _____

③ _____

_____

Sense: _____

④ _____

_____

Sense: _____

⑤ _____

_____

Sense: _____

⑥ _____

_____

Sense: _____

©1996 M. E. LEDBETTER

II. ORGANIZATION--Explain the organization of your details: by using **SENSORY IMPRESSIONS** (sights, sounds, smells, etc.), **SPATIAL ORDER** (from top to bottom, left to right, etc.), **EMPHATIC ORDER** (starting with the least important or striking element and ending with the most important), or **CHRONOLOGICAL ORDER** (ordered by time sequence).

_____

_____

_____

_____

III. REVISION--Cite evidence of the following from your paper:

A. VARIED SENTENCE BEGINNINGS/STRUCTURE--List **TWO** examples of sentences that do not follow the normal subject/verb pattern.
     Possible variations:
➡ **PREPOSITIONAL PHRASE** (In the morning)
➡ **ADVERB CLAUSE** (Since I was a child)
➡ **INVERTED ORDER** (Verb before Subject)
    (Whirling in my head **WERE WHEELS,** like a great clock.)
➡ **MODIFIERS AFTER WORD MODIFIED** (the boys, lazy and carefree)

① _____

_____

② _____

_____

B. ELIMINATION OF UNNECESSARY ADVERBS in favor of more **POWERFUL VERBS**--List two examples of powerful verbs from your paper. (Instead of "walked slowly"; use a verb such as "strolled.")

① _____

② _____

C. INCLUSION OF FIGURATIVE LANGUAGE--List two examples of figurative rather than literal language used in your paper and identify the type.

©1998 M. E. LEDBETTER

II. ORGANIZATION--Explain the organization of your details: by **SENSORY IMPRESSIONS** (sights, sounds, smells, etc.), **SPATIALLY** (from top to bottom, left to right, etc.), **EMPHATICALLY** (starting with the least important or striking element and ending with the most important).

_____

_____

_____

_____

III. REVISION--Cite evidence of the following from your paper:

   A. VARIED SENTENCE BEGINNINGS/STRUCTURE--List **TWO** examples of sentences that do not follow the normal subject/verb pattern.
      Possible variations:
      ➡ **PREPOSITIONAL PHRASE** (In the morning)
      ➡ **ADVERB CLAUSE** (Since I was a child)
      ➡ **INVERTED ORDER** (Verb before Subject)
         (Whirling in my head **WERE WHEELS**, like a great clock.)
      ➡ **MODIFIERS AFTER WORD MODIFIED** (the boys, lazy and carefree)

      ① _____

      _____

      ② _____

      _____

   B. ELIMINATION OF UNNECESSARY ADVERBS in favor of more **POWERFUL VERBS**--List two examples of powerful verbs from your paper. (Instead of "walked slowly"; use a verb such as "strolled.")

      ①_____

      ②_____

   C. INCLUSION OF FIGURATIVE LANGUAGE--List two examples of figurative rather than literal language used in your paper and identify the type.

① _____

Type:_____

② _____

Type:_____

D. AVOIDANCE OF CLICHÉS--Descriptive writing can be especially vulnerable to the use of clichés, rather than the use of fresh, original images. **TO PROVE THAT YOU HAVE AVOIDED CLICHÉS**, cite an image from your paper and write a cliché that could have been used by a less accomplished writer.

① Image:_____

_____

② Cliché:_____

_____

IV. PROOFREADING--After analyzing the types of errors marked on previous papers, **LIST YOUR THREE MOST PREVALENT MISTAKES** (run-ons, fragments, commas, etc.) and give evidence that you have proofread this paper to avoid these errors.

A. FIRST
① Error:_____

② Evidence:_____

B. SECOND
① Error:_____

② Evidence:_____

C. THIRD
① Error:_____

② Evidence: _____

Dominant Impression Game

①→ SHOWING PICTURES: Play a dominant impression "game" by asking the first person in each row to step into the hall to look at pictures, each of which has a distinct dominant impression. One picture might be of **RICH** kids or **POOR** sharecroppers or a **CRAZY, WILD** old woman. Each row leader sees only one picture.

②→ DETERMINING DOMINANT IMPRESSION: Ask the leaders to think of a dominant impression for their picture and then supporting details. For instance, the rich kids are in their **EXPENSIVE CLOTHES**, on a **YACHT**, dining on **GOURMET FOOD**.

③→ DESCRIBING PICTURES: After studying the pictures for details, the leaders come back into the room and **WHISPER THE DOMINANT IMPRESSION AND SUPPORTING DETAILS OF THEIR PICTURE** to the next person in their respective rows.

④→ PASSING INFORMATION: Each student in the row tells the person behind him or her what was heard. As the **INFORMATION GETS PASSED ALONG**, details--and even the dominant impression itself--usually are altered, as were the outcomes of "gossip" games in elementary schools.

⑤→ COMPARING DESCRIPTION TO PICTURE: After all rows have finished passing along the information about their pictures, the last person in each row tells what he or she has heard. **TO COMPARE THE FINAL VERSION TO THE ACTUAL PICTURE**, hold up each picture after each row has finished and discuss how the dominant impression and the details could be improved. The winning row(s) could receive "prizes."

Dominant Impression of Childhood Supported by Three Places

①→ BRAINSTORMING DOMINANT IMPRESSIONS: Ask students to **BRAINSTORM FIVE DOMINANT IMPRESSIONS** from their childhood (e.g., adventurous, secure, accomplished, pampered).

②→ SHARING IDEAS: As a class, **DISCUSS VARIOUS OPTIONS** before asking students to decide on one dominant impression for the assignment.

③→ BRAINSTORMING PLACES: Next, students should **BRAINSTORM A LIST OF THREE PLACES** where that dominant impression was apparent. For instance, if **SECURITY** were the dominant idea, perhaps the student felt secure in the **KITCHEN** with Mother cooking the family meal, in the father's **STUDY** reading books, and in the **WOODS** playing games with her friends.

④→ WEBBING SENSORY DETAILS: Now students are ready to make a **SENSE WEB** of their three places. Encourage students to mentally "return" to the three places of their childhood in order to more accurately envision specific details.

⑤→ FREEWRITING: After webbing, students can begin their **FREEWRITING**, making sure that each place supports their chosen dominant impression. The rough drafts should result in a multiparagraph descriptive essay centered on one dominant impression from childhood supported by three specific places.

⑥→ USING TEACHER MODEL: Included is an example of freewriting for the **FIRST WEB** cluster. Students may analyze the piece for use of **EFFECTIVE DETAILS**.

Sample Sense Web: Dominant Impression-- SECURITY

① KITCHEN

BRAINSTORMING:

➤ SIGHT
Mama gathering Grandma's silver from the drawers
Placemats from the cupboards
Old Blackie asleep by the sink

➤ SMELL
Strong chicory coffee
Bacon frying

➤ SOUND
The "grandfather" of a rocker rocking back and forth

➤ TOUCH
The way the cushion bunched up under my legs
The way the rocker's rungs held my feet just so

➤ TASTE
Bacon
Eggs
Biscuits
Hot tea
Ample pats of butter on toasted raisin bread
Freshly squeezed orange juice

WEBBING:

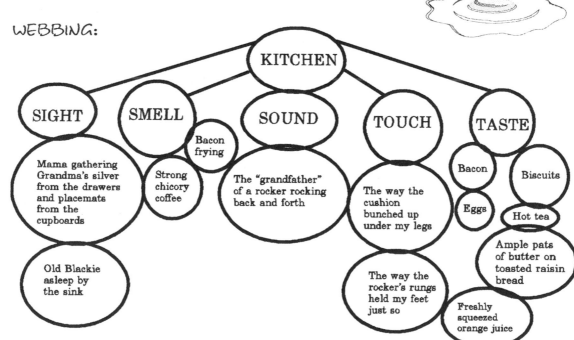

© 1998 M. E. LEDBETTER

② WOODS

BRAINSTORMING:

➤ SIGHT
Hundred-year-old pines like giant stakes

➤ SMELL
Aunt Emily's honeysuckle bush
Rosin fresh from the trees

➤ SOUND
Mama's calling me in for supper
Claudia's giggling
Ken's barking orders

➤ TOUCH
Running my hand over the gnarled pine tree with knots swollen and grown into its
bark like festering sores

➤ TASTE
Candies and cookies and anything we could "smuggle" across enemy lines for our foray
into "no man's land"

WEBBING:

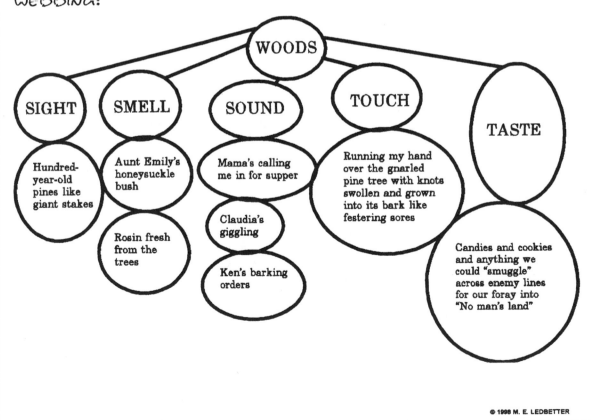

③ STUDY

BRAINSTORMING:

➤ **SIGHT**
Daddy amidst wall-to-wall books, nestled in his rust-colored easy chair

➤ **SMELL**
The sweet, cherry-wood smoke from the long Cuban cigars Uncle Chuck always brought back as gifts for Daddy

➤ **SOUND**
Daddy's favorite jazz or classical music coming from the console radio he kept covered with its original protective cloth

➤ **TOUCH**
The smooth, cold "world" of the globe as I spun it round and round

➤ **TASTE**
The Cokes and cookies or crackers and cheese Mama would bring us as respites from our math reviews or English lessons or simply to remind us that there was another world outside Daddy's study

WEBBING:

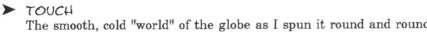

```
                          ┌──────────┐
                          │  STUDY   │
                          └──────────┘
       ┌──────────┬──────────┼──────────┬──────────┐
   ┌───────┐  ┌───────┐  ┌───────┐  ┌───────┐  ┌───────┐
   │ SIGHT │  │ SMELL │  │ SOUND │  │ TOUCH │  │ TASTE │
   └───────┘  └───────┘  └───────┘  └───────┘  └───────┘
```

SIGHT: Daddy amidst wall-to-wall books, nestled in his rust-colored easy chair

SMELL: The sweet cherry-wood smoke from the long Cuban cigars Uncle Chuck always brought back as gifts for Daddy

SOUND: Daddy's favorite jazz or classical music coming from the console radio he kept covered with its original protective cloth

TOUCH: The smooth, cold "world" of the globe as I spun it round and round

TASTE: The cokes and cookies or crackers and cheese Mama would bring us as respites from our math reviews or English lessons or simply to remind us that there was another world outside Daddy's study

Mama's Kitchen

Security, I felt the warmth of it every morning I pushed back the heavy, pocket, louvered door to our kitchen. Every morning I knew what to expect. Mama would have been up hours before the rest of us, making the strong, chicory coffee Daddy liked, gathering Grandma's silver from the drawer and placemats from the cupboard, letting the dog out and the fresh morning air in. I knew exactly where I'd find the newspaper and which sections would be on top, ready for Mama and me, and which would be saved for Daddy. And I see now--years removed from the luxury of waking up to that kitchen daily--that it's the finest gift a child can be given, that sense of sureness, the idea that people can be counted on, that what was yesterday--just like the bacon and eggs and biscuits and hot tea Mama prepared--will be there again today and tomorrow and every day after that. It was salve for any wound, a remedy for any childhood disaster, to know that each day could begin again with Mama in the kitchen and me by her side, spreading ample pats of butter on toasted raisin bread, pouring frothy, freshly squeezed orange juice into the special stemmed glasses used only for breakfasts, and setting them at aunts' and uncles' and cousins' places, for their presence was as sure as Mama's. I knew the feel of the old green rocker, the way the cushion bunched up under my legs, like the lumpy mattress in my attic playhouse, the way the rocker's rungs held my feet just so--away from cold winter linoleum or years of playful puppies eager to gnaw a little girl's big toes. And I knew to be careful not to

rock back too far, not to provoke the injuries that old grandfather of a thing had sustained over

decades of use, each and every one of us having perched at one time, mid-kitchen floor, rocking

back and forth, back and forth, as if the very movement would bring us closer to Mama, to our

center, to the activities of the kitchen. I knew all this those mornings long ago.

Ryan Rogers
Descriptive Essay: Dominant Impression
Supported by Three Places in Childhood

THE BOY WARRIOR

My imaginative childhood was not to be underestimated. It was usually violent: me, good, versus them, evil. Sometimes my imagination would get me into trouble, but of course, I had never meant to do wrong. My room, the yard, and the creek were three innocent places turned into places of turmoil, violence, and fear, thanks to the carrying out of my plans.

The yellow carpet in my room was worn thin from my pacing BACK

Repetition for Effect

AND FORTH, BACK AND FORTH, *like a tiger in a cage*. This is

Simile

where my imagination began. I'd fervently WHIRL the WHEELS in my head,

Alliteration

like a great clock, thinking of traps, fights, and what I'd wear in the

Simile

parade given in my honor. My old FAKE-WOOD-COVERED DESK was

Explicit Metaphor

now my TOP SECRET MILITARY DESK with hidden panels and drawers. The walls concealed poised crossbows, rifles, and poison darts. The door was a trigger point, and its opener was soon to meet his fate. The closet hid a tunnel to the army headquarters, and the goldfish in the aquarium held a high-powered microphone.

In my early childhood, the haven where I carried out my plans was

Alliteration

our yard. Its soft, GREEN GRASS provided a cushion for my Ninja fights against the evil sorcerers of the world. The two huge BUSHY CRAB-

Explicit Metaphor

APPLE TREES were no longer a source of sour fruit, but a MILITARY

POST that fought alongside G.I. Joe and He-Man. The HEDGES *Explicit Metaphor* that had

pricked me so many times turned INTO A BOMB SHELTER and an anti-

aircraft station. The BIRDS *Explicit Metaphor* OF THE SKY BECAME JETS, the WATER

Explicit Metaphor

BUGS in the rain puddles became NAVY SHIPS, and the ANTS *Explicit Metaphor* became

MARINES MARCHING TO BATTLE. The old refrigerator box was no

longer inhabited by insects, but was inhabited by me, the great pilot in his

state-of-the-art cockpit. Of course, the battlefield was limited, for the street

loomed out *Simile* *like candy in a store*, tempting, tempting me to neglect my

mother's rule and conquer it too. By the time the DARKNESS *Personification* OF

NIGHTFALL CAME THREATENING my empire, everything turned back to

normal, and I was no longer a great leader, but a little boy past his

bedtime.

As I got older, I was allowed to explore the creek. ARMED WITH MY *Participial Phrase*

SLINGSHOT, now a crossbow, I'd examine the NO-MAN'S LAND, THE *Implicit Metaphor*

BUBBLING WATERS of the creek. Any fish, bug, or snake was considered

enemy. LITTLE ISLANDS BECAME CONQUERED LAND, *Explicit Metaphor* and I

challenged anyone and everyone. I led a great army OVER THE KNEE-HIGH *Magic 3's*

WEEDS, OVER THE DEAD ANIMAL CARCASSES, AND OVER THE

DANGEROUS, TO-BE-AVOIDED ANT HILLS. Soon the cries of the damsel in distress turned to shrieks of, *Dialogue Inclusion* "YOUNG MAN, YOU'RE IN BIG TROUBLE!" I had lost my empire.

My imaginative childhood is long since gone, for I am usually too busy with homework and other activities of reality. However, every once in a while, as I enter my room, the yard, or the creek, I get that mischievous look in my eye once again.

Monica Prince
Descriptive Essay
(Written from Picture Prompt)

CAPE COD EVENING

Look at the collie, two lonely, old people, and the house surrounded by the serene fields. See the dog standing in the field while his owners watch him with contented expressions. See the peacefulness of the farm, which is evident through the fields and flowing grasses. See the old house which has signs of years of use in this serene environment.

The cedar trees in the pasture behind the house stand tall and reach for the breeze blowing high above them. A few catch the whispering wind and sway to and fro, dancing. The long yellow grass that surrounds the trees gives the place a heavenly appearance. Almost as if it were a field of cotton, the grass stretches itself to grow just one inch higher. Whistling winds and rustling leaves combine in a harmony of nature. Somewhere, a redbird sings happily among the branches of its cedar tree. The fields are serene by this old, well-worn farmhouse.

Sturdy, but worn with age, standing in the field is the two-story ivory house. On this house, large windows stand guard beside a tall wooden door. A decorative overhang shades the swinging door and concrete step that lead down to the butterscotch-colored grass. The inhabitants of the house have made this lonely place in the lonely woods homey and more alive. Instead of staying dark day and night, every morning shutters fly open and the sun comes in, in a tidal wave of gold light.

Sitting on the back step is an old man wearing a milky-white shirt and coal-black pants. In his hand he is holding a dog bone. He leans over cautiously and wonders whether or not to call his dog. Wearing a teal dress that overflows with color, his wife stands beside him, arms folded, hair neatly pulled back, and with a contented expression watches the dog. Neither one wants to break the peacefulness of the quiet morning. The orange and white collie stands in the sea of grass and stops, head up, ears alert, tail wagging. He pants from the heat of the lemon sun and stares into the woods. A dog's panting and a redbird's melody are  the only noises to be heard. The dog slowly closes its mouth as a marching band of birds, chirping away, arises from the trees and flies off. The complete chaos of the moment sends the dog's mind racing, and just as quickly as it began, it is over.

The old man, his wife and their dog, living in a peaceful old farmhouse in the country, are all with love in their hearts. To some the country may be lonely, but to them, it's home.

Patricia Eaton
Descriptive Essay: Dominant Impression
Supported by Three Places in Childhood

My Grandma's House

The best memories I have of growing up were at my grandma's house. When I look back on my childhood there, I realize that the large, rambling house at 15 Lathrop Street was full of happiness and love. Her special touches were everywhere, but my fondest thoughts revolve around the kitchen, the dining room, and the basement recreation room.

Her kitchen was bright yellow like the summer sun and was the center of our social gatherings. Family and guests were drawn to her kitchen like a magnet. The adults gravitated toward the warm smell of coffee wafting from the ever-busy pot on the stove. Our childhood friends knew there would always be fresh cookies, usually peanut butter, but sometimes chocolate-chip or sugar. There was always laughter in Opal's kitchen, mingled with music from her small radio, which sat on the pale-lemon Formica counter top. It was an old house, with floor grates arising from the behemoth furnace in the basement. In the winter, when I returned from school, I would stand over the kitchen grate and warm my bones while the melting snow made puddles on her immaculate floor. She never cared. She would finish making my cocoa, complete with three baby marshmallows, and ask me what I had learned that day. In the warmer months, she would open the windows to catch the breeze which made the curtains billow and float like the clouds passing overhead. On the breeze would be the rich perfume of her garden, full of roses and apples and pears and grapes. During those lazy summer days we drank lemonade while we snapped beans and made jelly and put up tomatoes for the next winter. When the shelves in the basement pantry were groaning with the burden of newly filled Mason jars, and the lid of the old white floor freezer would just barely close, we knew we were ready for another fall.

Next to the kitchen was her blonde oak dining room, chock-full of treasures. Covering one wall were old sepia pictures from Kentucky of aunts and uncles and great-grandparents. On the other three walls were her numerous mirrored shadow-boxes full of knickknacks from everywhere

she had visited. In the spring, we would gently carry them two
at a time to the kitchen for a warm, soapy swim. Every year I
would ask her about them, and every year she would tell me
their stories. There was a little ceramic lady from Canada and
a thimble from Nebraska and a tiny silver spoon from Florida.
On her buffet sat a huge silver refreshment service consisting of
a cream pitcher, sugar bowl and coffee urn that she and Grandpa
had received for a wedding present. She used it only during the holidays.
She made sure, though, it was always polished until you could comb your
hair in its reflection. In front of the bay windows sat the perfect place to
read and nap, an overstuffed turquoise settee covered with plump
embroidered pillows we had made together.

In one corner of the room was a large, free-standing bird cage, home of
Polly the parrot. Grandpa had taught Polly to call Grandma's little
Pekingese, Cookie. It drove the dog crazy, of course, and never failed to
make us laugh. Along one wall sat the blonde upright piano, where we
spent hours with our company playing and singing. The centerpiece of the
dining room was the table, covered with flowers, and crowned with a
gleaming crystal chandelier, which would tinkle gently given any breeze.

Finally, there was my favorite place of all, the basement recreation room.
Grandpa had remodeled the basement when my brother and I were quite
young so we would have a playroom. We had our own sofa, television, hi-fi
and ice box, and our friends were always welcome. Grandpa had put up
paneling and an acoustic ceiling so we could make all the noise we wanted.
The floor was black and white tile which he had laid out like a
checkerboard. When I practiced dancing, my tap-shoes on the tiles made the
most delicious sound! There was a storage closet full of grown-up, dress-up
clothes we used for costumes and a dresser with costume jewelry and high-
heeled shoes just for me. With our friends, we put on shows with acting
and singing and dancing and magic, which surely rivaled anything ever
seen on Broadway or the Grand Ole Opry. At least, that's what Grandma
and Grandpa said.

Growing up on Lathrop Street was an ideal childhood my brother and I
still discuss often and remember fondly. Grandma's cheerful and loving
personality filled her kitchen, her dining room, and her recreation room.
She touched many lives. She is sadly missed by all who had the privilege
to know her.

Todd Swaney
Descriptive Essay
Dominant Impression Supported by Three Places

THE GREAT ADVENTURES

As I look back on my childhood, I have to admit that I do not remember much, at least not in vivid detail. The parts I do remember, though, are the great adventures I used to have in my neighborhood.

I did not live in just any normal place. My neighborhood, if you could 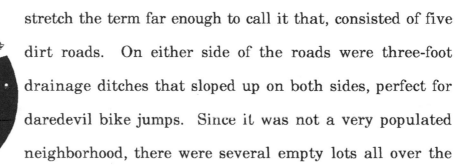 stretch the term far enough to call it that, consisted of five dirt roads. On either side of the roads were three-foot drainage ditches that sloped up on both sides, perfect for daredevil bike jumps. Since it was not a very populated neighborhood, there were several empty lots all over the place which called to me and enticed my adventurous soul. Three such lots that I remember are the grassy lot next to my house, the wooded lot across the street, and the huge field behind my neighborhood.

As far back as I can remember, my first great adventures took place in the overgrown lot next to my house. The grass stood three to four feet in some places, and *Personification* **THE WIND WOULD WHISTLE AN ALLURING SONATA** *Metaphor* as it passed over the tops of the tall weeds. Every summer my dad would take the push mower and create an *Metaphor* **ELABORATE LABYRINTH** for us kids to play in. Everyday it was the same game, hide-and-go-seek. I can remember feeling my heart beating as the game began. We would all run and hide throughout the maze. As the hunter counted to ten, I could feel my senses heighten. I remember how the coarse, dry grass would scuff my hands and knees as I **_Vivid Verb_ SLITHERED** towards base. I could hear the screams and yelps as **_Metaphor_ THE CUNNING HUNTER OVERTOOK THE WEAKER PREY**. As I drew nearer to base, my pulse quickened and I had to make a conscious effort to quiet my breathing. Suddenly, I could see something move around the corner of the path behind me, so **I WOULD SPRINT _Simile_ LIKE A CHEETAH** to the base ahead of me. As I entered the safe haven, my heart just short of bursting, I would let out a victory cry to announce to all my triumph.

As I grew older and taller, my ears grew deaf to the **_Metaphor_ SONGS OF THE FIELD NEXT DOOR** and tuned into the dense, wooded lot across the street. It had always seemed dark and forbidding, but now that I was a little older, I started to feel something different, the need to conquer. I remember how I would beg my dad to borrow his hand saw and sickle and how he would give me a huge lecture on the dangers of these sharp-edged objects and how I shouldn't come running to him if I sawed my leg off. **_Specific Details_ I SPENT AN ENTIRE WEEK GUTTING THE TINY FOREST OF VINES, TALL GRASS, OIL FILTERS, BEER CANS, AND THE BIGGEST PAIR OF WOMEN'S UNDERWEAR I HAD EVER SEEN IN MY LIFE.** Before my journey home across the street each day at twilight, I would look back at what I had done and would be filled with a feeling of satisfaction and a sense of accomplishment. Upon my arrival home, my mom would always fuss about my fresh scrapes and cuts and how if poison ivy got in there *Humor* **IT WOULD ROT MY ARM OFF** unless I got in the tub right now and took a bath. I could always expect to hear comments from my dad too about how maybe *Humor* **IF HE PLANTED SOME TREES IN MY ROOM I MIGHT GET THE URGE TO CLEAN IT UP SOMETIME, TOO**. Undaunted, I would return each morning until finally I had engineered three intersecting roads through the woods. I had created my domain, my safe haven, *Metaphor* **MY ESCAPE FROM THE SISTERS GRIMM**. In those woods, I would spend hours listening to the wind rustle the leaves, climbing trees and spying on nesting birds, and giving the occasional wild growl to scare away any *Metaphor* **PINK-FLOWERED GIRLS** who might be riding their bikes too close to my secret entrance.

When I grew big enough for a two-wheeled bicycle, *Personification* **MY GENTLE PATHS** through the woods soon became my *Contrast* **RIP-ROARING BMX TRACK**. *Personification* **MY BIKE AND I WERE BEST PALS**. It would take me wherever in the world I wanted to go, until I got to the end of the street, of course. As I became a skilled rider, wise of the ways of the road, my parents let me venture off throughout the neighborhood. I would fly down the road on my 5000 horsepower turbo scream machine, the wind through my hair, giving me an inner calm I had never felt before. One day out of the corner of my eye, I saw a yellow bulldozer in a field behind the neighborhood --someplace I had never been. Riding up the ditch towards the bulldozer, I

neglected to see the false mud bottom until the back of **MY NEW STAR**
Specific Details
WARS SHIRT WITH CHEWBACCA ON IT HAD BEEN BLOBBED WITH

GOOEY MUD. Still I rode on until I reached the vast dirt mounds that had

been created by the bulldozer. I never wondered why they were there--**I WAS**
Hyperbole
CERTAIN I HAD JUST DISCOVERED A NEW CONTINENT! Each mound was

different. Some had rocks, some were smooth, some were too steep, and some

were so soft you would just sink into them. I came to know each one so well

that I did not think twice about riding full speed over their tops and around

their sides. I would imagine that **I WAS ON A DIRT BIKE IN FRONT OF**
Hyperbole
THOUSANDS OF PEOPLE WHO WERE CHANTING MY NAME. One day when

I returned to my supercross track, I found it being cleared away with dump

trucks and men in bulldozers. It took them about a week to clear it all away.

Each day I would come after they left and ride around. It wasn't the same,

though. Now there were big ruts in the ground from truck tires, and the
Personification *Alliteration*
mounds were **FATALLY SCARRED FROM THE BITE OF THE BULLDOZERS**.

Now that I am grown up, the mounds have been gone for some time

and buried on top with new houses. The woods across the street were cleared

away to make room for a barn, and the tall, grassy field next door is a neatly

trimmed lawn. My adventurous spirit still thrives, though; only now my

bicycle has been replaced by a motorcycle. And I still explore

hidden dirt roads and trails whenever I get the chance. Only now

I am in my jeep. My friends always said that they would hate to

live way out where I did, but for me, it was the best place in the world.

Section 5:

HOW-TO WRITING

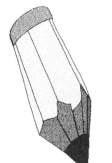

A Prewriting Game for How-To Writing

① BRAINSTORMING ACTIVITIES:

    A. Ask students to brainstorm a list of *five activities* they **LIKE TO DO** (e.g., read, play baseball, listen to music).

    B. Next, instruct them to list *five activities* they **DON'T LIKE** (e.g., cleaning their lockers, doing their homework, babysitting their little brothers or sisters).

    C. Finally, ask the class to list *five activities* that they **DO WITHOUT THINKING** (e.g., tying their shoes, walking to class, making a sandwich).

② LISTING STEPS: Students should first **CHOOSE ONE** of the ideas from their brainstormed lists. Next, they must **LIST THE STEPS** they think would be important if they were teaching someone how to do the activity. Finally, they need to **RECOPY** the steps **OUT OF ORDER** on another sheet of paper, purposefully not identifying the activity for the reader.

HOW TO TALK ON THE PHONE

A Prewriting Game
for How-To Writing, page 2

③   DISTRIBUTING PAPERS: After all students are finished scrambling the steps, **COLLECT** the papers and **DISTRIBUTE** them to the class, making sure no one gets his or her own paper.

④   SEQUENCING STEPS: Students must then try to **DETERMINE THE ACTIVITY** and the **STEPS IN THE ORDER** that they feel is correct, adding any additional steps that have been left out.

⑤   GUESSING THE ACTIVITIES: Students return papers to the owners, who may **READ THE STEPS** to the class in order for the class to guess the activities.

⑥   USING TOPICS: Students may use one of the ideas generated in class as the **TOPIC** for their how-to essay.

CREATING IMAGINATIVE HOW-TO ESSAYS

① → BRAINSTORMING TOPICS: Instruct students to **BRAINSTORM A LIST** of ten imaginative how-to topics (e.g., how to imagine, how to make dragons cry diamonds, how to make the sun rise).

② → SHARING IDEAS: Ask each student to **READ** his or her best one or two examples to the class.

③ → STUDYING MODELS: As a class, read the included student-written examples, **ANALYZING THE ELEMENTS** indicated. You might want to require a certain number of figurative language devices to be included and labeled.

④ → WRITING ROUGH DRAFTS: Students will then **CREATE** their own imaginative how-to essays.

Ryan Rogers
How-To Writing

How to Imagine

Question Intro
HAVE you ever wanted to soar like the wind, while sitting in a desk?

OR travel back in time to save a princess, while lying in bed? The key to this wonder called imagination is at the end of three simple steps: **PREPARING**, **CHOOSING A SPOT**, and **CHOOSING A TOPIC**. Though these steps might take time, the reward lasts a lifetime.

The first step to imagining is **PREPARING**. There are many materials which you must gather, a task that may take a few seconds or many years:

-the thoughts and opinions of a three-year-old

-the faith of a child

-the joy of new parents

Personification
-the patience of a sunrise

-the laughter of a new-found joke

Personification
-the tears of a golden stream

-the love of a mother

-the beauty of a rainbow

Once all the materials have been gathered, use them wisely, for they each have a special purpose. You must also relax, feeling all tension, stress, and discomfort **floating away on a huge cloud.** *Implicit Metaphor* All worries, doubts, and denials must be pulled out of your mind and heaped on the same cloud to float away to eternal disposal.

The next step is to **CHOOSE THE PERFECT AREA** where you will imagine. The **perfect place** *Repetition for Effect* is a king's castle. The **perfect place** is a simple kitchen. The **perfect place** is an office. The **perfect place**

© 1998 M. E. LEDBETTER

is your place. Whatever you want, whatever you need, is at your place. It could be as simple as a lake, or as extravagant as a royal palace in England. For many students, **it's in the _Humor_ middle of math class**.

The final step is ***CHOOSING THE PERFECT TOPIC***. The perfect topic is *Magic 3's* SAVING THE CITY, OR DEFENDING A MOUSE. It's FLYING LIKE THE WIND, OR SWIMMING LIKE A FISH. It's FLYING *Contrasting Elements* TO MARS, OR SWIMMING THE ATLANTIC. Your topic is the perfect topic. However, you must follow these simple guidelines: It must always bring you up, never bring you down. It must not be boring **like a _Simile_ five-hour sermon**. It can make you cry **like _Simile_ the tears out of the heavens**, or laugh **like _Simile_ a hyena in a cage**. You set the limits to the choices.

You are now ready to explore whatever you want. Use your imagination wisely, for it is a precious thing, not to be wasted. If you prepare correctly, choose the perfect place, and choose the perfect topic, the limits are as far as the horizon.

Christy Alexander
How-To Writing

How to Make the Sun Rise

Have you ever wanted to make the sun rise? Have you ever wanted to watch the golden beams of the sun touch housetops, but you couldn't? If you follow these steps, you can make the sun rise by **MAKING THE PERFECT SETTING, MAKING IT HAPPEN**, and **FEELING THE SUN RISE**.

First things first, the **PERFECT SETTING** needs to be made. Find mountains that reach into the heavens and sprinkle them with dandelions. Then make sure the sky is GHOSTLY BLACK, so the sun can work its true magic on the world. The temperature needs to be slightly colder than usual to make it pleasurable when the sun makes its first appearance. Once you have included these in your setting, you can move on to step two.

Now, all you have to do is **MAKE THE SUN RISE**. Whisper three simple words, and three only as long as they're simple, and MAKE SURE THE DAWN OF TIME CAN HEAR THEM. Cuddle up to the special someone beside you, for warmth, while sitting on the peak of the highest mountain in the valley. GUIDE THE SUN WITH YOUR HEART until IT PEEKS OVER THE MOUNTAINS AND SAYS GOOD MORNING TO THE WORLD IN A SPLASH OF GOLD. Yes, go ahead and make the sun rise.

So now that you've made the sun begin to rise, you'll want to **FEEL IT** as it makes its journey into the sky. First, you'll want to watch the flowers. Watch the frail buds of the morning-glories open up into a BLOSSOM OF COLOR as soon as the first thread of light EXALTS THEM IN ITS BRILLIANCE. Then you'll want to hear the mountains. You'll want to HEAR THE MOUNTAINS echo with song as a flood of light washes out the night. Also, you'll want to touch the sky. YOU'LL TOUCH IT WITH YOUR EYES, and they'll see the ENDLESS BLACK turn into soft shades of pink and peach with a hint of the blue that will soon break through all other colors. Yes, you'll want to feel the sun rise.

I bet you can picture the scene of a rising sun right now, but why not make it a reality? If you follow these steps in how to **MAKE THE PERFECT SETTING**, how to **MAKE THE SUN ACTUALLY RISE**, and how to **FEEL ITS FIRE**, then you can have your very own sunrise. Remember, if the setting is right, IT'S GUARANTEED TO WORK WITHIN TWENTY-FOUR HOURS OF THE TIME YOU SAY THREE LITTLE WORDS.

Amy Braselton
How-To Writing

How to Make a Dragon Cry Diamonds

I am here to tell you an important secret. You can make dragons cry diamonds. But, first you have to know the steps in fulfilling this quest. It will be a hard, dangerous journey, but if you listen to me and follow my directions, you will make it to this far and mystical place.

Dragons have been gone from the New World for centuries. They cannot see the purpose in hard, cold, modern machinery. They prefer to live *Elements of Fantasy* in the **LOST LAND OF THE OLD WORLD**. This place is far away from our sun's horizon, and there are only three ways to get there. First, **YOU CAN BORROW BUTTERFLY WINGS**. The brilliant splashes of colors may look like a nice way to get to the Lost Land, but it's actually the most dangerous. The wings tear easily, and you will fall to reality with a bang. But, you could always try to get there by floating on a cloud. Sitting on a *Implicit Metaphor* **PUFFY, WHITE, GOLDEN-LINED PILLOW OF SUNLIGHT** sounds delightful, but after awhile, it gets boring and slow. So, I personally suggest getting there by dreaming. Go to sleep at 12:05, when the moonlight becomes silver, and dream of fairies with their gold dust floating in a haze around their pink, frosted wings. Then suddenly you'll be there in a world filled with unicorns and glittering trees,

Implicit Metaphor

with a **CRYSTAL WATERFALL** and a purple sky and a temperature that stays at

Hyperbole

a perfect 75 degrees. Mermaids with silver tails swim in **POOLS OF CROCODILE**

TEARS. This is the land of lost things.

The second thing you must do to make a dragon cry diamonds is to

pick out your dragon. He must be blue-green scaled with purple eyes. He

will be the one that will give you what you want. To get him, you must

hide yourself, and he will pick up the object you are hiding in and make you

appear. You may decide **TO BECOME A MARBLE**, which is the best thing, since

DRAGONS LOVE MARBLES. To become one, you must think hard about them.

Onomatopoeia

Hear them clicking and see them rolling. Then **BANG**, you're a marble!

You could always decide to hide in a crystal, but dragons never really like

Elements of Fantasy

crystals because they are too ordinary. If you do want **TO BECOME A CRYSTAL**,

touch one while singing "Mary Had a Little Lamb." Then there's always the

Elements of Fantasy

decision of **BECOMING INVISIBLE**, although that is the worst thing to be

because dragons can't see you very well when you're invisible. However, if

Elements of Fantasy

you do choose to be invisible, **KISS A FAIRY'S WING**.

Now, you are on to your last step, saying the magic words or doing

the magic thing. You may decide to say, **"LALA DANGO,"** and be over with it

Humor

quickly. Or you could **TOUCH YOUR NOSE AND CLOSE YOUR EYES**. Or maybe if

you are daring enough, you could **HOP ON ONE FOOT WHILE RUBBING YOUR**

TUMMY. The dragon will start laughing so hard that he will have huge,

Implicit Metaphor

TEAR-SHAPED DIAMONDS coming out of his eyes.   When he is through, remember to thank him, and you will always be welcomed back.

These diamonds will always bring you good luck.   When you get back to reality, the diamonds will be gone, but only from sight.   They are really placed in your mind.   Since you *Elements of Fantasy* **WENT TO THE LOST LAND**, **PICKED OUT YOUR DRAGON**, and **SAID THE MAGIC WORDS**, you will forever be enjoying your diamonds.

NAME:_____ CLASS:_____ DATE:_____

RUBRIC FOR HOW-TO ESSAY

I. INTRODUCTION

A. Write your **THESIS STATEMENT** below. (Remember that this is the topic sentence for your entire paper and must include the subject, the mode, and the steps.)

_____

_____

B. To make sure the **"HOW-TO" STEPS** presented in your thesis statement are in **PARALLEL STRUCTURE**, list them below and explain the structure you are using (all nouns, all verbs, etc.).

① → _____

② → _____

③ → _____

*Explanation:_____

*Remember that the steps should be covered in the body paragraphs in the **SAME ORDER** that they are listed in the introduction.

II. BODY PARAGRAPHS--List five **SMILEY-FACE PASSAGES** and explain the **TYPES** (simile, metaphor, personification, repetition for effect, specific example/detail for effect, alliteration, etc.)

A._____

Type:_____

B._____

Type:_____

C._____

       Type:_____

D._____

       Type:_____

E._____

       Type:_____

III. *REVISION/PROOFREADING*

   A.   Explain your overall *TONE*. (Remember that this is the author's attitude toward his or her work and can range from serious to humorous, sarcastic to poetic, etc. Your tone needs to be *CONSISTENT* and clearly understood by your reader.)

      ① → Explanation of tone:_____

_____

_____

      ② → Revisions to achieve consistency:_____

_____

_____

   B.   Give specific examples of your *REVISION/PROOFREADING*:

      ① → _____

      ② → _____

      ③ → _____

Section 6:

LITERARY ANALYSIS

Writing
Literary Analysis Papers

①→ DETERMINING ASPECTS FOR ANALYSIS: One effective method of literary analysis is to ask students to decide on **THREE ASPECTS** of a work that they would like to analyze (or one aspect with three strong subdivisions). Remind students that the idea of literary analysis is to shed some light on a piece using the **STUDENT'S OWN PERSONAL INTERPRETATION** (combined with the ideas of literary critics if you require a more extensive analysis), **WHICH MUST BE SUPPORTED BY SPECIFIC QUOTES FROM THE TEXT**. Literary analysis is an excellent method of teaching a more advanced form of persuasion in that students are forced to find textual proof of their ideas and **INCORPORATE IT INTO THEIR OWN SENTENCES**.

②→ USING ANALYSIS WEB: After students have brainstormed (or been assigned) their three main points, they may use the **LITERARY ANALYSIS WEB** to outline their strategy. The web forces students to find their proof **before** they begin their rough drafts, allowing them to change a point if enough evidence cannot be found.

③→ USING EXCERPT CONTAINING COMMON ERRORS: Before students begin writing their papers, give them the **EXCERPT CONTAINING COMMON ERRORS IN LITERARY ANALYSIS** as practice in detecting and avoiding these sorts of mistakes.

④→ USING RESPONSE SHEET: After students write their initial rough drafts, assign partners, response groups, or response rows. The **RESPONSE SHEET FOR COMMON ERRORS IN LITERARY ANALYSIS PAPERS** provides structured feedback from peer groups and works as a useful proofreading/revisionary tool that can help student authors reshape their literary analyses.

LITERARY ANALYSIS WEB WITH QUOTED SUPPORT

TOPIC

1st Main Point	2nd Main Point	3rd Main Point

SUPPORT   SUPPORT   SUPPORT   SUPPORT   SUPPORT   SUPPORT   SUPPORT   SUPPORT   SUPPORT

(Write quotes for support on the lines.)

Excerpt Containing Common Errors
in
Literary Analysis Essays

Directions: The following is an excerpt from a student literary analysis of poetic devices used in Dylan Thomas's "Memories of Christmas." **In the blanks below, cite the errors from the paragraph according to the types listed and make the corrections in the paragraph itself.**

One type of poetic device Dylan used is imagery to tell you about his setting. This quote tells the reader it is Christmas and that it is snowing ":...the ice broke and the skating grocer vanished like a snowmen threw a white trap-door on that same Christmas Day" (page 1). This quote tells the place of the action, "All the Christmases roll down the hill towards the Welsh-speaking sea, like a snowball growing whiter and bigger and rounder, like a cold and headlong moon bundling down the sky that was our street" (page 1). Imagery is important.

① → **Incorrect tense/tense shift:** _____

② → **Incorrect reference to author:** _____

③ → **Incorrect point of view:** _____

④ → **Reference to "quote":** _____

⑤ → **Misuse of colon:** _____

⑥ → **Run-on:** _____

⑦ → **Lack of persuasive explanation:** _____

⑧ → **Incorrect footnote form:** _____

⑨ → **Inaccurate quoted material:** _____

Name:_____ Class:_____ Date:_____

Name of partner:_____

RESPONSE SHEET
FOR
COMMON ERRORS IN LITERARY ANALYSIS PAPERS

Directions: Proofread your partner's paper in terms of the errors listed below. If there is no error in a category, write **NONE**. If an error exists, write it on the appropriate line.

① → INCORRECT TENSE/TENSE SHIFT--(Remember to use present tense for literary analysis.)

----

② → INCORRECT REFERENCE TO AUTHOR--(for first reference, use author's first and last names; for all subsequent references, use last name only.)

----

③ → INCORRECT POINT OF VIEW--(Do not use first person singular--I, me--or second person--you.)

----

④ → AWKWARD BLENDING OF QUOTED MATERIAL/NO BLENDING OF QUOTED MATERIAL--(Textual support must be blended with your own words.)

----

⑤ → MERGING OF QUOTED MATERIAL RESULTING IN A RUN-ON--(To avoid a run-on, use a semicolon, a comma and conjunction, or a clause signal Remember that quoted material cannot stand alone.)

----

⑥ → LACK OF PERSUASIVE EXPLANATION--(quotes should be used to further your point. The reader should never wonder why a quote was used; the reason for its inclusion should be made apparent.)

----

⑦ → INCORRECT FOOTNOTE FORM--(Correct footnote form is author's last name and page number or page number alone if attribution has been given.)

----

⑧ → LACK OF PROOFREADING OF QUOTED MATERIAL--(Be sure quoted material is represented accurately.)

LITERARY ANALYSIS RUBRIC

I. ORGANIZATION

A. Introductory paragraph—

Write your **thesis statement**, the sentence that tells what your paper is about. Here you will list the three aspects to be covered.

Be sure to use the author's first and last names and **state the name of the piece** being analyzed. **Refer to the author by last name** (without titles such as "Mr." and "Dr.") all other times.

_____

_____

B. Three body paragraphs—

Each body paragraph must have a **topic sentence** that tells what the paragraph is about. Write each topic sentence below. Be sure to include **transition words/phrases**.

1st body:_____

2nd body:_____

3rd body:_____

C. Conclusion—

The conclusion must **restate the thesis** in a different way. Write your restated thesis below.

_____

_____

II. Persuasive support in body paragraphs

Each body paragraph must have enough persuasive support to persuade the reader to share your opinion about your topic, which means at least **two specific examples, preferably three.** The examples should not merely be presented but be stated in a **convincing manner.** Write a sample of a persuasive support from each body paragraph.

A. 1st body: _____

_____

B. 2nd body: _____

_____

C. 3rd body: _____

_____

III. PROOFREADING/EDITING

A. Blending of quoted material—

①→ Quoted material should be **blended with your own words** in a way that is easy for the reader to follow and that supports your thesis, such as in the following example:

Thomas's use of humor is evident in his treatment of the Prothero fire: "*There was no fire to be seen, only clouds of smoke and Mr. Prothero standing in the middle of them, waving his slipper as though he were conducting*" (2). ◄ *Place Period after Parentheses.*

Remember that **quotes cannot stand alone.**

② → Watch for **run-ons that can occur from incorrect blending**—(e.g., Thomas presents a collage of memories for his readers, "*One Christmas was so much like another, in those years...*").

The Comma

Causes a Run-On.

(A **colon or semicolon** could be substituted for the comma.)

③ → **Never refer to the quote itself**—(e.g., This quote says...).

④ → Be sure to include **page numbers** for quoted material.

➡ Write an example of a blended quote from your paper:

_____

_____

B. Verb tense—
Use present tense for literary analysis.
Proofread your work for present tense by listing five present tense verbs from your paper:

① _____   ② _____   ③ _____   ④ _____   ⑤ _____

C. Spelling—
Proofread for spelling errors by listing five spelling/vocabulary words from your paper and the **page numbers of the dictionary** where the word was found.

① → _____ (   )   ② → _____ (   )

③ → _____ (   )   ④ → _____ (   )

⑤ → _____ (   )

MCNALLY'S RISK,
Our Good Fortune

Who among us doesn't like a good mystery? After endless hours at work, where the biggest mystery might be who has been drinking coffee without paying into the coffee club, and after countless chores on the homefront, where the excitement for the day occurs when the mailperson leaves yet another ad for the Foley's Red Apple Sale as well as that second reminder from the Light Company, who wouldn't appreciate a good book, one that promises far more than our everyday lives hold for us? [Lawrence Sanders's <u>McNally's Risk</u>, *Thesis statement & 3 aspects* one of a series involving the infamous detective Archy McNally, fits the bill. Its *PLOT*, *CHARACTERIZATION*, and *STYLE* can make even the most jaded reader forget that he, like Archy, isn't the daring sleuth out on the case of the century.]

From the **FIRST** INCIDENT, when Silas Hawkin--a famous artist--is killed, a prime suspect cast of "who-dun-its" is assembled for us--from the quarreling duo of mother and daughter, " '*quote within a quote* **step-daughter,' the younger woman said in a Freon voice" (25)**, to the newest in a seemingly never-ending line of Archy's girlfriends to the enigmatic Hector Johnson, a man without a past. And if this first gruesome murder, where we, too, are **"*Blend quotes* spooked by the sight of the murdered artist, so pale" (51)** doesn't pose enough problems for our fearless McNally, to compound his worries he is asked to investigate the extraordinary beauty with whom he has fallen in love. We learn that not only are her connections less than honorable, but she is purportedly engaged to McNally's client, the **"Chinless Wonder himself, Chauncey Wilson Smythe-Hersforth" (16)**. Ah, the plot thickens. The final blow is yet another murder, this time that of Marcia Hawkin, the bereaved daughter of Silas. What? A dearth of excitement in our lives? Never, now that we've got Archy . . . <u>and</u> the missing painting <u>and</u> the characters posing as people they are not <u>and</u> the Father and Daughter pair pitted against each other--not to mention the untimely demise of several minor characters--it's all there and more. What's so much fun is that it's our puzzle to solve, with Archy's help.

BESIDES THE INTRIGUE, we can't help ourselves--we fall for the *PROTAGONIST*, Archibald McNally, Archy to his friends--and by the end of the book, those friends include us. Archy is fun--pure and simple. He eats too much, works too little, and enjoys every moment of it all; and his wit and charm make unraveling the plot a pleasure. He's rich and intelligent, but he doesn't use his advantages to make us feel inferior. Instead, we learn from him. Archy advises us about food, and, yes, the wealthy apparently <u>do</u> dine differently--if you count luncheons on an expense account, a daily cocktail hour, and meals prepared by a live-in chef: **"Dinner that night was another of Ursi Olson's specialties: medallions of veal, breast of chicken, and mild Italian sausages sauteed with mushrooms and onions and served with a wine sauce over a bed of fettuccine" (277)**. And his habit of talking to us, the readers, makes us care about his plight. We have an exchange of sorts with this character, as he explains to us that **"I must confess that I mention my daily labors so frequently because the record I keep becomes the source of these published accounts of** *Ellipsis & period* **my investigations . . . . I just don't want you to think**

I'm making it all up" (287). We're not detached observers but involved participants, thanks to Sanders's expert portrayal of the character of Archibald McNally.

IF SANDERS'S PLOT AND CHARACTERIZATION ARE NOT ENOUGH TO TOTALLY CAPTIVATE THE READER, then his ST⅄LE surely will provide the finishing touch. One noticeable stylistic device is his use of puns. After Archy has "gotten his man," so to speak, Archy and his attorney father settle down in the McNally study to provide the denouement of the novel for the readers and to indulge in a glass of wine for the beleaguered characters, at which point Archy confides to us that **"I was hoping for a cognac, but he poured glasses of wine. That was okay; any port in a storm"** (314). We, having lived through the whole ordeal of McNally's "risk" ourselves, right along with our hero, can only chuckle in approval-- one more thing Archy can do--make us smile. Of course, all along we knew he had it in him. His quips--everything from **"You must understand that you are required to pass a Gossip Aptitude Test before you are allowed to live in the town of Palm Beach"** (322) to **"I was simultaneously rapt and unwrapped"** (15)--combined with his use of figurative language, **"The air was choky, hard to breathe, and the sun gleamed waterily behind a scrim of clouds the color of elephant hide"** (286), prove that some detective novels can indeed offer more than fast-paced action.

If our jobs and our lives in general have lost their zest, or if we are of the opinion that a little added gusto never hurts, then Lawrence Sanders's <u>McNally's Risk</u> is a certain winner. The cover hints at "beauty, scandal, and suspicion," but as we read, we realize that there is ever so much more awaiting us . . . we have only to turn the page.

Karen Solis
Assignment: Literary Analysis of Dylan Thomas's "Memories of Christmas"
and "Holiday Memory"

Dashing Down Memory Lane

In his essays "Memories of Christmas" and "Holiday Memory," Dylan Thomas recaptures images from the past and delivers them to us in an upbeat, unusual fashion. *Thesis statement & 3 aspects* [Through the use of stylistic devices such as STREAM OF CONSCIOUSNESS, WORD PLAY, and FIGURATIVE LANGUAGE, Thomas presents us with a vividly expressive collection of childhood memories.]

FOR INSTANCE, in "Memories of Christmas," Thomas uses the stylistic device of STREAM OF CONSCIOUSNESS to lead us on a lively jaunt through a myriad of images as they surface in his mind. He likens the retrieval of thoughts from his memory to reaching into the snow and pulling up findings such as **"holly or robins or pudding, squabbles and carols and oranges..." (1)**. Again, as he describes the varied contents of his Christmas stocking over the years as a **"folded flag and a false nose and a tram-conductor's cap and a machine that punched tickets...a little hatchet, and a rubber buffalo, or it may have been a horse...and a**

celluloid duck . . ." **(3)**, visual images spill out before us. Similarly, in "Holiday Memory," Thomas begins his essay with a flood of thoughts: **"A tune on an ice-cream cornet. A slap of sea and a tickle of sand. A fanfare of sunshades opening"** **(304)**. He continues this pattern in a typical picnic beach scene where **"fathers spread newspapers over their faces, and sand fleas hopped on the picnic lettuce, and someone had forgotten the salt"** **(304)**. Images change quickly as he describes the action of the dogs among the hustle and bustle of the busy kitchen on holiday morning as they **"chased their tails in the jostling kitchen, worried sandshoes, snapped at flies, writhed between legs, scratched among towels, sat smiling on hampers"** **(305)**. As he "runs" us through an assortment of images, we are left breathless, yet ready for the next lap.

WORD PLAY is **ANOTHER** stylistic device Thomas uses to conjure up vivid images and impressions. In "Memories of Christmas," Thomas recaptures the essence of the winter-cold sea breaking onto shore when he writes of **"the ice-edged, fish-freezing waves" (1)**.   He touches the senses of sight and sound when he depicts several Christmases rolled into one as a **"wool-white bell-tongued ball of holidays" (2)**. A steady stream of action words instills a sense of activity as he remembers the **"thimble-hiding musical-chairing blind-man's-buffing party" (2)**. Other examples of word play are seen in "Holiday Memory." For instance, we can visualize the untanned ready-to-be-burned skin when Thomas speaks of **"fathers in the once-a-year sun" (306)**. Animals stubbornly parading in an endless tethered circle of a children's ride are remembered as **"foolish, mulish, religious donkeys on the unwilling trot" (306)**. The brown uniformity of the beach is recalled as the **"paper-bagged sand" (306)**.

As a **THIRD** method of stylistic device, Thomas incorporates various types of FIGURATIVE LANGUAGE to paint a vivid picture of his childhood for the reader. In "Memories of Christmas," he **personifies** the setting and atmosphere of the winter-laden town as he reveals its location by the **"Welsh-speaking" (1)** and **"carol-singing sea" (2)**. With the use of **similes**, the local neighborhood cats are transformed into exotic beasts of prey **"sleek and long as jaguars...spitting and snarling" (2)**. We are **visually** led through the sensational events of an unexpected fire on Christmas Eve at Mrs. Prothero's house and her subsequent reaction as he recalls her **"announcing ruin like a town crier in Pompeii" (2)**. Using **alliteration**, Thomas provides us with a humorous image of Mr. Prothero **"smacking at the smoke with a slipper" (2)**. Figurative language in the form of **alliteration** is also used in "Holiday Memory." Flowing phrases such as a **"whole harmonious, hollow minute" (304)** and the **"princely pastime of pouring sand" (306)** change otherwise ordinary moments into meaningful passages of time. Thomas uses a **simile** to describe a boy's lion as being as **"ferocious as a hearth-rug" (304)**, which counters the normal images that come to mind and, instead, reveals it as actually being old, worn, and bedraggled.

IN BOTH ESSAYS, the use of such stylistic devices allows Thomas to lead us on a lively excursion down memory lane while captivating our interest with vivid imagery and events along the way.

Allisa Brill
Assignment: "Rikki-tikki-tavi" Literary Analysis
Comparing and Contrasting

RIKKI-TIKKI-TAVI Analysis

In the exciting short story "Rikki-tikki-tavi," Rudyard Kipling compares and contrasts our brave hero, Rikki-tikki, and his hideous foes, the cobras. [Through APPEARANCE, PERSONALITY AND ACTIONS, and LOVE FOR HOME, Kipling presents a mental picture of three animals, all fighting for control over the garden.]

FIRST, the characters are continually compared and contrasted in their APPEARANCE. Rikki-tikki-tavi looks tame, but he can look mean when he is angry, **"rather like a cat in his fur and tail"(13).** Kipling also shows how he has a darker appearance by saying, **"Rikki-tikki-tavi felt his eyes growing red and hot"(16).** Nag, on the other hand, has a more sinister, evil appearance, as we can tell when **"inch by inch out of the grass rose up the head and spread hood of Nag, the big black cobra, and he was five feet long from tongue to tail"(15).** So, while two the felon and one their foe, their differences range farther than their appearances.

THEN, in their PERSONALITIES AND ACTIONS, they are also compared. Kipling shows Nagaina's aggressiveness when, **"just under him whizzed the head of Nagaina."** Rikki-tikki, too, is a fierce fighter as is seen when **"his eyes were red, and he held on as**

the body cartwhipped over the floor" and also when Rikki is "chattering with rage"(16). He seems to have a wild side, which somehow makes him even more of a hero.

LAST, something the three characters have in common is their *LOVE FOR THEIR INDIAN HOME*. This is proven when " 'Tricked! Tricked! Tricked! Rck-tck-tck!' chuckled Rikki-tikki. 'The boy is safe and it was I-I-I that caught Nag by the hood last night in the bathroom' " (21). We can tell Rikki-tikki-tavi loves his home because he is willing to risk his life for his human companions. Nag and Nagaina show their honor for their home as well, good or bad: " 'When the house is emptied of people,' said Nagaina to her husband, 'he will have to go away and then the garden will be our own again'"(17). This shows that the cobras do indeed like their home and will do anything to be in charge of it again. The snaky pair may also feel that their territory is invaded by the intrusion of Rikki-tikki. So, obviously, there are two sides to this story.

[*IN CONCLUSION*, Kipling does a great job comparing and contrasting the *APPEARANCE, PERSONALITY AND ACTIONS*, and *LOVE FOR HOME* of Rikki-tikki and the two evil cobras, Nag and Nagaina.] Kipling's love for India really shows in this adventurous short story, "Rikki-tikki-tavi."

Ginger Fisher
Literary Analysis

THE WOLVES OF WILLOUGHBY CHASE: An Analysis

Who hasn't needed an escape from days when everything seems to have gone wrong? Who couldn't use some humor to add spice to these tedious times? [Joan Aiken's The Wolves of Willoughby Chase is just what we all need. From the lovable BONNIE and other CHARACTERS' laugh-out-loud names and antics to the WOLVES themselves, this book is a wonderfully written comedy of tragedies.]

FROM THE FIRST CHAPTER we are affected by the humor as the main character, BONNIE, **"picked up a jug of warm water...and dashed Mrs. Slycarp full in the face" (5)**. From the beginning we know Bonnie's a head-strong young vixen who doesn't take any nonsense. Even after Mrs. Slycarp sends her and her cousin to live in a boarding house, she doesn't lose any of her spirit: **"She picked up a bowl full of rancid gravy and flung it right in the cook's face" (94)**. We laugh as we think to ourselves, "That serves the cook right for hitting her with a saucepan!" When Bonnie's cousin, Sylvia, becomes ill, we see another side of Bonnie, as **"Bonnie took a chance and ran upstairs to visit Sylvia who she found weak and coughing" (101)**. We cry along with Bonnie as Sylvia gets sicker and sicker, but Bonnie's already planned a daring escape!

AS IF BONNIE'S WITTY ANTICS AREN'T ENOUGH FOR US, Aiken has assembled an outrageous cast of CHARACTERS who aid and abet them on their escape into London. Bonnie and Sylvia almost get caught by Mrs. Brisket, **"a short, massive, smartly dressed woman" (84)** who owns the boarding house that evil Mrs. Slycarp dumps them in. We get misty-eyed, yet are still rolling in laughter, as the sick Sylvia and witty Bonnie jump into the back of an oncoming goose wagon when Sylvia gets too weak to travel. But, too, who discovers them? The faithful Simon, a long-lost friend. Seeing Sylvia sick, he takes them to Mr. Wilderness, **"an immensely tall man, wearing a blackened leather apron" (113)**, who lives by himself in the middle of nowhere. In a month, they are on their journey again. When they finally reach London, our sides still split in laughter from what happened along the way, they meet Mr. Gripe, **"a thin, worrisome, agitated, gray-haired man" (132)**, who is a whiny baby through and through. He hears of Mrs. Slycarp, and they turn right around to head back.

AIKEN HAS MORE LAUGHTER IN STORE FOR US as they head back through the territory of the WOLVES, a humorous additive to this story. They all get thrown around because **"if the wolves see a train slowing down, they're alert at once" (137)**, so the train is making all these sudden stops along the way. On the train ride, funny enough to make even the most solemn of readers dash off a smile, a window flies open and **"a wolf precipitated itself through the aperture thus formed" (146)**. What's more, surely intended to make our hearts race in fear, are Bonnie and Sylvia getting stuck outside the gates where **"nothing stood between them and those ruthless fiends" (152)**.

If we need a respite from that bad day, [then let BONNIE, a host of other assorted CHARACTERS, and the WOLVES in The Wolves of Willoughby Chase be the escape that once every so often we all need.] Aiken's masterpiece will have us all laughing so hard we will barely be able to turn the page.

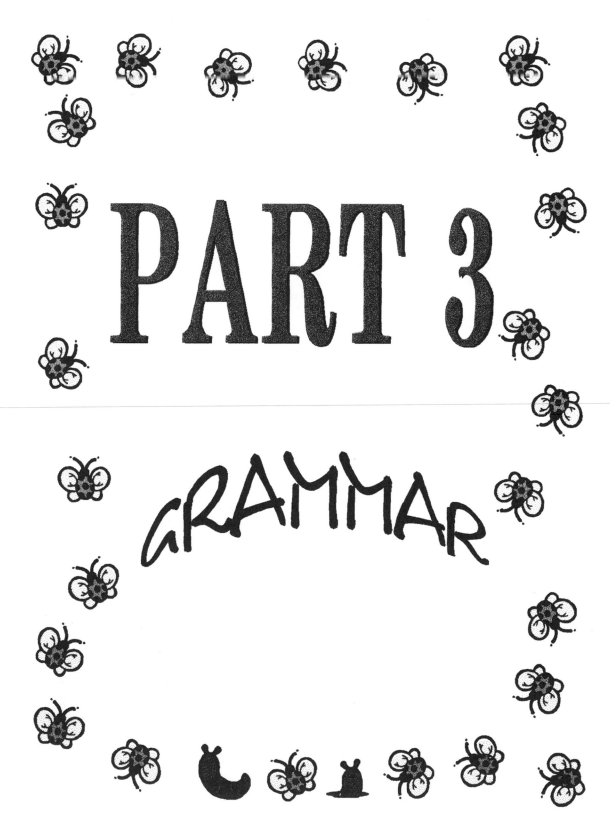

PART 3

GRAMMAR

PURPOSE OF CORRECTION SHEETS

①→ ADDRESSES INDIVIDUAL GRAMMATICAL WEAKNESSES: The purpose of the correction sheet is for students to address their own **INDIVIDUAL WEAKNESSES**, rather than to practice on errors they haven't made in textbook sentences they haven't written.

②→ PROVIDES INTERACTION WITH TEACHER PROOFREADING COMMENTS: Correction sheets force students to **INTERACT** with teacher-made comments and to come to an understanding of the **REASONING** behind the errors marked.

③→ FAMILIARIZES STUDENTS WITH RULES: Through correction sheets, students learn to **CATEGORIZE ERRORS** by types, to become more **FAMILIAR WITH THE RULES** for each type, and to make **FEWER ERRORS** overall.

USE OF CORRECTION SHEETS

① → MARK ERRORS ON STUDENT ESSAYS: **AFTER MARKING ERRORS** on student final drafts, hand out correction sheets.

② → DETERMINE ERRORS FOR STUDENTS TO CORRECT: **STUDENTS DO NOT NEED TO ADDRESS ALL ERRORS FOR EACH ASSIGNMENT.**

    A. Explain to students which types of errors they will correct for each assignment.

    B. Students will record the types of errors in the appropriate space on the Correction Sheet.

    C. For instance, one essay could serve as practice for correcting all **RUN-ONS, FRAGMENTS,** and **SPELLING** as well as one other error of the teacher's or student's choice.

    D. Next time, after a minilesson on **SUBJECT-VERB AGREEMENT** or **COMMA USAGE,** for example, add these types of errors to the list of items to be corrected.

③ → NUMBER THE ERRORS TO BE CORRECTED: Students must **NUMBER** only the errors chosen to be corrected for a particular assignment.

④ → STATE RULES: It is important to emphasize that **SPECIFIC RULES** must be written. For instance, students should specify which comma rule applies--**COMMA IN A SERIES, comma for an INTRODUCTORY ADVERB CLAUSE,** and so on.

➤ Provide students with **GRAMMAR HANDBOOKS,** a **CLASSROOM SET** of rules, or **INDIVIDUAL STUDENT NOTES** to assist them in finding rules that apply to their individual mistakes.

NAME_____CLASS_____DATE_____

Writing Assignment:_____

Corrections Required for This Assignment:_____

CORRECTION SHEET

On your **ESSAY** itself, **NUMBER AND HIGHLIGHT THE ERRORS TO BE CORRECTED FOR THIS ASSIGNMENT** (unless there are other specific instructions).

Then, on this **SHEET** do the following:

    a. I identify the **TYPE OF ERROR** (run-on, fragment, comma, spelling, etc.)
    b. Write the **SPECIFIC RULE** regarding the error.

    ☞ For **SPELLING ERRORS**, put **DICTIONARY NAME AND PAGE NUMBER** of correct spelling.
    c. **CORRECT THE ERROR. NEVER** write the **ERROR**.

1
A. _____

B. _____

C. _____

_____

2
A. _____

B. _____

C. _____

_____

3
A. _____

B. _____

C. _____

_____

CORRECTION SHEET, page ___

NAME _____

____

a. _____

b. _____

c. _____

_____

____

a. _____

b. _____

c. _____

_____

____

a. _____

b. _____

c. _____

_____

____

a. _____

b. _____

c. _____

_____

____

a. _____

b. _____

c. _____

_____

GRADING CORRECTION SHEETS

① → INDIVIDUALIZING THE GRADE:

A. Decide the **POINT VALUE** of the correction sheet.

B. If the correction sheet itself is worth **50 POINTS TOTAL**, and one student has made **10 ERRORS** that come under the types of errors to be corrected for this particular assignment, then each of his numbered corrections will count **5 POINTS**.

C. Another student, however, might have only **5 ERRORS**; therefore, her corrections count **10 POINTS** each.

D. **INDIVIDUALIZE THE GRADING SYSTEM** to correspond to the number of mistakes.

   Or ...

② → LIMITING THE NUMBER OF ERRORS TO BE GRADED: Another method is to grade only a **DESIGNATED NUMBER** of corrections for all students--for instance, 5 errors per person.

   Or ...

③ → ASSIGNING AN EFFORT GRADE: Tell students that you will spot-check their papers and assign **EFFORT GRADES**.

Teacher Model
Sample Persuasive Essay
Errors Marked for Correction Sheet

Let's Head to Seaside!

Hungry for fresh mahi mahi? *Longing for white sands and crystal clear water?* Tired of all work and no play?* Then let's head for Seaside, Florida. We can visit our favorite restaurant, enjoy the world-famous scenery, and participate in activities that will put Baytown light years away.

First, in terms of cuisine, aren't we ready for a change? How many times lately has our collective refrain been "This again?" when hot dogs, TV dinners, and everything and anything microwavable have been plopped down on TV trays in front of the six o'clock news? Then Bud and Alley's is for us. **We'll be dining beach side in an open-air bungalow, exotic fish, vegetables al dente, and salads with such unusual ingredients as arugula, endive, and shiitake mushrooms will be served with that perfect wine that we always enjoy.** (1) And don't forget espresso or cappuccino in the gazebo afterwards. What could be more romantic?

Besides all the culinary delights, Seaside's scenery would be a welcome relief. Instead of Gulf Coast's refineries rising in our polluted skies like giant, soot-blackened tinker toys, we'd have an unobstructed view of nature's best--clear blue skies broken only by steep-pitched rooftops of homes that not only are award-winning for their uniqueness but reminiscent of days long ago. Gone will be the monotony of neighborhoods we're used to, where each house resembles the next except for a curlicue here and a doodad there, and in its place will be winding, red-bricked streets and rainbow-

colored houses, some with gables and dormer windows, rooftop decks, and trilevel porches. And the terrain itself is unparalleled. When was the last time we've seen yards sprouting misshapen scrub oaks like some sort of beach-side modernistic sculpture? And grass, your dreaded enemy, is almost a thing of the past in Seaside. **Instead, wildflowers and sea grasses and sand--miles and miles of it--makes this town truly a Seaside paradise.** (2) Ready for some sightseeing?*

If fine dining and unprecedented scenery aren't quite enough to fill our postcards then the activities will be truly something we can write home about--if we have time, that is. (3) Your endless complaints of a thirty-mile drive to an "uninspired" municipal golf course will be forgotten. Seaside's neighboring town, Destin, offers courses unique enough for even the most jaded players. Soon you could be teeing off with the rich and famous. **One picture-perfect hole after**

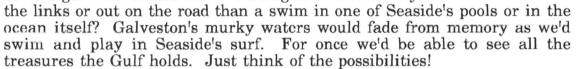

another as your backdrop.(4) What about biking?* How many times have we dreamed of following the ocean wherever it may lead--just you and I, and our trusty Schwinns. We could pack a picnic lunch, and the day would be ours--coasting along the seaside highway or following countless bike trails in and out of the city itself. Who knows, we just might strike up a conversation with Prince Charles, a fellow Seaside visitor and cyclist, as rumors go. And what's more relaxing after a hard day at the links or out on the road than a swim in one of Seaside's pools or in the ocean itself? Galveston's murky waters would fade from memory as we'd swim and play in Seaside's surf. For once we'd be able to see all the treasures the Gulf holds. Just think of the possibilities!

What do you say? Let's put away those frozen dinners, get out those travel brochures, and plan the **itenery (5)** for the best trip of our lives. Tennis anyone?*

(1) Run-on sentence
(2) Subject/Verb Agreement
(3) Comma
(4) Fragment
(5) Spelling

✳ Intentional fragments

NAME_____ CLASS_____ DATE_____

Writing Assignment: <u>Persuasive Essay: "Let's Head to Seaside"</u>

Corrections Required for This Assignment: <u>Commas, Run-ons,</u> Subject-Verb Agreement, Fragments, Spelling

CORRECTION SHEET
Sample

On your **ESSAY** itself, **NUMBER AND HIGHLIGHT THE ERRORS TO BE CORRECTED FOR THIS ASSIGNMENT** (unless there are other specific instructions).

Then, on this **SHEET** do the following:

    a. I dentify the **TYPE OF ERROR** (run-on, fragment, comma, spelling, etc.)
    b. Write the **SPECIFIC RULE** regarding the error.

    ☞ For **SPELLING ERRORS**, put **DICTIONARY NAME AND PAGE NUMBER** of correct spelling.
    c. **CORRECT THE ERROR. NEVER** write the **ERROR**.

1
A. <u>Run-on Sentence</u>

B. <u>One method of correcting a run-on is to use a period between the two sentences.</u>

C. <u>We'll be dining beach side in an open-air bungalow. Exotic fish, vegetables al dente, and salads...will be served with that perfect wine that we always enjoy.</u>

2
A. <u>Subject-Verb Agreement</u>

B. <u>Compound subjects joined by "and" require a plural verb.</u>

C. <u>Instead, wildflowers and sea grasses and sand--miles and miles of it-- make this town truly a Seaside paradise.</u>

3
A. <u>Comma</u>

B. <u>Use a comma after an introductory adverbial clause.</u>

C. <u>If fine dining and unprecedented scenery aren't quite enough to fill our postcards, then the activities will be truly something we can write home about--if we have time, that is.</u>

NAME _____

4
a. Fragment _____
b. One way to correct a fragment is to combine it with the previous sentence.
c. Soon you could be teeing off with the rich and famous, one picture-perfect hole after another as your backdrop.

5
a. Spelling _____
b. American Heritage, page 696 _____
c. itinerary _____
_____

___
a. _____
b. _____
c. _____
_____

___
a. _____
b. _____
c. _____
_____

___
a. _____
b. _____
c. _____
_____

Classroom Posters/Notes

①→ MAKING POSTERS/CLASS NOTES: Put students into groups to make large **POSTERS** for display or to write classroom **NOTES** listing **GRAMMATICAL RULES** and **SAMPLE SENTENCES** that will be helpful as year-round references.

②→ TEAMING UP FOR RULE WRITING: Divide students into teams, giving a **SPECIFIED NUMBER** of **RULES PER TEAM**. Each team must list the rules, compose sentences that serve as examples for each rule, and illustrate the sentences.

③→ HOLDING A CONTEST: Hold a **CONTEST** for best posters in each category to serve as display. Give extra credit or prizes.

④→ RELATING RULES TO THEMES, WORKS READ, FICTIONAL CHARACTERS, ETC.: For a further challenge, require students to **RELATE ALL SAMPLE SENTENCES TO A CERTAIN THEME**, a work read in class, or a fictional character. The point is that specifying the **SUBJECT MATTER** as well as the rule to be addressed requires students to meet two criteria.

⑤→ ASSIGNING INDIVIDUAL RULE WRITING: Instead of group work, students may work **INDIVIDUALLY**, each student doing all rules and writing original sentences that apply to his or her life.

⑥→ PREPARING QUIZZES: Use a sampling of student sentences as a class quiz over certain rules.

GRAMMAR PROJECTS

© 1998 M. E. LEDBETTER

How to Individualize Grammar Assignments

① → USING SENTENCES FROM CLASS CORRECTION SHEETS:
To check a class's understanding of various grammatical concepts throughout the year, use sentences gathered from individual correction sheets from all classes to form a **CLASSROOM CHECK TEST** on a particular error or errors. For example, you may keep a working list of fragments and run-ons as they occur in student writing.

➥ Students find these tests derived from student-written sentences **MORE RELEVANT** than obscure textbook-written sentences.

② → USING STUDENT-WRITTEN TESTS: Ask students to compose a "test" on a particular grammar skill for their neighbors. The actual class test can be derived from an **ASSORTMENT OF STUDENT-COMPOSED SENTENCES**.

➥ When students write proposed questions and answers, they become more familiar with grammatical rules and revisionary options.

Sentence/Fragment/Run-On Test
Sentences From Student Papers

On your scantron, mark **"A"** for **SENTENCE, "B"** for **FRAGMENT,** and **"C"** for **RUN-ON.**

1. Things like beaches, activities, and especially shopping.

2. It was great hearing from her!

3. When Cloyd first arrives, he is boiling mad.

4. Old Dan will not leave the tree, he refuses to go until the coon is caught.

5. The tall pines with their long, fresh-smelling needles.

6. Bobby and I went fishing he forgot his fishing pole.

7. It was a hot summer day, and I walked down the street to the city pool to take a swim.

8. Walter took Cloyd into the mountains for mining; he let the boy go exploring.

9. Lisa doesn't go crazy on bright days, however, she does on her dark days.

10. Lisa Shillings is a young girl who thinks she's going out of her mind, but her parents don't believe her.

11. The colors are like Christmas lights hanging from every inch of the house.

12. As soon as Teddy goes to sleep, "Rikki goes for his nightly walk around the house," this shows he is on guard for any problems that may happen.

13. You can sit on your back porch and hear the rush as the river passes by.

14. Next to their personality, which is different too.

15. It's like a never-ending maze.

16. It won't be that bad, he can view the beautiful rings that look like a Ferris wheel going around.

17. One of the very sad things that happens in this story.

18. Finally, the food, oh the food.

19. They're going to the concert I'm going to the basketball game.

20. Another way Rikki is curious is that when he roams the house he inspects everything.

21. Billy's hair is sticking straight up like the quills on a porcupine.

22. To draw attention away from Teddy.

23. He is loyal because he protects Teddy's family "as soon as Teddy goes to sleep he goes for his nightly walk around the house."

24. When Cloyd has faith that Blueboy can make it across the mud.

25. Fulfilling his dream.

26. For instance, when a young boy named Cloyd is out in the canyons and finds an ancient burial ground.

27. Boy, was I wrong it is a very interesting book.

28. Animals that are no thicker than a finger.

29. Icicles hanging from trees, houses, and signs.

30. Yes, Mom, I know what you're thinking you think I'm going to ask for something.

31. Finally, come the activities, Mom and Dad.

32. Our farm, where animals roam wild, and the country is as peaceful as the animals themselves.

33. This shows it's not the size that helps you win against all odds, it's the courage you possess.

34. Florida, such a nice place.

35. I give in; I surrender.

36. The humor, a number one item on my list.

37. The fresh breeze making our hair fly like millions of butterflies.

38. Just as a deer is surrounded by the illuminating glow of headlights from a massive motor home, just as the deer is paralyzed in fright, I am held rigid in the spot.

39. Along with the beach, I liked the electric parade, from way down the street the lights look like fireflies huddled together as if they were telling each other a secret.

40. These two girls, alike in many ways, contrasting in appearance and personality.

41. Billy's mother gently placing the bandage on Old Dan's wounds.

42. The house will be covered with snow and icicles, looking as if summer never existed.

43. Little ponds frozen solid along the sides of the parks and schools, where they can't see the fish.

44. While Anne tries to make friends, Matt hides himself.

45. When we're there, we can make our own things such as necklaces and bracelets, we can even make a watch out of a variety of beads.

46. Well, here's my chance.

47. The Illinois River is glistening from the bright light of the moon.

48. My sister is just the opposite.

49. Lying in my bed, images racing through my mind, I will sleep calmly every time a memory is evoked.

50. After church, we went to eat.

ANSWERS to

Sentence/Fragment/Run-On Test

Sentences From Student Papers

On your scantron, mark "A" for **SENTENCE**, "B" for **FRAGMENT**, and "C" for **RUN-ON**.

1. B	26. B
2. A	27. C
3. A	28. B
4. C	29. B
5. B	30. C
6. C	31. A
7. A	32. B
8. A	33. C
9. C	34. B
10. A	35. A
11. A	36. B
12. C	37. B
13. A	38. A
14. B	39. C
15. A	40. B
16. C	41. B
17. B	42. A
18. B	43. B
19. C	44. A
20. A	45. C
21. A	46. A
22. B	47. A
23. C	48. A
24. B	49. A
25. B	50. A

©1998 M. E. LEDBETTER

Grammar Integrated Into Literature

①→ USING WORKS READ IN CLASS AS SAMPLES OF GRAMMATICAL RULES: Students may find examples of various grammatical rules **USING WORKS READ IN CLASS**. Whatever the subject of class grammatical minilessons, ask students to analyze recently studied fictional or nonfictional works to serve as "famous" examples of the rule(s).

②→ USING WORKS AS EXCEPTIONS TO RULES: Students may also find **EXCEPTIONS** in published work--fragments, run-ons, grammatical "errors" for effect, and so on.

③→ REVIEWING RULES FOR DOCUMENTATION: Review rules for **INTERNAL FOOTNOTING & BIBLIOGRAPHIC ENTRIES** in conjunction with grammar minilessons by asking students to cite their sources.

④→ USING STUDENT-WRITTEN SENTENCES: Ask students to write original sentences related to the **SETTING, CHARACTERIZATION, PLOT, THEME**, etc., of a work that could serve as a **BASIS FOR A MINILESSON** on a grammatical concept. An example follows.

Comma Review: A CHRISTMAS CAROL

For the following sentences, **ADD COMMAS** where necessary and circle them. In the blank, **WRITE THE RULE** that applies.

_____ 1. Scrooge is a mean-spirited stingy and unbelieving old man.

➤ After you have punctuated the sentence with the necessary commas, rewrite the sentence without the conjunction **AND** for a more sophisticated method of dealing with adjectives. Without the conjunction, the comma rule would be **COORDINATE ADJECTIVE**.

_____

_____

_____ 2. Jacob Marley Scrooge's old business partner tries to warn Scrooge to change his ways.

_____ 3. The setting is London England Christmas Eve 1843 in various offices and homes.

➤ **ADDRESS AN ENVELOPE** to Scrooge (make up an address), from you (use your real address), on the back of this sheet.

_____ 4. Finally Scrooge declares that he will keep Christmas in his heart all year.

_____ 5. Adam get me the best bird at the poultry shop for the Cratchit family. (The comma rule here has to do with the fact that Adam is being directly addressed.)

⇒*REWRITE THIS SENTENCE* so that it is direct quotation.

_____

_____

_____ 6. When the Ghost of Christmas Past first visits Scrooge he thinks the ghost is a figment of his imagination.

_____ 7. Scrooge according to Marley will be visited by three spirits.

_____ 8. Scrooge says "Aren't the Union workhouses and Poor Laws still in effect?"

_____ 9. Scrooge doesn't believe in Christmas but he soon changes his mind.

_____10. *Write a sentence of your own about the play, punctuate it, and list the rule.

_____

_____

_____

Answer Key for

Comma Review: A CHRISTMAS CAROL

Series   1. mean-spirited, stingy,

                Scrooge is a mean-spirited, stingy, unbelieving old man.

Appositive   2. Marley, partner,

Addresses
Dates   3. London, England, Eve, 1843,

Introductory
Word   4. Finally,

Direct
Address   5. Adam,

                "Adam, get me the best bird at the poultry shop for the Cratchit family," Scrooge said.

Introductory
Adverb
Clause   6. Scrooge,

Interrupter   7. Scrooge, Marley,

Direct
Quotation   8. says,

Compound
Sentence   9. Christmas,

_____   10. Answers and rules will vary.

Avoiding Changes in Verb Tense

Authors must decide if they want to tell their stories in **PRESENT** or *PAST TENSE*. The advantage of **PRESENT TENSE** is that it is more **IMMEDIATE**; the reader is almost present, watching the action as it unfolds. *PAST TENSE*, on the other hand, allows a certain *DISTANCE* between the reader and the story. It removes the audience to a degree; the action is over and the reader knows it. Whichever tense authors use, they must be **consistent**--changing only if the narrative demands it for purposes of flashback, and so on.

For the following excerpt, **CIRCLE ALL PRESENT-TENSE VERBS**. On the lines below, write their *PAST-TENSE* forms.

Smoke squeezes its way out of the stainless steel oven, but no one notices. Mama is on the phone with Aunt Eileen, and Carol and I ☞ have been playing and like most kids we keep right on running in and out the back screen door. We almost snap the old thing off its hinges as we fling it open and bang it shut.

On one of our several trips in or out, we let Blackie, the outside dog, in. So we scramble from room to room. Carol misses him by a tail as he sprints under the dining room table. I grab a paw but come up empty-handed as he scoots under the Victorian loveseat and heads for the Queen Anne wingback. Finally Carol tackles him as he makes his way down the hall to Daddy's study.

With all the shenanigans, toast broiling in the stainless steel oven is forgotten until, with Blackie firmly in my grip, we make our way the length of the house, through the kitchen to the back door. Safely deposited on the other side, Blackie once again can be--as God ☞ has intended him, as Mama always says--an outside dog.

It is then we all notice the smoke.

✿✿✿

1. _____
2. _____
3. _____
4. _____
5. _____
6. _____
7. _____
8. _____
9. _____
10. _____
11. _____
12. _____
13. _____
14. _____
15. _____
16. _____
17. _____
18. _____
19. _____
20. _____
21. _____
22. _____
23. _____
24. _____
25. _____

☞ NOTICE: "Have been playing" is in **PRESENT PERFECT TENSE**, as it uses "have" with the present participle. Remember that changing to **PAST PERFECT TENSE** will involve changing the helping verb to "had."

ANSWERS to Avoiding Changes in Verb Tense

1. squeezed
2. noticed
3. was
4. had been playing
5. kept running
6. snapped
7. flung
8. banged
9. let
10. scrambled
11. missed
12. sprinted
13. grabbed
14. came
15. scooted
16. headed
17. tackled
18. made
19. was forgotten
20. made
21. could be
22. had intended
23. said
24. was
25. noticed

How to Use the Grammar Skills Chart

Use the **GRAMMAR SKILLS CHART** as an analysis worksheet to study various grammatical components of a **STORY** read in class or as the basis for a grammar **MINILESSON** highlighting one or two skills at a time. For example, ask students to prove their understanding of the following concepts:

1. FRAGMENT RECOGNITION--Students can cite examples used in the story and explain what they believe the author's intended effect is.

2. RUN-ON RECOGNITION--Students can identify a **RUN-ON** or a sentence that borders on being a run-on, or they may explain how the author combined sentences to avoid a run-on.

3. SENTENCE COMBINING--Students can cite particularly effective sentence structure and analyze combining techniques.

4. SUBJECT-VERB AGREEMENT--Ask students to find sentences that exemplify various subject-verb agreement rules (e.g., compound subjects, a subject separated from its verb by a prepositional phrase, an inverted order subject and verb).

5. VERB TENSE AND FORMS--Students can find effective verbs and determine their tense, emphasizing the need for tense consistency, or they can practice conjugating commonly missed verbs (e.g., lie, lay, rise, sit).

6. PRONOUN-ANTECEDENT AGREEMENT--To stress the importance of this rule, ask students to cite sentences that exemplify pronoun-antecedent agreement.

How to Use the Grammar Skills Chart, Continued

7. **PRONOUN USAGE**--An effective method to review pronoun usage is to ask students to locate examples of nominative, objective, and possessive cases. Students can then explain which sentences they might have written incorrectly and why.

8. **ADJECTIVE/ADVERB USAGE**--Correct adjective/adverb usage is more meaningful when applied to an actual narrative. Students can cite examples of effective usage.

9. **DOUBLE NEGATIVE RECOGNITION**--While most stories do not contain examples of double negatives, to prove their understanding of the concept, students can change sentences to contain a double negative, especially involving "hardly" and "scarcely."

10. **CAPITALIZATION**--Students can determine the rules for capitals used within a story (relationships, languages, etc.).

11. **PUNCTUATION**--Ask students to cite examples of various punctuation rules (e.g., introductory adverb clause, direct address, compound sentence).

12. **OTHER**--Other rules could involve citing examples of parallel structure, proper verbal usage, and so forth.

➜ Following the **GRAMMAR SKILLS CHART** is a sample **GRAMMAR SKILLS ANSWER KEY** for **MAUREEN DALY'S "SIXTEEN."**

GRAMMAR SKILLS

SKILL
FRAGMENT RECOGNITION
RUN-ON RECOGNITION
SENTENCE COMBINING
SUBJECT-VERB AGREEMENT
VERB TENSE AND FORMS
PRONOUN-ANTECEDENT AGREEMENT
PRONOUN USAGE
ADJECTIVE/ADVERB USAGE
DOUBLE NEGATIVE RECOGNITION
CAPITALIZATION
PUNCTUATION
OTHER

NAME_____ CLASS_____ DATE_____

GRAMMAR SKILLS
(Sample)

SKILL Taken from: Daly, Maureen. "Sixteen," <u>Scholastic</u>, 1937.	
FRAGMENT RECOGNITION	"Not because he *had* to but because he *wanted to*" (72).
RUN-ON RECOGNITION	"I can't remember what we talked about at first; I can't even remember if we talked at all" (72). [Avoidance of run-on]
SENTENCE COMBINING	"It was cold at first even with my skating pants on, <u>sitting on</u> <u>that heap of snow</u> . . ." (72). [Participial phrase]
SUBJECT-VERB AGREEMENT	"There <u>was</u> a <u>smell</u> of singed wool . . ." (71). [Inverted order]
VERB TENSE AND FORMS	Begins in present tense (know, listen), moves to past tense (was, were), and returns to present tense (is, know)
PRONOUN-ANTECEDENT AGREEMENT	". . . saddle <u>shoes</u> that look as if <u>they've</u> seen the world" (71).
PRONOUN USAGE	". . . I couldn't tell if <u>it</u> <u>was</u> <u>he</u> or my heart whistling out there in the night" (73). [Nominative case-subject complement]
ADJECTIVE/ADVERB USAGE	". . . they smelled so <u>queer</u> . . ." (71). [Adjective used after sense verb]
DOUBLE NEGATIVE RECOGNITION	"And I did<u>n't</u> have my Latin done, <u>either</u>" (71). [Avoidance of double negative]
CAPITALIZATION	Swiss, Slavic, Luxlike (Proper adjectives) Latin (Language) christmas (Holidays) ". . . and said, 'We'd better start home'" (72). [Direct quote]
PUNCTUATION	"See, that's how I know he wanted to take me home" (72). [Introductory word]
OTHER	". . . as if every little word <u>were</u> a secret" (72). [Subjunctive mood]

WORDS X FIVE

➔ REVIEWING PARTS OF SPEECH: The game WORDS X FIVE reinforces the differences among **PARTS OF SPEECH** and is particularly helpful as an introduction to an **ADJECTIVE/ADVERB USAGE** mini-unit.

① ➔ Give students a **BLANK CHART**, or they may draw one on their own papers.

② ➔ Instruct students as to which **HEADINGS** are required for each particular game. You may change the headings to fit the assignment.

    A. For instance, for a review on various parts of speech, use the headings **N**, **V**, **ADJ**, **ADV**, and **PREP**.

    B. For a more concentrated study of adjectives and adverbs, try the headings **ADJ**, **COMPARATIVE**, **SUPERLATIVE**, **ADV**, **SENTENCE USING ADV SUPERLATIVE**.

③ ➔ Give students a **SAMPLE LETTER** to use as practice to make sure they understand the requirements for each chart. For instance, if the headings are **N**, **V**, **ADJ**, **ADV**, and **PREP**, and the sample letter is **"U,"** acceptable answers could be **UMBRELLA**, **UNDERSTAND**, **UGLY**, **UNKNOWINGLY**, and **UNDER**.

④ ➔ Once students have had a chance to practice, select the actual **GAME LETTERS**. Allow **FIVE MINUTES** for students to fill in all blanks. The first five students to complete the chart correctly are the winners.

 ords X ive

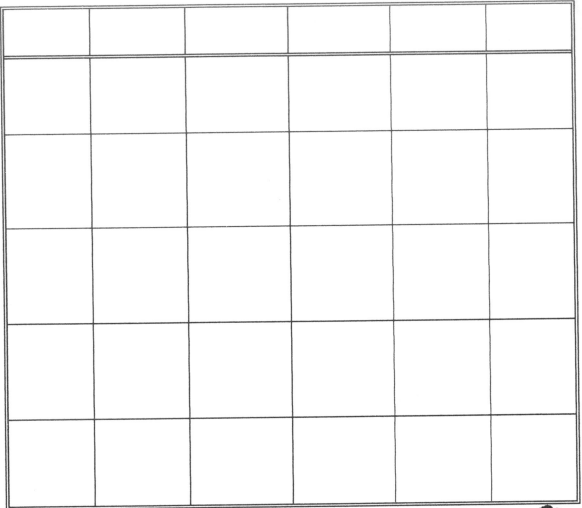

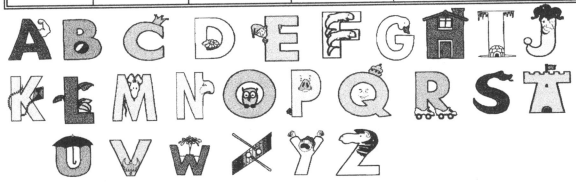

Words X Five

(SAMPLE)

	NOUN (Idea)	ADJECTIVE (Comparative and Superlative)	VERB (Action)	ADVERB (Comparative and Superlative)	PREPOSITION
A	ACTION	AGILE MORE AGILE MOST AGILE	APPLY	ANXIOUSLY MORE ANXIOUSLY MOST ANXIOUSLY	AGAINST
B	BATTLE	BEAUTIFUL MORE BEAUTIFUL MOST BEAUTIFUL	BEGRUDGE	BRIGHTLY MORE BRIGHTLY MOST BRIGHTLY	BEYOND
C	CIVILIZATION	CUTE CUTER CUTEST	CAJOLE	CALMLY MORE CALMLY MOST CALMLY	CONCERNING
D	DILIGENCE	DRY DRIER DRIEST	DIVIDE	DENSELY MORE DENSELY MOST DENSELY	DOWN
E	EVAPORATION	EASY EASIER EASIEST	ELOPE	EARNESTLY MORE EARNESTLY MOST EARNESTLY	EXCEPT

ROW GAME

➡ For a class activity with **ADJECTIVE/ADVERB USAGE**, ask students to play a ROW GAME.

① → **WRITE REQUIREMENTS:** On the board, write the order of the requirements, **ADJ**, **ADV**, for example.

② → **FIRST PLAYER ANSWERS:** Call out a letter, such as **"C."** The first student must think of an **ADJECTIVE** that begins with a **"C,"** such as **CUTE**.

③ → **SECOND PLAYER ANSWERS:** The next student must think of an **ADVERB** that begins with the **LAST LETTER** of the previous answer, in this case **"E."** For instance, an appropriate answer could be **EVENTUALLY**.

④ → **THIRD PLAYER TAKES TURN:** The third student must return to an **ADJECTIVE** that begins with **"Y,"** such as **YELLOW**.

⑤ → **DISCUSS RULES:** Set a **TIME LIMIT** and warn students **NOT TO REPEAT WORDS**. If a student is unable to answer, his letter goes to the next student.

⑥ → **USE VARIATIONS:** Variations include asking for **BOTH** the **ADJECTIVE** and **ADVERB** form of a word. For instance, **CUTE** and **CUTELY**. The next student can be required to make up a sentence that serves as a practice sentence for adjective/adverb usage--for example, **"SHE SMILED (CUTE, CUTELY)."** The next student must answer correctly--**CUTELY**. The sequence, then, is words, sentence, answer. Students may use paper if necessary to aid in their constructions.

Principal Parts of Verbs "Bee"

➡️ CONJUGATING VERBS: After a minilesson on principal parts of verbs, hold a **VERB BEE**.

① → Give the first student a **VERB TO CONJUGATE**. To expedite the **VERB BEE**, use a list of irregular verbs and call the words in alphabetical order.

② → For **PRACTICE** and to keep as **NOTES**, ask all students to write all forms of each verb given.

③ → The student may simply state the **THREE PRINCIPAL PARTS** of the verb, or she may use the verbs in a **SENTENCE** (e.g., I **LIE** down every day for a nap. I **LAY** down yesterday for an hour. I **HAVE LAIN** down every day this week).

④ → **IF A STUDENT MISSES** any part of the verb, the question goes to the next student.

⑤ → Award **PRIZES** to the **TOP STUDENTS**, perhaps the last three remaining.

Verb/Refrain Poems

① → BRAINSTORMING ACTIONS: Ask students to **BRAINSTORM A LIST OF ACTIVITIES THEY LIKE TO DO**, concentrating on specific **ACTIONS** (e.g., **CLIMBING** trees, **FISHING**, **PADDLING** canoes).

② → BRAINSTORMING REFRAINS: Then instruct students to **BRAINSTORM VARIOUS PHRASES THAT COULD SERVE AS REFRAINS** (e.g., as a child I did weird stuff).

③ → FREEWRITING POEM: Finally, assign a **100-WORD** (minimum) poem including at least **TEN SPECIFIC ACTIVITIES** and at least **ONE REFRAIN**. The poem that follows could serve as a springboard for ideas.

④ → CONJUGATING VERBS FROM POEM: As an **ADDENDUM ACTIVITY**, require students to make a list of their ten action verbs and conjugate them as a review of principal parts.

Jessica Haigus
Verb Poem
(Inclusion of ten specific actions/
  At least one refrain)

AS A CHILD

As a child, I did weird
stuff
Like
Climb trees and play with
Lizards.
Many girls would find lizards unappealing at age six,
But as a child I did weird
stuff

Like
Going fishing and catching pet bugs.
Many girls would find fishing unappealing at age seven,
But as a child I did weird
stuff

Like
Paddle canoes and have garage sales.
Many girls would find canoeing unappealing at age eight,
But as a child I did weird
stuff

Like
Play baseball and football.
Many girls would find sports
  unappealing at age nine,
But as a child I did weird
stuff

Like
Watch the news and listen to Pink Floyd.
Many girls would find Pink Floyd unappealing at age ten,
But as a child I did weird
stuff

Like
Chop wood and look at stars through a telescope.
Many girls would find chopping wood unappealing at age eleven,
But as a child I did weird
stuff

Like
Paint my toenails and chew sugarless gum.
Many girls--wait, yes--many girls would find that appealing at age
   twelve.
Now I am thirteen, and I like to do girl
stuff.

Isn't
That
Weird?

Capitalization Poems

① → REVIEW CAPITALIZATION RULES: As a class, **REVIEW CAPITALIZATION RULES**. As part of the review, require students to take **NOTES** on each rule and give a **PERSONAL EXAMPLE**.

② → ASSIGN POEM USING RULES: Ask students to **WRITE A POEM** incorporating a specified number of **CAPITALIZATION RULES**, **FOOTNOTING** the capitalized words and providing the **CORRESPONDING RULES** on a separate sheet.

③ → REQUIRE A SPECIFIED NUMBER OF SPECIAL DEVICES: For a further challenge, instruct students to include a designated number of **METAPHORIC DEVICES**, **"WILD" IMAGES**, and so forth, and to footnote them as well.

Helmuth Mayer
Capitalization Poem
(Incorporating 12 Capitalization Rules)

Tuesday, July 29

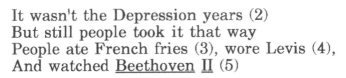

I still remember it clearly
It was Tuesday (1), July 29, 1986
I was twelve that year and my brother Jim eleven

It wasn't the Depression years (2)
But still people took it that way
People ate French fries (3), wore Levis (4),
And watched <u>Beethoven</u> II (5)

My mom worked at Charlie's Agency (6) and
My dad was Charlie, Private Investigator (7)

It was a regular day in Toronto (8)
Beggars on the streets
Preachers lecturing the Lord (9) and
Memorial Day Church (10) quiet as a reading room

My brother Jim was watching TV
And I was studying my literature that my ex-teacher
     gave out for the summer (11)
Then all of a sudden a knock was heard
So I raced to the door, hoping there was something fun at it

As I opened the door, I saw a seven-foot man, who apparently
   didn't notice
That I stood there with my bottom lip to my toes,
While he asked, "Can I use your phone?"
I replied anxiously, "Sure, Mr. Hakeem Abdul Olajuwon" (12)

After he used the phone, I asked him to sign a couple of my hats
Then he was off again
That was Tuesday, July 29, 1986

Liz Alexander
Capitalization Poem
(Incorporating 9 Capitalization Rules)

SHOES!

Karaza Hepfa Kalie McFruga
Came from the land of Spittin McGuga.

He was a shoemaker, good and kind,
That sort of person is hard to find.

He'd make Shadarack sandals and
   Terrifan tennies and Barakoo boots,
Out of Cartie's Apples, Kazoo Flickles,
   and Chipedo Roots.

He moved to Sadafarin
And built K.F.'s House of Shoe Wearin'.

He made shoes for Marazins and Kazeds,
People who were Greens, Pinks, and Reds.

He worked on Fizday, Jasday,
   and Ixday,
But never on Monday.

He made galoshes for Mayor Fred,
And hickory clogs for the Court of Kazed.

He made sneakers

For the author of Szxwatski's Thinkers .

He made slippers of topaz
For the writers of the Constitution of Glopaz.

Times were tough,
But never too rough.

He made South Polean Mukluks
For Henny Penny and her cluck ducks.

He made moccasins for the Indians
Who went to the Sipapu with all their kin.

He made gumshoes galore
And platforms and dress shoes and more!

And if you still think shoes are a bore,
Visit K.F.'s House of Shoe Wearin'.

275

Ryan Rogers
Capitalization Poem
(Incorporating 12 Capitalization Rules)

N-N-W

It stands alone in the underground shelter,
    its metal surface gleaming
It stands erect on its launch pad,
    counting down the seconds
On its side are stamped three letters,
    N-N-W
The three letters seem innocent alone, but
    their meaning sends chills to the bone
They stand for Nazi Nuclear Warheads ◄1,

    the return of the Third Reich ◄2 is here
The great warhead is not alone,

    27 others point to the West◄3

In the front stands the son of Marshal ◄4
    Hermann Goering, the one no one knew he had
He's the command of the Luftwaffe ◄5,

    and today is Christmas for the German ◄6,

For today the U.S. ◄7 shall fall,
But they won't be alone,
    Western Europe will tumble also

On this cold Sunday,◄8
    while people travel to church
They shall hear a great roar,
    then all will explode
The major cities of the world,
    that will be the target
Houston, New York, and Washington, too,
Minneapolis, London, Paris,
    the list continues
The Nazi ◄9 stands at the front,
    waiting for the countdown
To his chest he clutches a copy of Hitler's
    Mein Kampf ◄10

He raises his eyes to God,◄11
    praying for success
He presses the ten-second countdown,
    28 trap doors open
A great rumbling thunders,
    and the German ◄12 warheads take off
Take off toward destruction.

How to Use Poems to Review Grammar Rules

①→ USING POEMS TO REVIEW GRAMMATICAL ERRORS: Use the following poem, **"What's a Kid to Do,"** and its accompanying worksheet as an entertaining activity to review various grammatical errors.

②→ WRITING POEMS THAT INCLUDE GRAMMAR ERRORS: As an ***EXTENSION ASSIGNMENT***, ask students to write their own poems incorporating at least ***TEN ERRORS***. Require that students ***FOOTNOTE*** their intentional mistakes and include an addendum ***RULE SHEET***.

✿ ADDED REQUIREMENTS could include the following:
- ❤ a specified ***RHYME SCHEME***
- ❤ a predetermined ***METER***
- ❤ the use of ***TEACHER-ASSIGNED RULES***

What's a Kid to Do?

Teacher, teacher, help

I can't seem to understand

I thought I swimmed and singed and runned

Not swam and sang and ran

I was sure, I really was,

That I had wrote and spoke and saw

But then you say I hadn't

No, I hadn't, not at all

Teacher, teacher, help

What's a kid to do

Oh, teacher, teacher, please

My mind is in a stew

You mean I don't have tooths and foots

And I had thought I'd knew

You told us just today

It's days and weeks and years

Just add an "s" to what you've got

So mooses, sheeps, and deers

Teacher, teacher, please

What's a kid to do

Teacher, teacher, show me
I want to get it straight
I ain't a bad kid, no siree
I just want to participate
See, me and you will work it out
You'll be seeing that, just wait
Them old words will flow like water
They won't even hesitate
Teacher, teacher, please
What's a kid to do

Teacher, teacher, stick by me
I'm doing all I can
A capital here and a comma there
Now don't that beat the band
Oh, teacher, teacher, don't you see
I know what I will do
I'll study more harder and harder still
And I'll do it just for you
Teacher, teacher, friend of mine
Thanks to you I ain't behind

Analysis: What's a Kid to Do?

Using the poem **"What's a Kid to Do?"** and any necessary reference material, answer the following questions.

1. In the first stanza, the narrator of the poem is confused about forming **PAST** and **PAST PARTICIPLES** of six verbs. List the verbs and conjugate them correctly.

PRESENT	PAST	PAST PARTICIPLE (had, have, etc.)
A.		
B.		
C.		
D.		
E.		
F.		

2. In the second stanza, the narrator's frustration occurs when attempting to form **PLURALS OF NOUNS**. Find the five **IRREGULARLY FORMED** nouns from this stanza. Give their singular and plural forms.

SINGULAR	PLURAL
A.	
B.	
C.	

D._____

E._____

3. Also in stanza two, the narrator alludes to an *"S" RULE*. Explain the rule and cite the three examples from this stanza that are correctly formed using this rule.

A. *RULE*:_____

B. *EXAMPLES* from poem:_____, _____, _____

4. In the third stanza, the narrator's plea to the teacher contains three *GRAMMATICAL ERRORS*. Quote the errors and explain the rules.

	ERRORS	*RULES*
A.		
B.		
C.		

5. Quote an *IDIOM* from the fourth stanza and explain its meaning.

A. *QUOTE:* _____

B. *EXPLANATION:* _____

_____

→*EXTENSION:* Give three other *REAL-LIFE IDIOMS* not included in this poem.

_____

_____

_____

_____

6. Quote the mistake from the last stanza involving the **COMPARATIVE OF AN ADVERB**, explain the rule, and correct the error.

A. **QUOTE:** _____

B. **RULE:** _____

C. **CORRECTION:** _____

7. Quote two **FIGURATIVE LANGUAGE DEVICES** from the poem and state their **TYPES** (simile, metaphor, personification, etc.)

      EXAMPLES   **TYPES**

A. _____

B. _____

8. A. What is the **TONE** of the poem?_____

    B. **EXPLAIN** your answer, using at least two **QUOTED EXAMPLES** from the poem.

_____

_____

_____

9. Explain the **THEME** of the poem.

_____

_____

_____

10.   **EXTENSION**--State three other **GENERAL RULES** for forming **PLURALS OF NOUNS** and give two **EXAMPLES** for each.

A. **RULE**: _____

   EXAMPLES:_____&_____

B. **RULE**: _____

   EXAMPLES:_____&_____

C. **RULE**: _____

   EXAMPLES:_____&_____

ANSWERS TO

Analysis: What's a Kid to Do?

1.
   A. swim, swam, swum
   B. sing, sang, sung
   C. run, ran, run
   D. write, wrote, written
   E. speak, spoke, spoken
   F. see, saw, seen

2.
   A. tooth, teeth
   B. foot, feet
   C. moose, moose
   D. sheep, sheep
   E. deer, deer

3.
   A. Most nouns form their plurals by adding "s."
   B. days, weeks, years

4.
   A. "ain't"--not accepted usage
   B. "me and you"--incorrect pronoun case and courtesy rule
   C. "them old words"--incorrect adjective form

5.

   A. "beat the band"

   B. How unbelievable! What a surprise! (Answers may vary.)

Extension: Answers will vary.

6.

   A. "more harder"

   B. "More harder" is a double comparison. Use "er" to form comparatives of short words and "more" to form comparatives for longer words.

   C. harder

7.

   A. "them old words will flow like water"--simile

   B. "they won't even hesitate"--personification

8.

   A. humorous/frustrated

   B. Answers will vary.

9. The English language is confusing. (Answers will vary.)

10.

   A. When a word ends in "y" that is preceded by a consonant, change the "y" to "I" and add "es." If the "y" is preceded by a vowel, simply add "s."

   B. When a word ends in "sh," "ch," "x," or "z," or "s," add "es" to form the plural.

   C. For some words ending in "f" or "fe," change the "f" to "v" and add "es."

* Accept all correct answers.

If I Were in Charge of the World

① → BRAINSTORM THE PERFECT WORLD: Before reading **JUDITH VIORST'S "IF I WERE IN CHARGE OF THE WORLD,"** ask students to brainstorm the "perfect" world. Ask not only for **CONCRETE IMAGES** but **WILD** images and **SENSORY** images as well.

② → REVIEW GRAMMAR MINILESSON: Review a **GRAMMATICAL** concept, such as comma rules, and require students to include a specified number of examples in their poems.

③ → ASSIGN POEM: Instruct students to write a **100-WORD MINIMUM POEM** on the topic of being in charge of the world. Students must include as many **WILD, CONCRETE,** and **SENSORY IMAGES** as possible as well as **EVIDENCE OF THEIR GRAMMATICAL RULE(S)**.

④ → READ JUDITH VIORST'S POEM: After students have completed their version of a "perfect" world, read Viorst's poem. **COMPARE AND CONTRAST** student ideas with the author's.

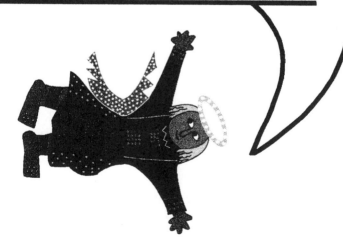

Allisa Brill
Mode: Refrain poem
       Including comma rules and specific images

IF I WERE IN CHARGE OF THE WORLD

If I were in charge of the world,
You would never find a hair
In your toothbrush
Or have a frog wet
In your hand.

(INTRODUCTORY CLAUSE)

(CONCRETE IMAGE)

If I were in charge of the world,
Vegetables would taste like candy bars,
And I'd make spinach and Brussels sprouts
Become extinct.

(COMPOUND SENTENCE)
(WILD IMAGE)

But, since I'm not in charge of the world,
These things will never happen.

If I were in charge of the world,
People wouldn't listen to heavy-metal music
Going full-volume on their boom boxes
Or eat an apple a day
To keep the doctor away.

(SENSORY IMAGE)

But, since I'm not in charge of the world,
These things will never happen.

If I were in charge of the world,
Dogs <u>really</u> would be a man's (and woman's) best friend,
And little kids would make more mud pies than any earthworm
Could possibly eat.

If I were in charge of the world,
You'd never have to fluff your pillow at night
Or put on insect repellent
To keep the mosquitos away.

But, since I'm not in charge of the world,
These things will never happen.

(INTRODUCTORY WORD)

If I were in charge of the world,
Meatballs wouldn't roll off your spaghetti
And get all dirty, and the little pieces
Of cheese and lettuce wouldn't
Fall out of your taco.

If I were in charge of the world,
Albert Einstein wouldn't be such a genius,
And Newton wouldn't have developed any of his laws.
They would have left that to me.

Because, if I were in charge of the world,
Some of these things really could happen.

Sentence Combining/ Varying Sentence Structure

① → USING STUDENT-WRITTEN SENTENCES: For a mini-lesson on **SENTENCE COMBINING/VARIETY**, use **STUDENT-WRITTEN SENTENCES** that could be revised using various approaches. Students may write sentences for the purpose of the combining exercise, or they may choose to use sentences from **PREVIOUS ESSAYS** that need restructuring.

② → REVISING SAMPLES: As a class, **REVISE A SET OF SAMPLE SENTENCES**, showing students options in combining.

③ → PRACTICING COMBINING METHODS: Using different sentences, **DIVIDE THE CLASS INTO GROUPS** for the purpose of **PRACTICING METHODS** learned. Instruct students not only to combine the sentences but to **ANALYZE THEIR APPROACH** as well.

Varying Sentence Structure

Combine **THE FOLLOWING TWO SENTENCES IN THE WAYS INDICATED BELOW. YOU MAY ADD AND DELETE WORDS AS NECESSARY. TRY NOT TO REPEAT ANY SENTENCES.**

The quiet, close-knit family sat on the porch. They watched the sun go down.

① → *-ing* word group (participial phrase) at **BEGINNING** of sentence:

_____

_____

② → *-ing* word group in **MIDDLE** of sentence:

_____

_____

③ → *-ing* word group at **END** of sentence:

_____

_____

④ → Adverb clause at **BEGINNING** of sentence:

_____

_____

⑤ → Adverb clause at **END** of sentence:

_____

_____

⑥→ **Adjectives** immediately ***FOLLOWING NOUN***:

_____

_____

⑦→ **Appositive** (actual word that will serve as the appositive will have to be added):

_____

_____

⑧→ ***NOUN*** followed by *-ing word group* (noun absolute):

_____

_____

ANSWERS TO

Varying Sentence Structure

Below are possible correct answers. Accept all correct answers.

1. <u>Sitting on the porch</u>, the quiet, close-knit family watched the sun go down.

2. The quiet, close-knit family, <u>sitting on the porch</u>, watched the sun go down.

3. The quiet, close-knit family sat on the porch, <u>watching the sun go down</u>.

4. <u>As the quiet, close-knit family sat on the porch</u>, they watched the sun go down.

5. The quiet, close-knit family sat on the porch <u>in order to watch the sun go down</u>.

6. The family, <u>quiet and close-knit</u>, sat on the porch, watching the sun go down.

7. The quiet, close-knit family, <u>the Smiths</u>, sat on the porch, watching the sun go down.

8. <u>The sun having already gone down</u>, the quiet, close-knit family sat on the porch.

Portfolio Assessment: Proofreading/Revising

①→ ANALYZING INDIVIDUAL REVISION PROGRESS: Students must **ANALYZE THEIR PROGRESS** in terms of **PROOFREADING AND REVISING** their papers. Ask them to review their portfolios, using the **Portfolio Assessment: Proofreading/Revising Sheet.**

②→ COMPILING GRAMMATICAL ERRORS CLASS ACTIVITY: After students complete their grammatical errors portfolio assessment, choose a sampling of student sentences regarding each rule to compile a **GRAMMATICAL ERRORS PROOFREADING WORKSHEET**. A sample assignment follows the Portfolio Assessment Sheet.

③→ REVIEWING REVISION TECHNIQUES: Put students into groups to **DETECT ERRORS** made by their classmates, **CATEGORIZE** them, and **REVISE/RECAST** the sentences.

④→ USING THE INDIVIDUALIZED RUBRIC: Assign the **Individualized Rubric** at any point throughout the year to serve as a reminder of students' most troublesome grammatical errors, the reasons for the errors, and possible strategies to prevent the occurrence of errors in future assignments.

PORTFOLIO ASSESSMENT:
Proofreading/Revising

ASSIGNMENT: Reviewing the works in your portfolio, **CITE EXAMPLES** of errors in the following categories by **WRITING THE COMPLETE SENTENCE** from your paper, **FOOTNOTING** the name of the paper and the page number, and **EXPLAINING** strategies you will use to avoid these types of mistakes in the future. If you have not made an error in a certain category, write an **ORIGINAL SENTENCE** that would exemplify this mistake and explain the corresponding rule.

EXAMPLE: RUN-ON RECOGNITION:

1. Victory and success and greatness weren't in the cards for me that year, I was twelve, my summer plans were fizzling like the Bay of Pigs Invasion ("One July Long Ago" 1).

2. Most of my errors involving run-on sentences were made by using a comma to join two sentences. I now realize that I have the following choices: a comma with a conjunction, a semicolon, a subordinate clause, or a period.

SKILLS
FRAGMENT RECOGNITION: 1. 2.
RUN-ON RECOGNITION: 1. 2.
SENTENCE COMBINING: 1. 2.
SUBJECT-VERB AGREEMENT: 1. 2.

VERB TENSE AND FORMS:
1.

2.

PRONOUN-ANTECEDENT AGREEMENT:
1.

2.

PRONOUN USAGE:
1.

2.

ADJECTIVE/ADVERB USAGE:
1.

2.

PUNCTUATION:
1.

2.

CAPITALIZATION:
1.

2.

OTHER:
1.

2.

OTHER:
1.

2.

Turtle
X-ing

Rule Sheet for PROOFREADING/REVISING

1. **RUN-ON**--A run-on sentence is two or more sentences improperly combined. (e.g., I like you, you like me.)

   Note: Four ways to correct a run-on are by using a period, semicolon, comma and conjunction, and dependent clause.

2. **FRAGMENT**--A fragment is a piece of a sentence, one that is missing either a subject, a predicate, or both. (e.g., Walking down the hall in my new shoes.)

3. **CHOPPY SENTENCES**--Choppy sentences are sentences that need to be combined. (e.g., I like Mr. Smith. He is my friend.)

4. **APOSTROPHES**--Apostrophes are used to show possession or to indicate a contraction. (e.g., Mary's book doesn't have a cover.)

5. **SEMICOLONS**--Semicolons are primarily used to separate two sentences (two independent clauses) of equal weight. (e.g., I went to Europe; she went to Texas.)

6. **COMMA FOR INTRODUCTORY WORD GROUP**--A comma is used to set off an introductory word group from the rest of the sentence. (e.g., As soon as the bell rings, the teacher will pass out the tests.)

7. **OMISSION OF COMMA FOR COMPOUND VERB**--A comma is **NOT** used to separate a compound verb. (e.g., She ran and jumped.)

8. **SUBJECT-VERB AGREEMENT**--Subjects should always agree in number with their verbs. (e.g., The list of students is in alphabetical order.)

9. **PRONOUN-ANTECEDENT AGREEMENT**--Pronouns should agree with their antecedents (the words to which the pronouns refer). (e.g., Each one of the girls did her work.)

10. **UNCLEAR PRONOUN REFERENCE**--A pronoun with no clear antecedent is said to have "unclear pronoun reference." (e.g., After Jill called Beth, she felt sad.)

Note: We don't know **WHO** felt sad--Jill or Beth.

11. **INCORRECT PRONOUN CASE**--Pronouns must be in the nominative, objective, or possessive case, depending on their use in a sentence. (e.g., She makes more money than I.)

Note: This sentence implies "more money than I **DO**."

12. **RESTRICTIVE VS. NONRESTRICTIVE CLAUSES**--A comma is used to set off non-restrictive (nonessential) clauses from the rest of the sentence. (e.g., Beth, who is my best friend, is president of the class.)

Note: We really don't need the adjective clause "who is my best friend."

13. **PARALLEL STRUCTURE**--The rule of expressing ideas in similar terms (all nouns, all verbs, etc.) is called parallel structure. (e.g., I like fishing, boating, and camping.)

Note: It is incorrect to say "I like fishing, to boat, and let's go sailing."

14. **INCORRECT OMISSION**--Omitting a word required for proper grammatical construction is called incorrect omission. (e.g., I have enjoyed and will always enjoy reading a good book.)

Note: It would be incorrect, for instance, to omit the word "enjoyed."

15. **REDUNDANCY**--Redundancy is unnecessary repetition of words or phrases. (e.g., It is 2 A.M. in the morning.)

> Note: The words "A.M." and "in the morning" mean the same thing.

16. **ILLOGICAL COMPARISON**--Illogical comparison is comparing dissimilar concepts. (e.g., His notes are better than Bill.)

> Note: His notes are not better than **BILL**. His notes are better than Bill's **NOTES**.

17. **ERROR IN VERB FORM**--An error in verb form occurs when an incorrect past tense or past participle is used. (e.g., I brang the note to class.)

> Note: The word "brang" is not the past tense of "bring."

18. **DANGLING MODIFIER**--A dangling modifier occurs when a word or phrase has nothing in the sentence to modify. (e.g., Walking down the street, a dollar bill was found.)

> Note: The **DOLLAR BILL** was not walking down the street.

19. **DOUBLE NEGATIVE**--A double negative occurs when two negative words are used in the same sentence. (e.g., I don't have no money.)

> Note: The words **SCARCELY** and **HARDLY** are also considered "negative" words.

20. **IS WHEN/IS WHERE CONSTRUCTION**--Something that is not a **TIME** or **PLACE** should not be defined as a time or place. (e.g., A real date is when someone pays for your meal.)

21. **COMMA FOR DIRECT ADDRESS**--A comma should be used to separate a noun of direct address. (e.g., **BILL**, please go get my purse.)

22. **HYPHEN FOR COMPOUND ADJECTIVE**--Use a hyphen in a compound adjective, two or more words working as one modifier in the sentence. (e.g., **SWEET-SMELLING** perfume, **SALT-FILLED** air)

23. **ADVERB USAGE**--Use adverbs to modify verbs, adjectives, and other adverbs. (e. g., Mother cooks **WELL** (not good). She's **REALLY** (not real) successful.)

24. **VERB TENSE CONSISTENCY**--Do not shift verb tense without reason. If one verb is in present tense, all verbs must be in present tense unless a change in time is necessary. (e. g., She **PICKED** up her doll as soon as she **GOT** (not gets) out of bed.)

PROOFREADING/REVISING: SENTENCES FROM STUDENT PAPERS

Using the **RULE SHEET**, list in the blanks to the left of the numbers the **TYPES OF ERRORS** contained in the sentences. Revise each sentence below.

_____1. The busy schedule crammed into available spaces create the perfect picture of hurried times.

_____

_____

_____2. His late night parties caused much uproar in the neighborhood.

_____

_____

_____3. Our two little naked bodies swimming around in a tub full of toys and playing games only kids could make up.

_____

_____

_____4. I had always liked Ken. He was the class clown. He used to get me in trouble in Mrs. Hockersmith's class.

_____

_____

_____5. We all look into our homemade pond and watch the tadpoles swim around like lost pups without a home.

_____

_____

_____6. He mowed the grass down real short.
(Contains two types of errors.)

_____

_____

_____7. We couldn't hardly blame her.

_____

_____

_____8. This didn't happen once, it happened two or three
times.

_____

_____

_____9. As a child, a visit to Mexico meant going swimming.

_____

_____

_____10. As I ran outside my lungs expanded with a breath of
fresh air.

_____

_____

_____11. I ran out into a huge field, and laid down in the deep
grass of the coastal plain. (Contains two types of
errors.)

_____

_____

_____12. Gradually opening my eyes, forcing the film off, amazed that I had slept so long.

_____

_____

_____13. Once I was in my room, minding my own business, when a little friend decides to join me.

_____

_____

_____14. "That's fine with me," she said, giving both Letha and I her infamous cold-shoulder treatment.

_____

_____

_____15. Father always said that I should remember three important rules about life: working hard, not to step on too many toes on my way up, and how to be a gracious winner.

_____

_____

_____16. Handing Dad screwdrivers and wrenches and pliers, the car was fixed in no time.

_____

_____

_____17. Its not that I hadn't noticed the sign. They were there all right, but they were written in some foreign language. How was I supposed to know which was the mens' restroom and which was the womens'?

_____

_____

_____18. After Grandma Verda left Laverne, she drove me back to school in her brand-new, two-toned Cadillac.

_____

_____

_____19. "What happened?" echoed a loud, thunderous voice.

_____

_____

_____20. She has never and will never love me.

_____

_____

_____21. I felt as if everyone had done their homework except for me. I was guilty, and I knew it.

_____

_____

_____22. An implicit metaphor is when you don't use a "be" verb to make your comparison.

_____

_____

_____23. Mom's tastes are not like Dad.

_____

_____

_____24. It's not as if I were used to saying, "Hey big boy want to help with the groceries?"

_____

_____

_____25. The narrator who grew up in Florida regularly put on a show for Northerners that "chugged down the sandy village road in automobiles."

_____

_____

ANSWERS to

PROOFREADING/REVISING

Sentences From Student Papers

1. **SUBJECT-VERB AGREEMENT**--The busy *SCHEDULE* crammed into available spaces *CREATES* the perfect picture of hurried times.

2. **HYPHEN FOR COMPOUND ADJECTIVE**--His *LATE-NIGHT* parties caused much uproar in the neighborhood.

3. **FRAGMENT**--Our two little naked bodies *WERE* swimming around in a tub full of toys and playing games only kids could make up.

4. **CHOPPY SENTENCES**--I had always liked Ken, the class clown, who used to get me in trouble in Mrs. Hockersmith's class.

5. **REDUNDANCY**--We all look into our homemade pond and watch the tadpoles swim around *LIKE LOST PUPS*. (*OR*. . . LIKE PUPS WITHOUT A HOME.)

6. **ADVERB USAGE and REDUNDANCY**--He mowed the grass *REALLY* short.

7. **DOUBLE NEGATIVE**--We *COULD HARDLY* blame her. (*OR* . . . We couldn't blame her.)

8. **RUN-ON**--This didn't happen once; it happened two or three times.

9. **DANGLING MODIFIER**--*WHEN I WAS A CHILD*, a visit to Mexico meant going swimming. (*OR* . . . As a child, *I THOUGHT* a visit to Mexico meant going swimming.)

10. **COMMA FOR INTRODUCTORY WORD GROUP**--As I ran outside, my lungs expanded with a breath of fresh air.

11. **ERROR IN VERB FORM and COMMA ERROR WITH COMPOUND VERB**--I ran out into a huge field and lay down in the deep grass of the coastal plain.

12. **FRAGMENT**--*I* gradually opened my eyes, forcing the film off, amazed that I had slept so long.

13. **VERB TENSE CONSISTENCY**--Once I **WAS** in my room, minding my own business, when a little friend **DECIDED** to join me.

14. **INCORRECT PRONOUN CASE**--"That's fine with me," she said, giving both Letha and **ME** her infamous cold-shoulder treatment.

15. **PARALLEL STRUCTURE**--Father always said that I should remember three important rules about life: **WORKING** hard, not **STEPPING** on too many toes on my way up, and **BEING** a gracious winner.

16. **DANGLING MODIFIER**--Handing Dad screwdrivers and wrenches and pliers, **I** helped him fix the car in no time.

17. **APOSTROPHES**--**IT'S** not that I hadn't noticed the signs. They were there all right, but they were written in some foreign language. How was I supposed to know which was the **MEN'S** restroom and which was the **WOMEN'S**?

18. **UNCLEAR PRONOUN REFERENCE**--After leaving Laverne, **GRANDMA VERDA** drove me back to school in her brand-new, two-toned Cadillac.

19. **REDUNDANCY**--"What happened?" echoed a **THUNDEROUS** (OR . . . **LOUD**) **VOICE**.

20. **INCORRECT OMISSION**--She has never **LOVED ME** and will never love me.

21. **PRONOUN-ANTECEDENT AGREEMENT**--I felt as if everyone had done **HIS** or **HER** homework except for me. I was guilty, and I knew it.

22. **IS WHEN/IS WHERE CONSTRUCTION**--An implicit metaphor does not use a "be" verb in its comparison.

23. **ILLOGICAL COMPARISON**--Mom's tastes are not like **DAD'S**.

24. **COMMA FOR DIRECT ADDRESS**--It's not as if I were used to saying, "Hey, **BIG BOY**, want to help with the groceries?"

25. **RESTRICTIVE VS. NONRESTRICTIVE CLAUSES**--The narrator, **WHO GREW UP IN FLORIDA**, regularly put on a show for Northerners that "chugged down the sandy village road in automobiles."

After assessing previous works in your PORTFOLIO, determine which types Of errors you have most often made and list them below. Use these as a guide for revisions of your current essay.

Individualized Rubric

I. Most prevalent type of error:

_____

_____

   a. Explain what you think caused you to make the error:

_____

_____

_____

   b. Give proof that you are revising/proofreading to correct this type of error in your current essay:

_____

_____

_____

_____

2. Second most prevalent error: _____

   a. Cause:_____

   _____

   _____

   b. Prevention:_____

   _____

   _____

   _____

   _____

3. Third most prevalent error: _____

   a. Cause:_____

   _____

   _____

   b. Prevention:_____

   _____

   _____

   _____

   _____

Proofread
Carefully

PART 4

LITERATURE

How to Chart Literature/Reading Tests

①→ RECORDING TEST GRADES: After each test, students keep track of their literature/reading scores by recording the **DATE**, **TITLE** of test, and **GRADE** on the RECORD OF LITERATURE/READING TESTS.

②→ CHARTING SKILLS MASTERED: Next, on the LITERATURE/READING SKILLS sheet, students chart the **SKILLS MASTERED** as well as the **SKILLS MISSED** for each test.

✪ For example, on **TEST 1** (Application Test / "Rikki-Tikki-Tavi") the student mastered three **plot/sequential order** questions, and one each of **characterization**, **point of view**, **theme**, **fact**, **figurative language**, **external conflict**, and **symbolism**.

✪ **SKILLS MISSED** were **opinion**, **supporting detail**, and **internal conflict**.

③→ CONFERENCING: Since the chart provides a PICTURE of **WEAKNESSES** as well as **STRENGTHS** of the student, teachers can use the chart to determine a program for individual student improvement.

④→ USING INDEPENDENT READING RECORD: Students may also chart the books they have read **INDEPENDENTLY**. **TESTS**, **ESSAYS**, and **OTHER PRODUCTS** may be assigned and recorded for a specified number of books depending on course/curriculum requirements.

QUALITY ASSURANCE

© 1998 M. E. LEDBETTER

NAME_____CLASS_____DATE_____

RECORD OF
LITERATURE/READING TESTS

	DATE	SELECTION	GRADE
TEST 1			
TEST 2			

	DATE	SELECTION	GRADE
TEST 3			
TEST 4			

	DATE	SELECTION	GRADE
TEST 5			
TEST 6			

NAME_____CLASS_____DATE_____

RECORD OF
LITERATURE/READING TESTS
page 2

	DATE	SELECTION	GRADE
TEST 7			
TEST 8			

	DATE	SELECTION	GRADE
TEST 9			
TEST 10			

	DATE	SELECTION	GRADE
TEST 11			
TEST 12			

NAME_____CLASS_____DATE_____

SAMPLE RECORD OF LITERATURE/READING TESTS

	DATE	SELECTION	GRADE
TEST 1	8/24 1994	*Application Test /"Rikki-Tikki-Tavi"*	90
TEST 2	9/19 1994	*"Caleb's Brother"*	100

	DATE	SELECTION	GRADE
TEST 3	10/24 1994	*Ordinary Princess*	90
TEST 4	11/30 1994	*"Thanksgiving Hunter"*	100

	DATE	SELECTION	GRADE
TEST 5	12/6 1994	*Jingo Django*	87
TEST 6	1/5 1995	*"A Christmas Memory"*	95

NAME_____ CLASS_____ DATE_____

LITERATURE/READING SKILLS

SKILL	TEST 1	TEST 2	TEST 3	TEST 4	TEST 5	TEST 6
1. PLOT/SEQUENTIAL ORDER						
2. SETTING						
3. CHARACTERIZATION						
4. TONE/MOOD						
5. POINT OF VIEW						
6. THEME/MAIN IDEA						
7. CAUSE/EFFECT						
8. FLASHBACK						
9. INFERENCE						
10. FACT/OPINION						
11. SUMMARIZATION						
12. RECOGNITION OF SUPPORTING FACTS/DETAILS						
13. LOGICAL CONCLUSIONS						
14. PREDICTING OUTCOMES						
15. CHART/GRAPH INTERPRETATION						
16. FIGURATIVE LANGUAGE						
17. CONFLICT						
18. SYMBOLISM						
19. IRONY						
20. OTHER						

NAME-------------------------------CLASS---------------DATE-----------

LITERATURE/READING SKILLS
Page 2

SKILL	TEST 7	TEST 8	TEST 9	TEST 10	TEST 11	TEST 12
1. PLOT/SEQUENTIAL ORDER						
2. SETTING						
3. CHARACTERIZATION						
4. TONE/MOOD						
5. POINT OF VIEW						
6. THEME/MAIN IDEA						
7. CAUSE/EFFECT						
8. FLASHBACK						
9. INFERENCE						
10. FACT/OPINION						
11. SUMMARIZATION						
12. RECOGNITION OF SUPPORTING FACTS/DETAILS						
13. LOGICAL CONCLUSIONS						
14. PREDICTING OUTCOMES						
15. CHART/GRAPH INTERPRETATION						
16. FIGURATIVE LANGUAGE						
17. CONFLICT						
18. SYMBOLISM						
19. IRONY						
20. OTHER						

NAME_____ CLASS_____ DATE_____

Sample LITERATURE/READING SKILLS

SKILL	TEST 1	TEST 2	TEST 3	TEST 4	TEST 5	TEST 6
1. PLOT/SEQUENTIAL ORDER	+ + +				+	+ Climax
2. SETTING		+ + +	+ +	+	+	+Time xPlace
3. CHARACTERIZATION	+	+	+		+ +	
4. TONE/MOOD		+ + +	+			
5. POINT OF VIEW	+	+				
6. THEME/MAIN IDEA	+	+		+	+	+
7. CAUSE/EFFECT					+	
8. FLASHBACK		+		+		+
9. INFERENCE					x	+
10. FACT/OPINION	+ Fact x Opinion	+ Fact + Opinion	+ Fact + Opinion			
11. SUMMARIZATION		+	+	+		
12. RECOGNITION OF SUPPORTING FACTS/DETAILS	x			+		+ +
13. LOGICAL CONCLUSIONS					+	
14. PREDICTING OUTCOMES		+	+		+ +	
15. CHART/GRAPH INTERPRETATION						
16. FIGURATIVE LANGUAGE	+	+ +	+	+ + +	+ + x	+ + +
17. CONFLICT	xInternal + External	+ +	+ +	+ +	+ +	
18. SYMBOLISM	+			+		+
19. IRONY			x	x		+
20. OTHER			xImagery	+Imagery		+ Rep for effect + Specific Detail

+ =Correct   X =Incorrect

NAME:_____ CLASS:_____ DATE:_____

INDEPENDENT READING RECORD

	TITLE OF BOOK	AUTHOR	DATE	MODE/GRADE
1				
2				
3				
4				
5				
6				
7				
8				
9				
10				

How to Use Literature/Reading Skills Sheet
As
Generic Literature Tests

The **LITERATURE/READING SKILLS SHEET** provides students with a CONSTANT REMINDER of the skills they are expected to master. On this form, students will find space to write evidence of a particular skill--either in the form of **QUOTED MATERIAL FROM THE TEXT** or in the **STUDENT'S OWN WORDS**. ✱The sheet has the following uses:

①→ CHECK TEST: The sheet can serve as a **check test** (or as an application worksheet) for a **SHORT STORY** or **NOVEL CHAPTER**.

A. After a reading assignment, assign students certain **SKILLS TO SUPPORT**. For instance, require students to address only **FIVE** or **TEN** skills for a quick review, or assign **ALL** of the skills for a more in-depth analysis of the piece.

B. This works well as a **GROUP** or an **INDIVIDUAL** assignment.

How to Use Literature/Reading Skills Sheet
As
Generic Literature Tests, page 2

②→ WORKING NOTES: The sheet is also useful for "Working Notes" on stories and novels. Ask students to keep track of **APPLICABLE LITERARY TERMS** as they read and to support their choice with **WORKING NOTES**.

A.   For instance, an applicable term for Chapter 1 of <u>Dandelion Wine</u> could be SETTING--*"Summer 1928 began."*

B.   WORKING NOTES can also reveal an **EPIPHANY** on the part of the reader.

 ❶ Initially, for example, in the Honeysuckle Ladies Lodge chapter of <u>Dandelion Wine</u>, the student reader might cite **CONFLICT** involving Elmira Brown vs. Clara Goodwater-- two women pitted against each other.

 ❷ As the chapter ends, however, the student could also cite Clara's promise to "use my magic for nothing but good," suggesting that all along the struggle has been more complex, one involving Woman vs. Witchcraft.

 ❸ The WORKING NOTES, then, reflect the **PROGRESSION** of the student's literary understanding.

Literature/Reading Skills

| 1. PLOT/SEQUENTIAL ORDER |
| 2. SETTING |
| 3. CHARACTERIZATION |
| 4. TONE/MOOD |
| 5. POINT OF VIEW |
| 6. THEME/MAIN IDEA |
| 7. CAUSE/EFFECT |
| 8. FLASHBACK |
| 9. INFERENCE |
| 10. FACT/OPINION |

11. SUMMARIZATION

12. RECOGNITION OF SUPPORTING FACTS/DETAILS

13. LOGICAL CONCLUSIONS

14. FUTURE OUTCOME/PREDICTION

15. GRAPH/CHART INTERPRETATION

16. FIGURATIVE LANGUAGE

17. CONFLICT

18. SYMBOLISM

19. TONE

20. OTHER

How to Use
Generic Literature Quizzes

① PERSON/PLACE/THING/IDEA--Students always enjoy an alternative to the conventional test. This quiz allows them to choose a **CHARACTER**, an **EVENT**, a **THING**, and an **IDEA** that <u>they</u> feel are important and to support their reasoning.

   A. The test can serve as a **CHAPTER** or **SECTION** quiz for a novel, allowing students to analyze key elements as the story progresses.

   B. OR give the quiz as a **CULMINATING** test for a novel or short story. More detailed instructions could require that students write a **LITERARY ANALYSIS** paragraph for each element, weaving **SEVERAL** quotes with their own words.

   C. Illustrations can be more elaborate in the form of mobiles, booklets, collages, etc.

② NOVEL TESTS--After students have studied a novel, assign one or more of the generic novel **TESTS**.

   A. The **TESTS**, given in the form of **OPEN-BOOK TESTS**, provide students with an opportunity to search for textual material to use to their advantage and to practice internal documentation.

   B. A **CLOSED-BOOK TESTING**, on the other hand, forces students to rely on a detailed as well as a more expansive reading of the text.

Literature Quiz
Person/Place/Thing/Idea

① → Write the **NAME** of your book:_____

and the **AUTHOR**:_____

② → Write the **PAGE NUMBERS** on which you will be tested:_____to_____

③ → You must choose an important PERSON (other than the protagonist), a PLACE, a THING, and an IDEA from your reading (only from the pages indicated above). These should be **ELEMENTS THAT YOU BELIEVE ARE SOMEHOW ESSENTIAL OR INTERESTING OR NOTEWORTHY**.

④ → Using your book, find a **QUOTE** for each that would support your reason for choosing this aspect.

⑤ → **EXPLAIN IN YOUR OWN WORDS** how each of these four aspects is an important element in the book.

⑥ → Draw a **PICTURE** to represent each.

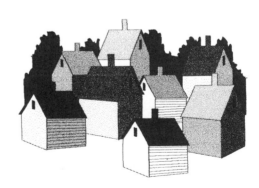

© 1998 M. E. LEDBETTER

NAME_____CLASS_____DATE_____

NOVEL TEST: SETTING

TITLE OF BOOK: _____*AUTHOR:*_____

1. State the **PRIMARY SETTING** of the novel and explain why you think the author uses this time and place. Give specific examples in your reasoning.

   a. *SETTING*: *TIME*--_____

   PLACE--_____

   b. *REASON*: _____

_____

_____

_____

2. Draw a **MEMORABLE SCENE** from the book and explain why it is one that will remain with you. You may choose to explain in the form of **LABELING PARTS OF THE SCENE** or **INCLUDING CONVERSATION "BUBBLES"** that would exemplify the importance.

NOVEL TEST: CHARACTERIZATION

TITLE OF BOOK:_____AUTHOR:_____

1. Choose two *adjectives* that best describe the *protagonist* (the major character) and give specific proof of each by referring to an incident when the character exhibited these traits.

CHARACTER:_____

    a. ADJECTIVE:_____

      PROOF:_____

_____

_____

    b. ADJECTIVE: _____

      PROOF:_____

_____

_____

2. **Choose two adjectives** that best describe the **Antagonist** (the adversary) and give specific proof of each by referring to an incident when the character exhibited these traits.

*CHARACTER:_____

   a. ADJECTIVE:_____

      PROOF:_____

      _____

      _____

   b. ADJECTIVE:_____

      PROOF:_____

      _____

3. Pretend you are the protagonist. Write a **DIARY ENTRY EXPLAINING WHAT YOU LEARNED FROM YOUR EXPERIENCE**--in other words, the **THEME** of the story. Remember not to sum up the plot of the book but rather tell the **LESSON LEARNED**.

Dear Diary,

Today I learned _____

_____

_____

_____

Love,

_____(CHARACTER'S NAME)

NOVEL TEST: CONFLICT

TITLE OF BOOK:_____**AUTHOR:**_____

1. If **CONFLICT** is a struggle between opposing forces, **PICTORIALLY REPRESENT** and **LABEL A MAJOR EXTERNAL conflict** clearly enough so that someone who has not read the book can understand the problem.

2. Explain an **INTERNAL conflict** in the book by writing a **NOTE** from a **CHARACTER'S POINT OF VIEW**, stating his or her problem and giving specific instances. The note should be written to an appropriate character in the book.

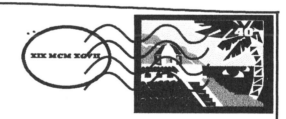

NAME_____CLASS_____DATE_____

NOVEL TEST: TERMS

*TITLE OF BOOK:*_____

*AUTHOR:*_____

1. Choose three **LITERARY TERMS** (cause/effect, fact/opinion, symbolism, mood/tone, inference, prediction, flashback, etc.) and *EXPLAIN HOW THEY PLAY A PART IN THE STORY*.

   a. *TERM*:_____

      EXPLANATION:_____

      _____

      _____

   b. *TERM*:_____

      EXPLANATION:_____

      _____

      _____

   c. *TERM*:_____

      EXPLANATION:_____

      _____

      _____

© 1998 M. E. LEDBETTER

2. To prove your understanding of *FIGURATIVE LANGUAGE,* as well as your familiarity with the text, do the following:

(1) COMPOSE three examples of figurative language that could have been included in the book. Remember to be consistent with the *TONE* of the story.

(2) Explain in which *SECTION* the examples could have been used. Be sure to use a different section for each example.

(3) Tell the *TYPE OF FIGURATIVE LANGUAGE DEVICE* that you have created (i.e., simile, implicit metaphor, explicit metaphor, personification, hyperbole). Each example must represent a different device.

(4) Demonstrate the effectiveness of the figurative language by writing corresponding *LITERAL VERSIONS* as a contrast.

a. *EXAMPLE 1*:

1.*FIGURATIVE*:_____

_____

2.*SECTION*:_____

_____

3. *TYPE*:_____

4. *LITERAL*:_____

_____

© 1998 M. E. LEDBETTER

b. EXAMPLE 2:

    1. FIGURATIVE:_____

_____

    2. SECTION:_____

_____

    3. TYPE:_____

    4. LITERAL:_____

_____

c. EXAMPLE 3:

    1. FIGURATIVE:_____

_____

    2. SECTION:_____

_____

    3. TYPE:_____

    4. LITERAL:_____

_____

DON'T FORGET

NOVEL TEST: BOOK REVIEW

TITLE OF BOOK:_____

AUTHOR:_____

1. Pretend you are a **BOOK REVIEWER**. Write a **BLURB** for the cover of the book. You will need to introduce the **CHARACTERS** and explain the **CONFLICT** without giving away any secrets. Remember that the idea is to entice the readers to buy the book by giving just enough **SUMMARY** to whet their appetites.

_____

_____

_____

_____

_____

_____

_____

_____

_____

_____

2. On a scale of zero to ten, *RATE YOUR BOOK* and specifically explain your rating, giving *THREE SPECIFIC EXAMPLES* from the text.

RATING:_____

EXAMPLE 1:_____

_____

_____

*EXAMPLE 2:*_____

_____

_____

*EXAMPLE 3:*_____

_____

_____

3. Briefly **COMPARE OR CONTRAST** this book to another literary work you have read. Give two specific examples of ways they are different or similar.

EXAMPLE 1:

_____

_____

_____

_____

EXAMPLE 2:

_____

_____

_____

_____

ADAPT, ADAPT, ADAPT!

HOW TO ADAPT LITERATURE ASSIGNMENT SHEETS

In the teacher pages preceding each literature assignment are **SUGGESTIONS FOR ADAPTING THE ASSIGNMENTS TO OTHER STORIES**. For instance, if a particular curriculum does not include the play Monsters Are Due on Maple Street, the VOCABULARY APPLICATION SHEET can be used as a **MODEL** for constructing a **SIMILAR ASSIGNMENT** based on stories that are used.

Creating VOCABULARY APPLICATION SHEETS
Involving Higher Level Thinking Skills

① → **USING VOCABULARY APPLICATION SHEETS:** After students have defined vocabulary words for a story, use application sheets that require students to prove their **UNDERSTANDING** of their new words by **APPLYING THE TERMS TO ASPECTS OF THEIR OWN LIVES**.

② → **WRITING VOCABULARY APPLICATION QUESTIONS:** **STUDENTS MAY WRITE THE QUESTIONS** for other students to answer.

A. Assign each **STUDENT** or each **GROUP** a certain number of **TEACHER-CHOSEN WORDS** from the text about which to write questions.

B. Or ask that each student or group **CHOOSE WORDS** on their own. Any overlapping of words would simply give more practice in application since the questions regarding the words would be different.

C. Require **SAMPLE ANSWERS** for each question.

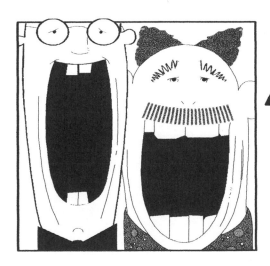

MONSTERS ARE DUE ON MAPLE STREET
by Rod Serling

VOCABULARY APPLICATION

Now that you have **defined** your vocabulary words, you must **apply** your knowledge of them in order to really understand them.   In **complete sentences** answer the following questions, using your notes and a dictionary if necessary.

①→   Name the first **INTELLIGIBLE** sound you made as a baby. (If you don't remember or if your parents haven't talked about it a million times, make a guess.)

_____

_____

②→   Name something that could be said to be **REPETITIVE**.

_____

_____

③→   Superman's life is based on **OPTIMISM** since he believes he can help good triumph over evil.

   a. Name another famous character whose life is based on **OPTIMISM**.

_____

_____

b. Do you live your life based on **OPTIMISM** or its antonym, pessimism, which is the tendency to view things in the gloomiest possible way?

_____

_____

c. Give an example of your **OPTIMISM** or pessimism.

_____

_____

④→ **a.** In school, what could your teachers try to **INSTILL** in you?

_____

_____

b. In church, what could the minister try to **INSTILL** in you?

_____

_____

⑤→ When you tell your teacher that you didn't finish your homework because your little brother doesn't like cabbage, she'll say that your argument has no **VALIDITY**. What will she mean?

_____

_____

⑥→ Name a TV character who could be said to be **DEFIANT**. (Or tell when **you** are defiant.)

_____

_____

⑦→ What could you do that would display **ANTAGONISM** toward another person?

_____

_____

⑧→ You can do something reasonably, or you can do something **INEXPLICABLY**. Name something you can do **INEXPLICABLY**.

_____

_____

⑨→ In <u>The Beauty and the Beast</u> what **METAMORPHOSIS** has occurred? (If you haven't watched this movie, name a **METAMORPHOSIS** you have undergone.)

_____

_____

⑩→ **INCISIVE** does not refer to sharpness as in the sharpness of a knife but to a sharp mental perception, one that cuts straight to the heart of a subject. For instance, after reading a play such as <u>Monsters</u> . . . , make an **INCISIVE** comment about the message of the play:

_____

_____

CREATING STUDENT-INTERACTION READING SHEETS

① → USING INTERACTION SHEETS: The point of an interaction sheet is for students to be **ACTIVELY ENGAGED** in the text. The sheets can be done as a **CLASS**, reading aloud and stopping to analyze together; as a **SMALL-GROUP** activity; or **INDIVIDUALLY**, with each student working at his or her own pace.

② → DEVELOPING YOUR OWN INTERACTION GUIDES: When constructing similar guides, find **"STOPPING PLACES"** where it is necessary for students to assess or respond to what has happened previously to make **FUTURE ACTIONS MORE MEANINGFUL**. Questions that are generally earmarked for class discussions can be used to generate **WRITTEN RESPONSES** so that **EACH STUDENT** is given an opportunity to express his or her understanding of the text thus far.

③ → TEACHING STUDENTS TO WRITE INTERACTIVE QUESTIONS: Call on a student to read a passage orally. Stop the student at an appropriate place and ask for volunteers to formulate a question based on the **SIGNIFICANCE** of the passage. Direct students to **WRITE** their answers, giving each person more practice in literary response.

④ → USING MODEL: Following is an example of a Student-Interaction Sheet for "Nancy" by Elizabeth Enright.

STUDENT INTERACTION "NANCY"

In order to comprehend a story, readers must CONTINUALLY INTERACT WITH THE TEXT, that is to say, be **active readers** involved with the story, as opposed to passive readers. To practice this skill, **READ THE STORY**, briefly stopping at the pages indicated, and interact with the piece as it has been revealed up to that point.

BEFORE YOU BEGIN READING:

1. BRAINSTORM TWO ENVIRONMENTS that you know personally that contrast and list elements of those environments that differ. For example, your **grandma's house** (in the country; cows/chickens/pigs; old-fashioned, rambling two-story with porches) **vs. your house** (in a subdivision; "inside" dog; compact, modern ranch with deck).

_____ vs._____

① → _____

② → _____

③ → _____

Stop at p. 230 (b), "But once she did."

2. Quote one thing you've learned about **Fiona's appearance, personality, and environment:**

    a. Appearance:_____

_____

b. Personality:_____

_____

c. Environment:_____

_____

Stop at p. 231 (b), "On the outskirts of the town..."

3. Quote the sentence that shows **what Fiona is compared to as she goes on her adventure:**

_____

_____

4. Explain why this is a good comparison. **What would Fiona have in common with this thing?**

_____

_____

Stop at p. 238 (a), " 'Fee-ona Farmer!' "

5. Quote an example of appearance, personality, and environment of **the people and the house that Fiona comes upon** that is a contrast to her own.

a. Appearance:_____

_____

b. Personality:_____

_____

    c. Environment: _____

_____

After finishing the story:

6. **Explain the "poetry"** in the passage that begins "She had never been homesick before . . ." (239) and ends with "Blackie's purr to throb against her chest."

_____

_____

7. Explain how this paragraph is the **theme** of the story.

_____

_____

_____

_____

8. If all the elements in the story are contrasting, **what element could be said to be the same about both** environments? In other words, on a comparison/contrast chart, what would you enter as the **similarity?** Quote an example from both environments:

    a. Fiona's environment:

_____

_____

    b. Fadgins' environment:

_____

_____

9. Write to Learn--Write a paragraph telling **what you've learned from this story**.

_____

_____

_____

_____

_____

_____

_____

_____

_____

_____

_____

_____

_____

Enright, Elizabeth. "Nancy." <u>Projection</u> <u>in</u> <u>Literature</u>. Ed. Robert C. Pooley et al., Glenview, Illinois: Scott, Foresman, 1967, 228-240.

How to Use Fluencies for Short Stories

① → **IDENTIFYING WITH STORY:** The idea of this type of assignment is for students to recall ***THEIR OWN EXPERIENCES*** on a certain theme or topic with which a story deals. Students are usually more interested in a piece when they see some sort of ***PERSONAL RELEVANCE*** and when their literary appetite has been whetted by the sharing of classroom anecdotes.

② → **ASSIGNING THE FLUENCY:** Give the fluency writing topic ***BEFORE READING THE STORY*** to increase student interest or ***AFTER READING THE PIECE*** to serve as summation of the lesson. Remind students that the idea of a fluency is to ***FREEWRITE*** their thoughts as quickly as possible, letting their subconscious ideas surface without being overly hampered by grammatical restraints.

③ → **USING MODELS:**

A. Following is a ***FLUENCY*** for the short story "Nancy" by Elizabeth Enright.

B. A ***GENERIC FLUENCY*** has been included; it may be used with any short story in an effort to ***PERSONALIZE*** the piece for the student reader. The generic fluency can be modified for use after the story is read.

Fluency for "Nancy"

ONE WAY AN AUTHOR REVEALS CHARACTER IS BY DESCRIBING HIS OR HER ENVIRONMENT.

FIONA FARMER is a lonely only child, who lives with her parents, her nurse, and her grandparents in a spotless, elegant old home attended by two maids. Her environment is almost a prison of decorum.

UNTIL...

She meets the **FADGINS**, a poor, fun-loving family with enough kids, animals, and freedom to last Fiona a lifetime ... OR AT LEAST UNTIL HER NURSE FINDS HER.

Think about contrasting environments that you know--either your own or that of friends or relatives.

Write for *FIVE MINUTES*, describing both environments.

FLUENCY

Title of Story:_____ Author:_____

BEFORE READING A STORY, we--as readers--can take steps to "ready" ourselves for the literary experience. By recalling certain **EVENTS**, **CHARACTERS**, and **LESSONS** in our very real lives, we can often more effectively **IDENTIFY** with aspects of a fictional piece.

Your teacher will use the following **GUIDE** to describe various elements of **PLOT**, **CHARACTERIZATION**, and **THEME** of the story you will be assigned to read.

✎You will write a **FIVE-MINUTE FLUENCY** about each of the following aspects.

1. PLOT--In this story a **SIGNIFICANT EVENT** is

_____

(Your teacher will briefly describe the event for you.)

RECALL A TIME when you or someone you know had a **SIMILAR EXPERIENCE**. If you have not had the experience, **EXPLAIN WHY** or why not **OR WRITE YOUR OWN FICTIONAL ACCOUNT** of a similar experience you could have had.

_____

_____

_____

_____

~~~~~~

~~~~~~

~~~~~~

~~~~~~

~~~~~~

2. CHARACTERIZATION--Remember that an author reveals information about a character by describing the character's **APPEARANCE, INNER THOUGHTS** and **FEELINGS, SPEECH, ACTIONS, ENVIRONMENT,** and **WHAT OTHERS SAY**.

The **PROTAGONIST** in this story is _____.
(Your teacher will describe the major character for you.)

DESCRIBE A PERSON you know who is **SIMILAR TO THE FICTIONAL CHARACTER** or else a person who is the very **OPPOSITE** of the character.

~~~~~~

~~~~~~

~~~~~~

~~~~~~

~~~~~~

~~~~~~

~~~~~~

~~~~~~

~~~~~~

3. THEME--We all learn **LESSONS** from life. In this story, one lesson the character learns is

~~~~~~.

(Your teacher will explain one lesson for you.)

RELATE TO THIS THEME by giving a **BRIEF ANECDOTE** about how this same message has played a part in your life.

~~~~~~

~~~~~~

~~~~~~

~~~~~~

~~~~~~

~~~~~~

~~~~~~

~~~~~~

©1996 M. E. LEDBETTER

Creating a Journal Project for Novels

① → USING JOURNAL PROJECTS: A journal project is an entertaining method of **INTRODUCING** various modes of writing or as a **CULMINATING ACTIVITY THAT SERVES AS A REVIEW OF ALL MODES**.

② →. SUPPORTING WITH EXAMPLES FROM TEXT: Not only does a project of this nature require students to focus on different types of writing done throughout the year but it forces students to make **TEXTUAL ASSOCIATIONS** as well.

③ → CREATING A PRODUCT: Students enjoy creating a **PRODUCT** in addition to the written journal entry. Hold a **CONTEST** for the most unusual/effective/interesting **JOURNAL FORM**.

④ → USING AN EXAMPLE: Following is an example of a journal project for Ray Bradbury's <u>DANDELION WINE</u>.

NAME:_____ CLASS:_____ DATE:_____

DUE DATE:_____ POINTS:_____

Dandelion Wine: Journal Project

In **Dandelion Wine**, Douglas Spaulding keeps a **journal**, which chronicles his rituals and ceremonies as well as his discoveries and revelations of the summer of 1928 in Green Town, Illinois.

As readers, *we* learn that we, too, have our own **TIME MACHINES**, namely our parents and grandparents and virtually anyone who has ever taken us back in time to their "Ching Ling Soos" and "Pawnee Bills" and "Civil War" days.

Our **JOHN HUFFS** might not have moved away yet, but they have committed other transgressions against us that have hurt as deeply. **TAROT WITCHES** and **LONELY ONES**? Maybe not. But we've had our *own* injustices--whether real or imagined--our *own* fears and indescribable illnesses with or without a **MR. JONAS** by our side.

And careening down *our* streets are our own versions of **MISS ROBERTA** and **MISS FERN** in their **GREEN MACHINE**, and next door someone very much like **LEO AUFFMANN** is hammering away at something very much like a **HAPPINESS MACHINE.**

And out back in the garden of that three-story Victorian are **BILL FORRESTER** and **HELEN LOOMIS** enjoying tea, and over there across the fence **GRANDPA** is extolling the virtues of lawn mowing . . . that is, if only we take time to see them, to recall *our impressions* of *our own times* that never again will be the same.

Assignment:

✎Just as Douglas records his rites and discoveries, you will keep a journal for the **WEEK** of _____. (Your teacher will assign the time period.)

✎Include **EACH** of the following types of entries, which should be a **MINIMUM OF 100 WORDS EACH**.

✎Cite a corresponding associated passage and page number from the book.

1. A **descriptive entry** of an OUTDOOR SCENE at the beginning of-- _____ (week of the project)--to correspond to Douglas's time in the cupola, waking up the town for the first day of summer [e.g., "It was a quiet morning, the town covered over with darkness and at ease in bed" (1)].

2. A **narrative entry** involving a PERSON that reminds you, on some level, of someone Doug knows--your own Time Machine story perhaps or a Clara Goodwater/Elmira Brown relationship or John Huff episode. The possibilities are endless.

3. A **narrative/descriptive entry** involving an EMOTION akin to something Douglas experiences--fear of the Lonely One, sadness at the deaths Douglas sees all around him, even love that Douglas realizes Bill and Helen feel for each other.

4. A **persuasive/narrative entry**--Doug tries to persuade his father that last year's tennis shoes have lost their magic; the children convince Mrs. Bentley that she was never young. What is your ARGUMENT?

5. A **comparison/contrast entry** involving RITES/CEREMONIES vs. DISCOVERIES/REVELATIONS. Doug records all the firsts of summer--things summer always holds for him--but this year he makes another column for ideas that have never really occurred to him. Maybe, he writes, his father and grandfather don't know everything and the reason that parents and kids do not agree is simple--they're of different races. What are *your* Rites and Discoveries?

6. A **descriptive entry** signifying the end of _____ (your project week)--["Everything runs backward now. Like matinee films sometimes, where people jump out of water onto diving boards" (238)].

Rubric:

①→ **Creativity/Figurative Language**--your writing style.

②→ **Footnoted references to book**--The association between your entries and aspects of the book should be made clear.

③→ **Illustrations**.

④→ **Mechanics**--grammar (run-ons, fragments, spelling, etc.).

*Ideas for form:

①→ Journal--homemade book

②→ Scroll

③→ Letters in box

④→ Mobiles

⑤→ Stand-up folding book

⑥→ Collage

⑦→ Computer banner and entries

⑧→ Book of letters

⑨→ Postcards

Bradbury, Ray. Dandelion Wine. New York: Bantam Books, 1975.

How to Design
Group Projects for Novels

① → MATCHING SKILLS TO CHAPTERS: Create a project by **DETERMINING DOMINANT LITERATURE/READING SKILLS** (e.g., flashback, logical conclusion, conflict) **FOR CERTAIN CHAPTERS**. For instance, **ONE SECTION** might emphasize **CONFLICT**; therefore, one group's project could produce an **IN-DEPTH ANALYSIS** of a central struggle between opposing forces inherent in that chapter.

② → DOCUMENTING SUPPORT: Students gain practice in **LITERARY ANALYSIS** by supporting their opinions with specific, **DOCUMENTED EXAMPLES FROM THE TEXT**.

③ → DISTRIBUTING ASSIGNMENTS: Cut out assignments and put on **INDIVIDUAL CARDS** so that groups can draw a card for a particular assignment.

④ → MAKING PRESENTATIONS: Heighten class interest with the use of **PICTORIAL REPRESENTATIONS** that can be displayed in the room and enjoyed by other classes. **CLASS PRESENTATIONS** of the projects serve not only as a **REVIEW OF LITERARY TERMS BUT AS A REVIEW OF WRITING MODES** as well.

Group Projects for DANDELION WINE

TIME MACHINE

"COLONEL FREELEIGH"

1. Prove that Bradbury uses the *FLASHBACK TECHNIQUE* in the Colonel Freeleigh chapter (80-87). You will want to support your theory with *QUOTATIONS FROM THE TEXT.*

2. Draw the *TIME MACHINE* and label the places it visits.

3. Each student will draw an ***INDIVIDUAL TIME MACHINE*** of his or her past, describing places where he or she could time travel.

"THE GREEN MACHINE"

1. Define the concept of *LOGICAL CONCLUSION* and apply it to this chapter by using quoted material from the text.

2. Write the *NEWSPAPER ARTICLE* that Roberta and Fern fear they will see based on their logical conclusion. Remember that newspaper articles are in *INVERTED PYRAMID STRUCTURE,* the five *"W'S" (WHO, WHAT, WHEN, WHERE,* and sometimes *WHY)* appearing in the first paragraph, followed by increasingly less important details. *DRAW A PICTURE OF THE GREEN MACHINE* to accompany the article.

3. Each student will write a *NEWSPAPER ARTICLE* based on a story about something he or she has often feared.

"THE TROLLEY"

1. This chapter contrasts trolleys to buses. Write a DESCRIPTIVE COMPARISON/CONTRAST PAPER based on as many quoted contrasts as possible from the text and at least one comparison that could have been included if Bradbury had gone into more detail. You will want to use mostly original ideas supported by some quoted material. Remember to write in Bradbury's style.

2. DRAW A PICTURE to accompany your paper.

3. Each student will write a DESCRIPTION OF SOMETHING HE OR SHE WOULD MISS, if it were suddenly to be eliminated or replaced, just as the town will miss the trolley. (See last major paragraph on p. 101 for model.)

"JOHN HUFF"

l. Prove that Bradbury uses at least three methods of CHARACTERIZATION in his description of John Huff. Support your theory with quoted material from the text.

2. DRAW A PICTURE and label parts that will further prove your point.

3. Each student in the group will write a CHARACTERIZATION of someone he or she knows based on Bradbury's model on p. 102.

"MRS. GOODWATER"

l. Prove that Bradbury uses INFERENCE when Elmira Brown concludes that Mrs. Goodwater is a witch. You will want to support your theory with quoted material from the text.

2. DRAW A PICTURE that will include ALL THE DETAILS you point to in your paper.

3. Each student will write a paper giving INFERENCE CLUES about some aspect of his or her life.

Bradbury, Ray. <u>Dandelion</u> <u>Wine</u>. New York: Bantam Books, 1975.

How To Integrate Research Skills

① → INTEGRATING RESEARCH INTO LITERATURE STUDIES:
Students can do a **MINI-RESEARCH UNIT** on *SHORT STORIES* or *NOVEL CHAPTERS* to review research techniques and to emphasize that careful readers ask questions as they read. They learn that it is fun to find *ANSWERS* to their *"REAL-LIFE" QUESTIONS*.

② → PROVIDING SOURCES: Schedule a day in the *LIBRARY*, pull sources and set up a *MINILIBRARY* in the classroom, or ask students to gather material themselves for classroom *PACKETS*.

③ → USING TEXT TO GENERATE QUESTIONS: The *RESEARCH ASSIGNMENT SHEET* illustrates how the text of a short story (e.g., "Rikki-Tikki-Tavi") can *GENERATE SPECIFIC QUESTIONS* for students to research and document.

RESEARCH

Objectives:

I. To provide an opportunity to practice research skills of
LOCATING ANSWERS to specific questions
generated from class/individual readings, TAKING
NOTES, and DOCUMENTING SOURCES.

2. To integrate **READING** (from short stories, novels, nonfiction, etc.) **WRITING**, and **RESEARCH** skills.

ASSIGNMENT:

① → From the reading, **QUOTE TEN PASSAGES THAT GENERATE QUESTIONS** that you
are interested in and would like to find more information about regarding
certain topics. Each quotation should be placed on a separate note card
with an internal footnote designating the page of the quotation. At the
bottom of the note card, **STATE THE QUESTION THAT YOU WILL RESEARCH**.

② → Research the answers to the questions, **DOCUMENTING SOURCES** according
to MLA guidelines on separate bibliographic cards. You may find several
answers from a single source, but a total of at least three sources must be
used for the assignment.

③ → On another note card, **WRITE THE ANSWER TO THE QUESTION IN CORRECT NOTE
FORM**, using either **COMBINED NOTES** (summarizing in your own words and
including some of the source's exact wording when appropriate or
necessary) or **SUMMARY NOTES** (condensing the words of the source and
expressing them in your own words). Be sure to avoid **PLAGIARISM** (word-
for-word notes) as well as **"NEAR" PLAGIARISM** (near-quotations).

Sample Assignment from **"RIKKI-TIKKI-TAVI"**:

① → Sample quotation and question from reading;

> Quotation from text:
>
> "'Good gracious,' said Teddy's mother, 'and that's a wild creature! I suppose he's so tame because we've been kind to him'" (14).
>
> Question :
>
> Are mongooses really tame?

② → Bibliographic card:

> A
>
> Goodwin, George G. "Mongoose," <u>Collier's</u> <u>Encyclopedia</u> (1980),
>   Vol. 16, 456-458.

③ → Note Card:

> A, 457
>
> Indian mongooses--
>   easily tamed--usually make nice pets if taken young
>
> can kill rats, mice, venomous snakes

How to Construct Tests that Integrate Research and Literary Analysis

① → TESTING RESEARCH SKILLS: To further **INTEGRATE THE STUDY OF RESEARCH SKILLS WITH THE STUDY OF A NOVEL**, ask students to **FIND** information about the novel's author, the novel itself, background information regarding the setting of the book, political movements, and so forth, and **DOCUMENT** it appropriately as part of the testing situation.

  A. Use this exercise as an **INTRODUCTION** to the novel and as a **REVIEW** of research skills, OR . . .

  B. Incorporate the research questions into a **CULMINATING TEST**. Even if previous classroom discussion revealed some of the testing information, students must still **FIND** the information, put it in proper **NOTE FORM**, and **DOCUMENT** it correctly.

② → TESTING LITERARY ANALYSIS SKILLS: Give students practice with **LITERARY ANALYSIS** by asking them to **SUPPORT** or **REFUTE** ideas expressed in **LITERARY CRITICISM ARTICLES**, citing specific examples from the novel itself as "proof" of their opinions. Use either articles that students themselves must locate or ones that can be made available to all students.

③ → TESTING STUDENT KNOWLEDGE OF WRITING MODES: Incorporate a **REVIEW OF WRITING MODES** into the test by asking students to create an additional, **ORIGINAL CHAPTER** for the book **(NARRATIVE/DESCRIPTIVE)** or to **SELL** the book to the class **(PERSUASIVE)**, and so on.

APPLICATION/SYNTHESIS TEST
ON
THE LITTLE PRINCE

I. BIBLIOGRAPHIC INFORMATION--Using your MLA GUIDE, make three **BIBLIOGRAPHIC CARDS**, one for each reference you will be using. *Your teacher will provide you with the various references for this assignment.

A. **Encyclopedia:**

B. **Book:**

C.   **Specialized Dictionary** (for cross-reference of author who is likened to **Saint-Exupéry**):

II.   BIOGRAPHICAL INFORMATION ABOUT AUTHOR--Using the **EXCERPTS FROM THE LIBRARY MATERIAL** and a **DICTIONARY** when necessary, find the following information about the author. At the end of each listing, write an **INTERNAL FOOTNOTE** to indicate your source.

A.   **Pronunciation and diacritical markings** for the author's name:_____ (   )

B.   **Age of author** when he was reported missing:_____ (   )

C.   **Interests** besides writing and flying:

_____ & _____ (   )

D.   **Writer** he has been likened to (compared to):

_____ (   )

E.   **Information about writer** in previous question-- Use dictionary to cross-reference:

_____

_____ (   )

F. **Vocation** during war:

_____ ( )

G. **Quote a** statement that proves that the author could easily have dealt with the realm of fantasy.

_____

_____

_____

_____ ( )

III. LITERARY COMMENTARIES--Using the excerpts from the library material, a dictionary, your notes, and the text of **The Little Prince**, answer the following questions.

A. **Prove the validity of the following statement using at least three specific, quoted examples from the novel:**

"Besides the ideals of duty and self-transcendence, the idea of 'becoming,' or striving to reach one's full potential, is central to Saint-Exupéry's philosophy, and images of growth fill his works" (Bryfonski, Dedria, and Sharon K. Hall, eds. Twentieth-Century Literary Criticism. Detroit: Gale Research, 1979).

In other words, *EXPLAIN HOW THE NOVEL EXEMPLIFIES THE CONCEPT OF "GROWTH" OR "BECOMING."* Remember to introduce quotations from the text with words of your own.

_____

_____

_____

_____

_____

_____

_____

_____

_____

_____

B. Using at least three specific, quoted examples from the novel, support the belief that "Saint-Exupéry developed a highly individualistic style of lyrical, poetic prose."

In other words, argue for the *POETIC QUALITY* of the work.

_____

_____

_____

_____

_____

_____

_____

_____

_____

_____

_____

IV.   CREATIVE DESCRIPTIVE/NARRATIVE--On his journey, the Little Prince meets many people from various planets who teach him lessons. ***WRITE A NEW CHAPTER THAT COULD BE INCLUDED SOMEWHERE IN THE NOVEL THAT INTRODUCES AN ENTIRELY NEW CHARACTER WHO TEACHES OUR PROTAGONIST YET ANOTHER LESSON ABOUT LIFE.***

RUBRIC:

A. **Stylistic devices/language** appropriate to tone of existing work

B. Inclusion of **figurative language**

C. **Lack of grammatical errors**

EXTRA CREDIT:
Illustration to accompany chapter

How to Use
Vocabulary Project for Novel

① → MAKING WORDS RELEVANT: Vocabulary becomes **MORE FUN** and **MORE MEANINGFUL** when the words come alive for students.

② → USING VOCABULARY PROJECT FOR NOVEL: When assigning a novel, give students the **Vocabulary Project for Novel sheet**, which outlines the assignment for them.

A. The **Twenty Words** give students practice in being more analytical readers. Instead of skipping over words they don't know, they will try **CONTEXT CLUES** and other **WORD-ATTACK SKILLS** to derive their meanings. If a word is still indecipherable to them, they may choose to add it to their **PERSONAL VOCABULARY LISTS**.

B. The original **Context Clue** passage further emphasizes the importance of this skill by asking students to **CONSTRUCT** a passage rather than merely analyze one.

C. The **Personal Identification** and **PERSONIFICATION** assignments **PERSONALIZE** the words and are fun to share with the class.

D. The **ILLUSTRATION** can be used as a bulletin-board vocabulary study for the class.

E. STUDENT SAMPLES have been included as models for classroom use.

© 1988 M. E. LEDBETTER

369

Vocabulary Project for Novel

Title of Book:_____

Author:_____

Project Due Date:_____

ASSIGNMENT:

①→ As you read, choose **twenty vocabulary words** from your novel. For each word, complete the following:

    A. *QUOTE THE PASSAGE* that contains the word; document the excerpt, using an *INTERNAL FOOTNOTE* that gives the page number.

    B. *DEFINE THE WORD* as it is used in the passage.

    C. *LIST THE APPROPRIATE PART OF SPEECH*.

②→ Choose *FOUR WORDS FROM THE LIST* in order to complete the following assignments:

    A. **Context Clue**--Write an original passage (50-word minimum) that contains a context clue to the meaning of the word.

    B. **Personal Identification**--Write a paragraph (100-word minimum) that illustrates *THREE REASONS* why you personally identify with a word.

    C. **Personification/Character Sketch**-- Write a descriptive paragraph (150-word minimum) that personifies a vocabulary word. Remember the **_SIX METHODS OF CHARACTERIZATION_**: appearance, actions, speech, inner thoughts and feelings, what others say, and environment.

D. **Illustration**--Illustrate the meaning of one vocabulary word by using an original drawing, pictures from magazines, and so on. Define the word and/or write an original sentence using the word as further examples of meaning.

③→ **Extra Credit**: Extra credit may be obtained by doing one or both of the following:

A. Quoting, defining, and identifying the part of speech of ten more vocabulary words.

B. Choosing another word for which to write a second context clue, personal identification, personification, or illustration.

Kesa Whitley
Vocabulary Project for Novel
Personal Identification

BRUTAL

If there is one word that is totally opposite of me, it is **BRUTAL.** For one thing, I am kind to my animals. I cringe when I think of my next-door neighbor who picks up his cats or dogs by their tails and swings them over his head. He lets go only after numerous times round and round, sending them flying down the street, howling on their fall. Most of the time, I also try to be nice to my brother. I don't walk down the street, holding him in a headlock and beating him on the back. And, of course, I try my best to keep other people's property in one piece. Never would I be the one to break rulers on people's heads, chew on their markers, destroy all their papers, bite their crayons in half, and spit them out on other people's desks.

If there is one word that is totally opposite of me, it is **BRUTAL.**

Christy Alexander
Vocabulary Project for Novel
Personification

SPLAYED

SPLAYED walks into the room, tripping over her feet and holding her arms awkwardly at her sides. She finally stumbles over to the dictionaries, managing to carry one back to her seat at the end of the row. She flips through the pages, reading intensely and snorting at funny words. SPLAYED'S dictionary suddenly flies across the room, knocking her classmate out cold. "Did I do that?" her manly voice asks. She falls out of her seat once again and trips over to the art supplies. Such big feet, such a big palette of finger paints, such a mess. She stumbles out of the classroom, thinking about what a dunce she is. It just doesn't pay to be SPLAYED.

At home, SPLAYED leans back on her bed, away from all the normal people, away from all the people she isn't. Sighing, she looks to the wall for comfort, at the picture of her hunk, Steve Erkel. Carefully, oh so carefully, she reaches for a CD and tries to put it on the player. "*%+*&$@!" Thirteen dollars in little pieces on the floor. "Well, I'll try the radio," she thinks. Nothing but static, static, static. "Okay," she thinks, "I'll play my oboe." She opens the case to her instrument, and a stack of broken reeds awaits her. "!@#$%^&*!" she screams. It just doesn't pay to be SPLAYED.

*SPLAYED = awkward or awkwardly formed; clumsy

Jessica Nelson
Vocabulary Project for Novel
Personification

ANVIL

ANVIL is the dark, sweaty man at the workshop. He is the one who maybe isn't that important to some, but others can't live without him. He shapes anything anyone needs. His hands are burned from the fire every time someone comes around for something to be made.

His surrounding is a fiery workplace with lots of tools and machines. Loud noises of hammers banging, saws, drills, and people all over the place make his head ache.

After a long day he lies down, rests, and gets ready for the next day's work. He aches all over and burns so badly that not even the arctic blizzards could cool him off.

When the next morning comes, it is time for work again, but before he goes, he eats his breakfast, always a healthy one, full of vitamins to keep him strong.

When he arrives at the workshop, there are already orders waiting for him. His first one is to make a horseshoe for a horse trainer. With a 12 P.M. deadline, he gets right to work. Once again he is at the mercy of the dreadful fire.

The noises start, and the work begins again for **ANVIL**, the dark, sweaty man at the workshop.

Camie Curry
Vocabulary Project for Novel
Personification

PLIABLE

PLIABLE, a skinny, pale twelve-year-old girl, has no friends at her middle school in "the Big Apple." Her busybody parents have no time for her with their complex schedule.

One Thursday, just as always, PLIABLE sat alone, at the third to the last table in the cafeteria. But suddenly, the Coolieo group walked up to her and sat down. All during lunch they talked, but PLIABLE kept to herself and talked very little. Then, out of the blue, the Coolieo girls' leader asked if she would join in with their group. She joined them, with much excitement.

After a while, her "A's" started looking like "F's" and she was always dragging into class late. But to her, none of it mattered; she was popular now, cool, and hip and part of a group . . . wasn't she?

One day after school, the Coolieo girls got together at the worn-down warehouse on Billian Avenue. When PLIABLE arrived, fashionably late, the rest of the gang was smoking. She walked in and they offered her a cigarette. At first she refused, but soon afterwards she gave into the peer pressure.

Her parents slowly found out about PLIABLE's school and after-school problems. They got her help and helped her to regain her looks and get her grades back to normal.

Today, thanks to the help PLIABLE received in her childhood, she is a student counselor. She works at being friends with all the students. She helps them shape their lives into what they want to be.

Kesa Whitley
Vocabulary Project for Novel
Personification

OBSTINATE

OBSTINATE is a stubborn boy who only does what he wants. He never turns in his homework, but instead sits around drawing doodles on a blank sheet of paper that was supposed to be a language assignment from the HBJ book on adjectives and adverbs.

At home he is difficult to manage and never minds his parents, only doing what he wants or feels like doing. His room is always messy with clothes and toys and whatever hobby currently interests him strewn all over the now invisible floor. His speech is terrible, but he "ain't" worried "hisself."

In his mind, nothing else matters but himself, and he doesn't care about what others think or say about him. People say he is hard to manage. When he does come around, he never likes anyone's ideas anyway and only plays the games he wants to. His parents say that maybe by the time he gets past age ten, he will grow out of this stage or phase.

Meanwhile, his clothes are mismatched, his socks are different colors, and his never-tied shoes are caked with mud. Maybe his parents are right; he may change his ways when he reaches age eleven. Or maybe not.

How to Create
SHORT-STORY ACTIVITIES

① → USING GENERIC GROUP ACTIVITIES FOR SHORT-STORY UNITS:

A. At the conclusion of a single short story or a short-story unit, put students into **GROUPS** of four or five, if possible.

B. Ask a representative from each group to **DRAW** for one of the following model assignments.

C. Require that each student write at least the rough draft on his or her own paper, discussing answers and **INDIVIDUALLY** recording the consensus of the group.

D. Groups should **PRESENT** their completed projects to the class, soliciting class involvement when applicable.

E. Give students individual or group **GRADES**.

② → CREATING SUPPLEMENTAL GENERIC ACTIVITIES:

A. Determine the **SKILLS** that are to be emphasized for a particular unit. **VOCABULARY, PLOT ANALYSIS, COMPARISON/CONTRAST, NEWSWRITING, POETRY**, and **FIGURATIVE LANGUAGE** are included as sample models.

B. Compose assignments that students can apply to most stories either as a **REVIEW OF SKILLS** or as an **INTRODUCTION TO NEW TERMS**.

C. Allow students to write assignments to add to the **CHOICES** for the class.

SUGGESTIONS

WORDS! WORDS! WORDS!

①→ Choose **TEN VOCABULARY WORDS** from the story.

②→ Look up the **DEFINITIONS AND PARTS OF SPEECH** in the dictionary.

③→ Create a **WORKSHEET** that allows fellow classmates to practice vocabulary usage in a creative way. Include questions such as the following:

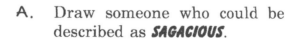

A. Draw someone who could be described as **SAGACIOUS**.

B. What TV character could be referred to as **DEFIANT**?

C. Do you live your life based on optimism or **PESSIMISM**? Explain.

④→ Make a **CROSSWORD PUZZLE** using all ten words. Include their parts of speech with the definitions.

⑤→ Make **ANSWER KEYS**.

PLOT IT!

①→ Make a **PYRAMID PLOT GRAPH** of the story.

②→ Be sure to place the events in order and to include at least **SIX RISING ACTIONS** of major importance, **ONE CLIMAX**, and **ONE FALLING ACTION**. All events should be summarized in your own words.

③→ After proofreading, make the final graph on **BUTCHER PAPER**. **ILLUSTRATE** at least three of the actions with drawings.

④→ Make a set of **INDEX CARDS** for the class to practice the skill of sequencing. Place one action on each card. Ask for volunteers to arrange cards. (This class participatory exercise will precede the presentation of the group's final graph.)

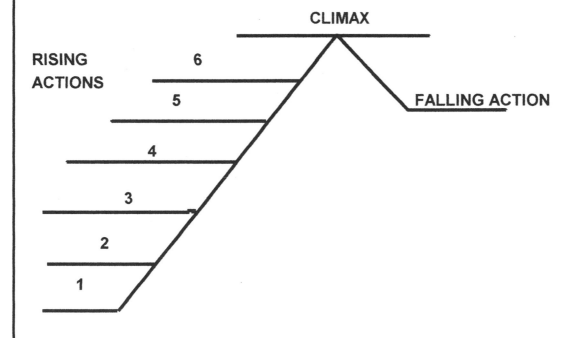

CLIMAX

RISING ACTIONS

6

5

4

3

2

1

FALLING ACTION

COMPARISON/CONTRAST CHART

①→ Make a *COMPARISON/CONTRAST CHART* of some aspect of the story, (or compare/contrast aspects of several stories) using the formula *S,S,D* (Similar, Similar, Different) or *D,D,S* (Different, Different, Similar). Compare/contrast the aspects using *THREE CATEGORIES*, such as appearance, personality, and so on. *EACH* category must include *AT LEAST THREE DETAILS*, which should be *QUOTED* from the text whenever possible.

②→ Transfer your chart to butcher paper, *ILLUSTRATING EACH CATEGORY*.

③→ Choose *ONE* of the categories and write a *PARAGRAPH* comparing or contrasting the two topics selected.

SAMPLE CHART

FORMULAS: SIMILAR, SIMILAR, DIFFERENT OR DIFFERENT, DIFFERENT, SIMILAR	CATEGORIES: APPEARANCE, PERSONALITY, etc.	_____(1) TOPICS COMPARED (people, places, things, ideas)	_____(2) TOPICS COMPARED (people, places, things, ideas)
_____ FORMULA	_____ CATEGORY	1. 2. 3.	1. 2. 3.
_____ FORMULA	_____ CATEGORY	1. 2. 3.	1. 2. 3.
_____ FORMULA	_____ CATEGORY	1. 2. 3.	1. 2. 3.

READ ALL ABOUT IT!

① → Pretend this story really happened. Turn fiction into nonfiction by writing a **NEWSPAPER ARTICLE** about it.

② → **STUDY AT LEAST THREE STRAIGHT NEWS ARTICLES** from newspapers in order to model your sentence structure after that of real-life journalistic writing.

*Remember that newspaper articles are written in **INVERTED PYRAMID FORMAT**, which means that the most important parts (who, what, when, where, and sometimes why) are revealed in the first paragraph. The remaining paragraphs reveal the less important details. Remember that your **HEADLINE** is important.

③ → Draw a **PICTURE** to accompany the article.

④ → For effect, articles may be **MOUNTED ON AN ACTUAL NEWSPAPER**, the title of which could be changed to fit the short story.

⑤ → For extra credit, create **A CARTOON OR WANT AD** that also applies to the story.

MOST IMPORTANT INFO=
WHO WHAT WHEN WHERE WHY

LESS IMPORTANT DETAILS

LEAST
IMPORTANT
INFO

POETRY!

① → Write a poem of **AT LEAST 150 WORDS USING THE THEME OF THIS STORY.**

② → You may incorporate the story line itself, or you may choose to write about an entirely different **SUBJECT.**

③ → Your poem may be free verse or rhymed, but make sure it is in **POEM, NOT PARAGRAPH, FORM.**

④ → Use and **IDENTIFY AT LEAST TEN FIGURATIVE LANGUAGE DEVICES** (simile, metaphor, personification, etc.).

⑤ → **ILLUSTRATE** your poem.

FIGURATIVE LANGUAGE PASSAGES

① → **QUOTE TEN FIGURATIVE LANGUAGE PASSAGES** from the story.

② → Rewrite the passages in **LITERAL LANGUAGE**, in other words, plain language devoid of all the special wording.

③ → On butcher paper, make a **CHART** that clearly shows the difference between figurative and literal language.

④ → Create a **WORKSHEET OF FIVE MORE PASSAGES** that could have been used in this story. Use the names of the major characters and the situations but your own figurative language. Then, ask the class to **REWRITE YOUR PASSAGES IN THEIR OWN LITERAL LANGUAGE**.

⑤ → Make an **ANSWER KEY**.

FIGURATIVE
VS.
LITERAL

More Practice with POETIC LANGUAGE

①→ USING THE POETIC LANGUAGE SHEET: To provide students with more experience in understanding figurative language passages, use the **Poetic Language Sheet** in conjunction with the study of "Memories of Christmas" by Dylan Thomas. The sheet asks students to do the following:

A. CATEGORIZE the passage quoted (simile, metaphor, etc.),

B. EXPLAIN the meaning of the passage, and

C. REWRITE it in literal terms.

②→ ADAPTING TO STORY STUDIED: Using the **POETIC LANGUAGE SHEET** as a model, ask students to **FIND POETIC PASSAGES** in their own literature unit as well as to identify the type, explain the meaning, and rewrite in literal terms.

© 1998 M. E. LEDBETTER

384

Poetic Language

The following excerpts are from DYLAN THOMAS'S "MEMORIES OF CHRISTMAS." In order to understand and appreciate the difference between *LITERAL AND FIGURATIVE LANGUAGE*, do the following:

A. First, *IDENTIFY THE TYPE OF POETIC DEVICE USED* (simile, metaphor, personification, etc.). A quoted piece might not be a *FIGURATIVE LANGUAGE* device per se; rather, it could be an example of a *STYLISTIC DEVICE* such as repetition for effect, which can add a rhythmical quality to the work. Several passages might contain more than one device.

B. Next, *EXPLAIN THE REASONING BEHIND THE DEVICE*. For example, if it is a SIMILE or a METAPHOR, state the two elements being compared. If it is a PERSONIFICATION, identify which human trait is being attributed to what inanimate object.

C. Finally, *REWRITE THE PHRASE LITERALLY*--devoid of the beauty of its poetry but retaining its meaning. You might need to refer to the passage to recall Thomas's original intent.

①→ "All the Christmases roll down the hill towards the Welsh-speaking sea..." (1).

Device:_____

Explanation:_____

_____

Rewrite:_____

_____

_____

© 1998 M. E. LEDBETTER

②→ "All the Christmases...stop at the rim of the ice-edged, fish-freezing waves, and I plunge my hands in the snow and bring out whatever I can find..." (1).

Device:_____

Explanation:_____

_____

Rewrite:_____

_____

_____

③→ "In goes my hand into that wool-white bell-tongued ball of holidays..." (2).

Device:_____

Explanation:_____

_____

Rewrite:_____

_____

_____

④→ "Sleek and long as jaguars and terrible-whiskered, spitting and snarling they would slink and sidle over the white back-garden walls, and the lynx-eyed hunters, Jim and I, fur-capped and moccasined trappers from Hudson's Bay..." (2).

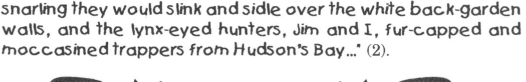

Device:_____

Explanation:_____

_____

Rewrite:_____

_____

_____

⑤→   "We were so still, Eskimo-footed arctic marksmen in the muffling
       silence of the eternal snows--eternal, ever since Wednesday..."
       (2).

Device:_____

Explanation:_____

_____

Rewrite:_____

_____

_____

Thomas, Dylan. "Memories of Christmas." The Norton Reader. Ed. Arthur
    M. Eastman. New York: W. W. Norton, 1992. 1-5.